Bible
Speaks
today

T0334446

the message of

1 AND 2 SAMUEL

Series editors:
Alec Motyer (OT)
John Stott (NT)
Derek Tidball (Bible Themes)

the message of

1 AND 2 SAMUEL

Personalities, potential, politics and power

Revised edition

Mary J. Evans

INTER-VARSITY PRESS
36 Causton Street, London SW1P 4ST, England
Email: ivp@ivpbooks.com
Website: www.ivpbooks.com

First published 2004
Reprinted 2006, 2008, 2010
This edition published 2022

British Library Cataloguing-in-Publication Data
A catalogue record for this book is available from the British Library.

ISBN 978-1-78974-373-9
eBook ISBN 978-1-78359-646-1

Set in 9.5/13pt Karmina
Typeset in Great Britain by CRB Associates, Potterhanworth, Lincolnshire
Printed and bound in Great Britain by Ashford Colour Press Ltd, Gosport, Hampshire

Produced on paper from sustainable sources.

*Inter-Varsity Press publishes Christian books that are true to the Bible
and that communicate the gospel, develop discipleship and strengthen the church
for its mission in the world.*

*IVP originated within the Inter-Varsity Fellowship, now the Universities and Colleges
Christian Fellowship, a student movement connecting Christian Unions in universities
and colleges throughout Great Britain, and a member movement of the International
Fellowship of Evangelical Students. Website: www.uccf.org.uk. That historic association
is maintained, and all senior IVP staff and committee members subscribe
to the UCCF Basis of Faith.*

for
Isobel and Ron, Elaine, Brad and Kathleen
with love and with thanks

Contents

Bible Speaks today

GENERAL PREFACE

The Bible Speaks Today describes three series of expositions, based on the books of the Old and New Testaments, and on Bible themes that run through the whole of Scripture. Each series is characterized by a threefold ideal:

- to expound the biblical text with accuracy
- to relate it to contemporary life, and
- to be readable.

These books are, therefore, not 'commentaries', for the commentary seeks rather to elucidate the text than to apply it, and tends to be a work rather of reference than of literature. Nor, on the other hand, do they contain the kinds of 'sermons' that attempt to be contemporary and readable without taking Scripture seriously enough. The contributors to The Bible Speaks Today series are all united in their convictions that God still speaks through what he has spoken, and that nothing is more necessary for the life, health and growth of Christians than that they should hear what the Spirit is saying to them through his ancient – yet ever modern – Word.

ALEC MOTYER
JOHN STOTT
DEREK TIDBALL
Series editors

Author's preface

The historical books of the Old Testament are sometimes seen more as fruitful sources for pictures, whether classical oil paintings of David and Bathsheba or children's drawings of David and Goliath, or for Sunday school lessons, than as appropriate or potent material for sermons. It is with the conviction that the books of Samuel are a vital part of God's Word, and that the stories are full of teaching which is dynamically relevant for believers of all ages, that this book is written. My hope is that readers will be as excited and challenged by the material as I have been and will be stimulated to learn much more from the text itself than can be contained in these pages.

I'm very grateful to IVP for the privilege of having been able to spend even more time immersed in Samuel in recent months, and especially to be able to focus on the area of application. In particular, my thanks are due to Alec Motyer, whose stimulating and encouraging criticism has had a great influence unacknowledged elsewhere, and to Philip Duce for his continuing support. I am also grateful to Kate Vine for her part in the production of the map which helps to locate the many places mentioned in Samuel.

As always, I need to express my debt and my gratitude to students and colleagues who provide constant stimulation, and to my family and friends for their continuing love and encouragement. This time I want to make particular mention of my aunts and uncles, to whom this book of significant stories is dedicated, and who have played a significant part in my own story.

MARY J. EVANS

Chief abbreviations

AB	Anchor Bible
CBQ	*Catholic Biblical Quarterly*
ESV	English Standard Version, Anglicized (2001)
ET	English translation
Int	*Interpretation*
IntB	The Interpreters' Bible
JBL	*Journal of Biblical Literature*
JETS	*Journal of the Evangelical Theological Society*
JSOT	*Journal for the Study of the Old Testament*
JSOTSup	Journal for the Study of the Old Testament Supplement Series
NCB	New Century Bible
NIBC	The New International Biblical Commentary
NICOT	New International Commentary on the Old Testament
NIV	New International Version, Anglicized (2011)
OTL	Old Testament Library
TOTC	Tyndale Old Testament Commentaries
TynBul	*Tyndale Bulletin*
VE	*Vox Evangelica*
VT	*Vetus Testamentum*
WBC	Word Biblical Commentary

Select bibliography

This list includes works referred to in the footnotes by the author's surname, or surname and date, and recommended further reading.

Ackroyd, P. R., *The First Book of Samuel* (Cambridge: Cambridge University Press, 1971).
——, *The Second Book of Samuel* (Cambridge: Cambridge University Press, 1977).
Alter, R., *The David Story* (New York: Norton, 1999).
Anderson, A. A., *2 Samuel*, WBC 11 (Waco: Word, 1989).
Baldwin, J., *1 and 2 Samuel: An Introduction and Commentary*, TOTC (Leicester: Inter-Varsity Press, 1988).
Brueggemann, W., *First and Second Samuel*, Interpretation: A Bible Commentary for Teaching and Preaching (Louisville: John Knox, 1990).
Caird, G. B., 'The First and Second Books of Samuel', in G. A. Buttrick et al. (eds.), IntB, Vol. 2 (Nashville: Abingdon, 1953).
Clines, D. J. A. and T. C. Eskenazi (eds.), *Telling Queen Michal's Story: An Experiment in Comparative Interpretation*, JSOTSup 119 (Sheffield: Sheffield Academic Press, 1991).
Craigie, P. C., *The Book of Deuteronomy*, NICOT (Grand Rapids: Eerdmans, 1976).
Davis, D. R., *1 Samuel: Looking on the Heart* (Fearn: Christian Focus, 2000).
Eaton, M. A., *1 Samuel* (Tonbridge: Sovereign World, 1996).
——, *2 Samuel* (Tonbridge: Sovereign World, 1996).
Evans, M. J., *1 and 2 Samuel*, NIBC (Peabody: Hendrickson, 2000).
Gordon, R. P., *1 and 2 Samuel* (Sheffield: JSOT Press, 1984).
——, *1 and 2 Samuel: A Commentary* (Exeter: Paternoster, 1986).

Hertzberg, H. W., *I & II Samuel*, OTL (ET) (London: SCM, 1964).

Hester, D. C., *First and Second Samuel* (Louisville: Geneva Press, 2000).

Jensen, I. L., *First and Second Samuel* (Chicago: Moody Press, 1995).

Jones, G. H., *The Nathan Narratives*, JSOTSup 80 (Sheffield: Sheffield Academic Press, 1990).

Kirkpatrick, A. F., *The First Book of Samuel* (Cambridge: Cambridge University Press, 1888).

——, *The Second Book of Samuel* (Cambridge: Cambridge University Press, 1889).

Klein, R. W., *1 Samuel*, WBC 19 (Waco: Word, 1983).

Knight, D. A., 'Deuteronomy and the Deuteronomists', in J. A. Mays et al. (eds.), *Old Testament Introduction: Past, Present and Future* (Edinburgh: T. & T. Clark, 1995).

Laney, J. C., *First and Second Samuel* (Chicago: Moody Press, 1995).

Mauchline, J., *1 and 2 Samuel*, NCB (London: Oliphants, 1971).

McCarter, P. K., *I Samuel*, AB (New York: Doubleday, 1980).

——, *II Samuel*, AB (New York: Doubleday, 1984).

Miller, P. D., *Deuteronomy* (Louisville: John Knox Press, 1990).

Provan, I. W., *1 and 2 Kings*, NIBC (Peabody: Hendrickson, 1995).

Introduction

Samuel is a storybook and storybooks are meant for reading! A good storybook might be challenging or comforting, exciting or calming, sad or happy, but it is always readable. The books of Samuel are no exception to this rule. They were written not as academic textbooks suitable only as examination material for scholars, but as storybooks for ordinary people, telling the life history of Israel. They are a very palatable way for believers to understand what it means to be a believer, Israelites what it means to be an Israelite and kings what it means to be a king. It is more than time for the books of Samuel, along with the other Old Testament historical books, to come down off the shelves and get back into the hands (and heads and hearts) of the ordinary people of the twenty-first century. This ordinary believer has revelled in the challenge of getting inside the texts and it is my great hope that any readers of this book will be stimulated more than anything else to read again the books of Samuel both for themselves and to others.

1. What do we do with stories?

Within the books of Samuel there is a whole variety of styles and forms. We find poetry, prophecy, genealogy, government personnel records and military honours lists. However, the vast majority of the material is in the form of narrative; the story of real people in real situations. There are battle stories, telling of Israel's continuing campaign to seek and ensure independence from external power blocs, of internal fights for supremacy between national and local rulers, and of individual fights to overcome the personal gremlins of pride or fear or jealousy. There are family stories of births, marriages and deaths, of love and hate, of rivalry, violence and rape, of friendship and loyalty. There are stories that centre on women and on men, on children, on young people, on the elderly. There are stories from the town and stories from the country. There is a particular and continuing focus on stories about the ruling families within Israel, but this does not exclude an interest in ordinary people, and one might say that one of the points that the writers are trying to get across is that rulers are indeed ordinary people.

If we are to take the books of Samuel seriously as the word of God, then we must take seriously this concentration on the telling of stories. A large section of Old Testament Scripture is dedicated to these records of how God's people lived their lives, of how they related and failed to relate to God and to one another, and, probably more importantly, of how God was active not only in the lives of individuals but in the life of the nation of Israel as well. So the question arises as to what we are supposed to do with these stories. Surely for those of us who want to assert that Samuel, along with the rest of Scripture, is 'God-breathed and is useful for teaching, rebuking, correcting and training in right-eousness' (2 Tim. 3:16), the point is that these are more than mere accurate accounts of past events. So much energy can be expended on defending the historical validity of the events described that we forget to question why these stories are being told. Surely to speak of the truth of Scripture in Samuel is to do more than just assert the accuracy of the record.

In every story that deals with the history of a people there are two key elements. First, there are the events themselves; the things that happened. Some of the events recorded in Samuel are said to be at God's command or in line with God's purposes; others most definitely were not. It would be possible to suggest that some of the stories are being told as examples, so later readers can imitate the behaviour and attitudes of the main characters. It is very clear, however, that not all the happenings described can be seen in that way. In this context we have to recognize the presence and significance not only of the characters described but also of the back-ground figures of the narrators, the storytellers. The second element in the telling of a story is the interpretation of the events. How and why are the narrators telling a particular story in any given way, emphasizing this element and underplaying that? These are not objective records stating facts and facts alone, they are stories told with a purpose. It is no accident that in the Jewish canon these books form part of the section called the Former Prophets. This is preached history and as such provides superb source material, maybe in method as well as in content, for modern preachers!

Modern scholars increasingly recognize that there is no such thing as the objective recording of history, and the books of Samuel are not even presented as an attempt to do that. There were national records kept for that purpose. Although the books of Samuel refer on occasion to such records, the accounts within them perhaps have more similarity to the court pages of a national newspaper than they do to the official records of, say, the proceedings of Parliament or of Congress. They tell about relationships and emotions, about enthusiasms and failures, about decisions and the failure to make decisions. We are not presented with a comprehensive picture. Particular events have been selected and presented in particular ways to make particular points; other events have been omitted altogether. Sometimes the reason for the selection of a particular story, or for its being told in a particular way, is very clear and the writers themselves present easily digestible conclusions. Sometimes the direction the writer wants his readers to follow is less obvious; nevertheless many clues are provided and the reader is left in no real doubt about where the story is leading.

However, sometimes the clues appear to be missing. It is as if the writer is deliberately challenging the readers to engage with the stories themselves, to think about the events and to come to personal conclusions as to their significance. The readers are being told, in effect, 'You've read the law, you've heard the prophets, you know who God is and what it means to relate to him, so what do you make of this? Don't just read this story – get inside it, interact with it in the light of what you already know about God and his purposes.' The challenge is twofold: on the one hand, to work out what was in the writer's mind as he recounts the story, and on the other hand, to interpret the accounts personally and to ask, 'What relevance does this story have for me and for those I am teaching?'

There is also a third element to take into account when reading historical books, one that is particularly important for the teacher and the preacher, and that is making sure that there really is a relationship between the first and second elements, that the point is genuinely drawn out of the story and not just read into it!

To seek to meet a challenge like this is demanding but also very exciting. It is demanding because it involves getting to grips with the whole of

Scripture, making sure that we really have read the 'law and the prophets' and that we do know what it means to relate to the God they reveal. In particular, it involves putting the story we are looking at in the context of all the other stories told within the books of Samuel and beyond. It is only as we identify the interests of the author throughout the book, and the themes that are being drawn out, that we can hope to understand what it is that we might learn from the individual passage. Because the interpretation of stories like these is often open-ended, there will be more instances of 'maybe' and 'perhaps' and 'probably' than when we are dealing with passages that contain more explicit teaching. It is in recognition of this open-endedness that a 'Questions to ponder' section has been added at the end of each chapter. None of this means that a story can be made to say anything one likes. The author's interests and concerns in the whole document provide a firm control; but it does explain how and why Paul and James can read the same story and see different emphases in it (Gal. 3:6ff.; Jas 2:20ff.). They were undertaking the same challenge that we are called to deal with.

It is exciting because the story itself is exciting and we are called to enter into it, to wrestle with it, to get into the minds and hearts of both the characters and the narrators, to see and feel God at work in the accounts. It is also exciting because the storytelling is masterful. We marvel at the remarkable perception and sensitivity of the writers, inspired by God no doubt, but with their own interests and abilities too. Not only do the writers describe the behaviour of the characters, but, as the stories unfold, we are given real insight into their personalities. At the end of the book we feel we know Samuel, Saul and David, and not only them but Hannah, Joab, Jonathan, Michal and others too. We understand something of what made them tick, of why they made certain decisions and not others. We can grasp how Tamar or Absalom or Mephibosheth felt as they sought to come to terms with what happened to them. The narrative skill is exhibited also in the way these stories appeal to women as well as men. This is done not just by including stories of women, but by concentrating on issues of relationship.

It is worth repeating that if we are to take the books of Samuel seriously as the word of God, then we must take seriously the fact that God chose to speak to us through stories.

2. A historical and literary perspective

The books of Samuel do not exist in historical or literary isolation. Historically, they contain the story of what happened to God's people during the lifetimes of Samuel and David. This follows on directly from the accounts of life in the land during the time of the judges and, more distantly but nevertheless very significantly, from the calling of Abraham through the time of bondage in Egypt, the calling of Moses and the wilderness wandering up to the entry into the land described in Joshua. It precedes the continuing history of life during the time of the monarchy found in 1 and 2 Kings and parallels the account of David's kingship found in 1 Chronicles. This parallel material proves to be helpful in identifying the major interests and concerns of both books. Sometimes they are clearly using the same sources and the wording is almost identical. At other times they present the same events but in different ways and with different emphases. On yet other occasions they choose to include or omit different stories. Chronicles is more concerned with the organization of the kingdom of Israel and its religion, and there are more genealogical lists and structural details than we find in Samuel. The focus in Chronicles is on David as king and what is happening in the kingdom, whereas Samuel is interested in David as a person and what is happening in his life.

In both a literary and a historical sense the books of Samuel are linked with Joshua, Judges and 1 and 2 Kings. There are common interests and common themes, emphasized by their joint title, the Former Prophets, in Hebrew tradition. Theologically there are also strong links between these books and Deuteronomy, and in recent times these historical books have also become known as the Deuteronomic History.[1] The writers of Deuteronomy and of Samuel have a common passion for God and his kingdom. They share a deep concern for the development of the nation as a community of God's people, they have the same understanding as to

---

[1] It is clear that at least the final editors of Samuel and Kings were aware of the content and the interests of Deuteronomy. What is less clear, at least to some, is whether Deuteronomy should be seen as the introduction to the history, the pre-existing document which had helped to formulate the views and ideas of the writers of Samuel and Kings, or as the conclusion to the history where the views and ideas that have developed in the writing of the history and in the observation of the monarchy are eventually brought together. The issue of the dating of Deuteronomy is fully discussed in most commentaries (e.g. P. C. Craigie, *The Book of Deuteronomy*, NICOT [Grand Rapids: Eerdmans, 1976]; P. D. Miller, *Deuteronomy* [Louisville: John Knox Press, 1990]); cf. D. A. Knight, 'Deuteronomy and the Deuteronomists', in J. A. Mays et al. (eds.), *Old Testament Introduction: Past, Present and Future* (Edinburgh: T. & T. Clark, 1995).

what is required in terms of ritual and there is often even a common phrasing.[2]

Finally, we should not forget that in both a literary and a historical sense there are strong links between this account and the New Testament. The links with the stories of Jesus, 'great David's greater son', are perhaps obvious, but there are also strong connections with the New Testament's presentations of what it means or should mean to live life as part of the community of God's people.

3. Who wrote Samuel?

The question of authorship is complicated. The storyteller plays a very significant role in the narratives and it is possible to discern a common thread throughout the books. Nevertheless, what we have in Samuel is clearly a composite document and it is not easy to work out what is meant by 'author'. There is no doubt that in the final production 1 and 2 Samuel form one volume that is in itself part of the larger history that also includes 1 and 2 Kings. The Septuagint, the Greek version of the Old Testament, puts them together as the four books of Kingdoms or Reigns. Clearly someone, perhaps several people, was involved in the production of the final document, bringing together all the material. This final editing could not have taken place until after the completion of the events recorded in Kings and so it is possible that these editors worked during the exile. However, it is also very likely that much of the material in 1 and 2 Samuel had reached almost its final form well before then and could have been brought together as a document as early as the reign of Solomon. Both the final editors and the earlier editors have a claim to authorship.

It is also clear, however, that there was a range of written documents used by these editors and many of the stories are told in a way that strongly suggests eyewitness accounts. The original producers of the individual records and tellers of the individual tales also have a claim to authorship.

The books of Samuel cover the full lifetimes of Samuel and of David and therefore no single person could have observed everything. The Chronicler states in 1 Chronicles 29:29: 'As for the events of King David's reign, from beginning to end, they are written in the records of Samuel the seer, the

---

[2] E.g. 1 Sam. 1:3–4 and Deut. 12:5–7, 17–18; 1 Sam. 8:1–5 and Deut. 16:18–19; 1 Sam. 17:32 and Deut. 20:1–4; 2 Sam. 1:22 and Deut. 32:42; 2 Sam. 7:23–24 and Deut. 4:32–38; 2 Sam. 22:3 and Deut. 32:4, 37.

records of Nathan the prophet and the records of Gad the seer.' It is a strong possibility that records like these were used within the final production. We have no evidence that individual sections ever existed separately, but a number of distinct segments within the books can be identified, linked either to separate time periods or to specific characters. Chapters 1–15 of 1 Samuel focus first on Samuel (chapters 1–7) and then on Saul; 1 Samuel 16 – 2 Samuel 5 deals with the history of David's rise, and 2 Samuel 9 – 20 with the continuing story of David's time in power. There may be a separate ark narrative used in 1 Samuel 4 – 6 and 2 Samuel 6. The text of 2 Samuel 21 – 24 appears to have been gathered from a number of separate sources.

In the end, it is virtually impossible to tell just how many different sources were used[3] and in what manner they were brought together. It is remarkable, given this variety and complexity, that the final document comes across in such a unified and comprehensible way.

4. Underlying themes

Each of the individual sections and stories has its own interests and concerns, which we will explore as we consider them in more detail. However, certain issues and ideas form recurring motifs within the books and could be identified as themes. It is worthwhile setting out some of these in advance to provide a context in which to read the text as a whole.

a. Government: who rules the people?

There is no doubt that the books of Samuel have a real interest in politics. Virtually all of the material has some link, direct or indirect, with the question of who is to be seen as the leader of God's people, Israel. Sometimes this involves theological considerations as to how the leadership impinges on God's rule of the people and what kind of responsibility the leader has for the spiritual life of the nation. Sometimes it involves the

---

[3] Any study of possible sources for Samuel is made more difficult by a series of problems that exist within the Hebrew Masoretic text. There are a number of instances where there appear to be errors of transmission and the Hebrew phrase is now unintelligible. The Greek translation, the Septuagint, does not suffer from these problems and for that reason many English translations have preferred the Septuagintal wording on a number of occasions. It is interesting that both the Hebrew fragments from Samuel found at Qumran and the text of parallel passages in Chronicles also reflect the text of the Septuagint. This does support the view that there was some particular problem of transmission in the copying of the Masoretic text of Samuel. The problem should not be overestimated, but most of the more extensive commentaries provide further details of these textual difficulties (e.g. Klein, pp. xxvi–xxviii, or Mauchline, pp. 33–34).

more practical issues of the succession – who is to be the next leader – or the implications of the current leadership and how a particular person functions in his role, whether that is as priest or prophet, judge or king.

b. Characters: individuals are interesting

There is also no doubt that the writers of Samuel have a deep interest in people. The characters presented are not simply there to enable the reader to make sense of particular historical events. They are taken very seriously as people. Both their personality and their potential are fully explored. We learn of their hopes and fears, successes and failures, ambitions and dreams, action and indecisiveness. All of them are seen as people who are responsible for their own actions and who are accountable for their own decisions. They are also people who are understood by God and for whom God cares. It is a very worthwhile exercise to follow some of the characters through the accounts, watching out for aspects of their personalities that the writers focus on and for the way in which their behaviour is critiqued as well as recorded.

c. Control: manipulation and people-management

One of the main concepts that links all the stories in these books and all the other interests of the writers is that of power. There is of course a significant focus on the power of God, his right to rule and his ability to carry out his own plans and purposes. Israel's God Yahweh is the one who brings security to the nation. God is the one who anoints and appoints rulers and kings. He is the one who gives Israel a future, who rewards and who punishes. But alongside this there is also an interest in human power that goes far beyond a presentation of information about the identity of the nation's leaders. There is an exploration of the nature of power, of how it can and should be used, of how it has been and most definitely should not have been misused and abused. The ways in which people manipulate and exercise control over others are examined and commented on. It is possible to see this theme as one of the main reasons for the selection of this particular group of stories and for the method in which they are presented.

d. Gospel: obedience, relationship and covenant

Behind and alongside all these concerns is the central emphasis that Samuel shares with the rest of the Old Testament, and indeed with the

New Testament too, on God and his kingdom. This is a story of people and of a people who are in relationship with God. The writers clearly understand and present what it means to be in such a relationship and what the implications are for those who ignore the demands and responsibilities involved. These stories are preached rather than merely told. The presentation of the Davidic covenant in 2 Samuel 7 is in the context of an understanding of the covenant relationship that was initiated at Sinai. The stories of the appointment of a king are told in the context of a search for one whose leadership would reflect God's own character in such a way that the whole people would be able to reflect God's character before the surrounding nations. The psalms in 1 Samuel 2 and 2 Samuel 22 function as bookends ensuring that the whole story is read in the context of the God who turns the world's values upside down, the living Rock who gives power to the weak, transforms failures and longs to bless those who serve him.

So, we have politics, personality and potential, power, preaching and prayer. These books provide a fascinating insight into so many elements of human life lived in God's world. It would indeed be a tragedy if these accounts were set aside as simply ancient history with only marginal relevance for today.

1 Samuel 1 – 4

1. Hannah: the powerless woman

1. Hannah's (missing) child (1:1–28)

There is no preliminary discussion or editorial introduction to the books of Samuel. We are plunged straight into a family story. From the beginning the writer's interest in people is clear, as is his conviction that one can learn of God's ways and character from his dealings with the lives of individuals. There are three initial characters: a man, Elkanah, and his two wives, Hannah and Peninnah. The writer of 1 Chronicles 6:33ff. apparently presents Samuel and Elkanah as coming from a levitical family, but it seems to state here that Elkanah was from the tribe of Ephraim. It is possible that the Chronicler was associating Samuel in particular with the Kohathite levitical clan because of the significant part he played in the religious leadership of Israel.[1] However, it is also possible that Elkanah was a Levite who happened to live in Ephraim. The amount of biographical information given here about Elkanah would normally indicate that he was a significant person within his own area. Polygamy was not particularly common in Israel but it was not unusual for a wealthy person to take a second wife, particularly if the first wife was childless. The order of the women's names in verse 2, with Hannah being placed first and then last, suggests that she was the first wife, although it may just be an indication that she is the real focus of the writer's interest.

a. Rights and responsibilities in family life (1:1–3)

Elkanah is portrayed as a sincere man who sought to do the right thing in his family and in his religion. His polygamy is mentioned without

---

[1] Cf. Caird, p. 877.

comment, as are all the other polygamous situations recorded in Samuel and Kings, not least David's own marriages. However, here as there, by presenting the resulting tensions, the writer could be encouraging readers to draw their own conclusions about the wisdom of such marriages. Genesis 2:24 and Jesus' reference to that verse in response to a question concerning divorce seem to make it crystal clear that what God intended from the beginning was for marriage to be between one man and one woman (Matt. 19:3–12; Mark 10:1–12). There may be no explicit discussion about the ethics of polygamy within the Old Testament, but it is still possible to state that polygamy was clearly not the right way forward for God's people. In today's society, the supposed 'right to have children' is seen as the overriding factor in a whole range of ethical questions on which the Bible makes little or no explicit comment. The use of donor sperm or embryos, genetic manipulation and surrogate motherhood are among the issues today that need serious reflection in the light not only of specific verses of Scripture but of stories like this one. What is possible or even what is legally permissible may not necessarily be what is right or what is best!

The main issue under discussion is introduced right at the beginning: *Peninnah had children, but Hannah had none* (2). The mention of Hannah's childlessness immediately brings to mind the situations of Sarah or Rachel, and the way in which their childlessness and subsequent childbearing had such an effect on their lives (Gen. 11:30; 29:31 – 30:24). This connection causes us to question whether Hannah's barrenness is not the final chapter in her story. The facts of Peninnah's fertility and Hannah's infertility are simply stated, but they had a major impact on the whole family, as we see when the writer skilfully opens a window onto their family life. They were concerned to keep the covenant and so every year they travelled to Shiloh *to worship and sacrifice to the Lord* (3). Whether this was at the time of the national festivals or privately in order to keep a vow (21) is not clear. What should have been a happy family occasion was, for the women at least, a time of particular jealousy and deep unhappiness. The writer's insight into the thoughts and feelings of these women is remarkable. The obtuseness that we see in both Elkanah and Eli seems typical of the attitudes of the men of the time, and indeed of many times, towards women, but the writer, almost certainly a man, is able to observe, present and critique that obtuseness. The books of Samuel as a whole present a series of power struggles between those men who are seen as the most significant figures within the nation. But we begin with the story of a barren woman whose childlessness leaves her powerless even within her own family situation. It seems certain that this is a deliberate attempt to encourage the reader to think further about life, about the significance of individuals and about what real power is.

b. Fair shares for all the family – of goods and of attention? (1:4–7)

Elkanah's polygamy may be questionable, but there is no doubt of his other qualifications as a good family man. He wanted to ensure that his whole family was treated properly and was involved in the sacrificial procedures. Peninnah and all her children were given a portion of meat – possibly to sacrifice, but more likely as their share in the fellowship meal (Lev. 7:11–18) which was part of the sacrificial procedure. Hannah was given a special portion[2] *because he loved her* (5). It appears that Elkanah was aware of Hannah's pain and wanted to do something to help, but his action only exacerbated the situation. It is not stated explicitly that Peninnah was not loved in the same way as Hannah, but the implication is certainly there. One cannot help feeling sympathy for Peninnah, however reprehensible her cruel taunting. If she was a second wife, married only to give Elkanah children, then the double portion emphasized her secondary status as much as it emphasized Hannah's perceived failure as a woman and a mother. This sad situation brings to mind Sarah's jealousy of Hagar (Gen. 16 and 21) and the intense rivalry between Rachel and Leah (Gen. 30). In this instance, the position of both women is unenviable and the writer seems to invoke sympathy for both.

c. Appreciating another's point of view (1:8)

As for Elkanah, he could observe the pain but did not really understand it. Because Peninnah had many children including several sons, Hannah's childlessness, to her an unbearable tragedy, was for him simply a minor inconvenience. It did not matter to him that she was childless, so why should it matter so much to her? He loved her, and he did not mind that she did not have children. Surely that was enough? For Hannah, daily reminded by Peninnah's very existence that for him love without children most certainly had not been enough, his attitude might even have rubbed

---

[2] The exact way in which Hannah's portion was different from the rest is not clear, but the NIV's *double portion* does convey the sense of specialness.

salt in the wound. Perhaps if he had said 'Don't you mean more to me than ten sons?' rather than 'Don't I mean more to you?', Hannah might have been a little more convinced. Elkanah seems to have been incapable of seeing Hannah's position from anything other than his own perspective. It is tremendously encouraging to all who feel their misery is not understood, not just women, to know that the account itself, and, more especially, the Lord who stands behind the account, does not share Elkanah's limitations. It is a challenge to all of us to try to get beyond our own perspective and see through the eyes of those loved ones whom we would seek to comfort.

d. Prayer: sharing, pleading, accepting – and eventually bringing peace (1:9–10)

The depth of Hannah's misery is clearly portrayed. *In her deep anguish Hannah prayed to the Lord, weeping bitterly* (10). Elkanah did not understand and she had no recourse but to turn to God. She believed that he was the one who had 'closed her womb' (5) and he was the only one who had the power to open it. As the same situation had happened year after long year, it is likely that Hannah had poured out her soul to God many times before. She takes it for granted that God will understand the situation and her unhappiness and that he is ready to listen to her. Maybe she knew from past experience that it brought some relief simply to express how she felt. We should never underestimate the importance of prayer in sharing our thoughts and feelings, miseries and joys with the one who understands all. On this occasion, we know that Hannah's deepest desire was met, but her continued coming suggests that she had found help even on those occasions when there seemed to be no response.

Hannah clearly acknowledged that her childlessness was in some sense a result of God's action – or inaction. He had closed her womb. Within her cultural background it seems to have been virtually impossible for anyone to envisage the possibility that God may have had a purpose, perhaps one that might even bring great blessing, in allowing childlessness to continue. One wonders if Hannah could have coped better with her situation if she could have accepted that possibility. Maybe the temporary relief that her prayers brought her in the past resulted in part from a reaching out to such a thought, but it is clear that she was never able to grasp it fully. For today's childless believers, still bound by cultural pressures but with greater awareness of the variety of God's purposes than was possible for those of

Hannah's time, it may be worth asking the question whether in their case God has indeed 'closed the womb' for a purpose. Fertility treatment can be seen as a God-given opportunity, but it is not the only way forward. Sometimes many years are wasted in desperate *weeping* (10), seeking one treatment after another, when acceptance of the situation might have brought both peace and fulfilment by another route. It is not always an easy thing to discern when it is right to keep wrestling in prayer, as Hannah did here, and when it is right to recognize, as Paul did (2 Cor. 12:7–9), that sometimes we should cease praying for a situation to change and accept that God's grace is sufficient for us within that situation.

e. Pastoral responsibilities (1:11–20)

Eli, elderly, overweight and very short-sighted (4:14–18), was sitting by the door of the temple.[3] Perhaps he was dozing and Hannah's silent lips were partially an attempt not to waken him. His lack of pastoral sensitivity would be more understandable if he was a little befuddled from having just woken up; nevertheless it should probably be seen as blameworthy. James tells us that those who set themselves up as teachers will 'be judged more strictly' (Jas 3:1) and those who take on pastoral responsibilities will similarly be held accountable for their failures. However, Eli did respond well when Hannah began to speak to him and he grasped then what was really going on. He gave her his blessing and Hannah gained a new sense of peace in her heart. It was not that Eli's prayers were more likely to be answered than her own. Nowhere in the Old Testament is there any indication that the prayers of priests or prophets are more likely to be heard than those of other believing Israelites. It may be that Eli's response confirmed her assurance that God had heard and understood her desperate outpourings. It was probably this assurance that gave her peace, rather than any real conviction that this time she really would have a child. Prayer is about relationship. Talking with God enables us to understand a little better what it means to relate to him and to rest a little more easily in the knowledge of his presence. Praying with others can be particularly helpful in this regard. Silent prayer before God can be a great blessing, but God often uses the sharing of that prayer with others to bring reassurance and comfort to a grieving heart. Christian leaders should take

---

[3] Shiloh was not actually a temple but it was a significant shrine, a semi-permanent building which housed precious religious objects including the ark of God.

very seriously their responsibility to pray with those who come to them for help. It is sometimes easy to dismiss desperation as drunkenness or some other blameworthy factor, when a listening ear, a kind word and a shared prayer might bring welcome relief.

In this instance, the peace that prayer brought to Hannah enabled her to regain her composure enough to eat something and to participate in worship with the family, presumably including Peninnah, before they all returned home. There was apparently no immediate change in Hannah's circumstances, but *in the course of time* (20) she did at last conceive and Samuel was born. His name, as so often in Old Testament times, relates to the circumstances of his birth. It sounds rather like the Hebrew phrase which means 'heard by God' and Hannah certainly saw herself in that category. The phrasing *the* LORD *remembered her* (19) is not all that common in the Old Testament and puts Hannah alongside Noah, Abraham, Rachel and the whole people of Israel in Egypt (Gen. 8:1; 19:29; 30:22; Exod. 2:24). This desolate woman was as much in God's mind as the great patriarchs of his chosen people.

f. Taking promises seriously (1:21–28)

Whatever vow Elkanah had made (21), he took it very seriously. Although for the next few years Hannah did not accompany the family on their regular visits to Shiloh, there was no question of the others not going. Hannah also took her own vow seriously. It would have been possible to forget what she had said in her distraught state, or to set it aside as unnecessary literalism. But Hannah had been very aware of what she had said and had clearly meant it. Making promises to God is a serious matter. Ecclesiastes 5:1–7 includes a discussion of this matter and concludes that 'it is better not to make a vow than to make one and not fulfil it'. Perhaps we should listen more carefully to the prayers (including those that are part of worship songs) that we voice or that are voiced on our behalf. Committing ourselves to being holy, or to giving God the whole of our lives, is not just a way of making us feel good about ourselves as we sit in a worship service. It has serious implications for our everyday life and behaviour.

Hannah's prayer of dedication, recorded in verse 11, could be seen as an attempt to bribe God. In exchange for the privilege of motherhood, Hannah would give God a child to serve him. However, although there must have been an element of self-interest in Hannah's desire for a son, this was not necessarily the whole story. If we really understand God's goodness and really appreciate God's gifts, then there bubbles up inside an almost uncontrollable urge to respond in the fullest way we can imagine. God's love inspires in us both gratitude and consecration. It is possible that Hannah's deepest desire was not simply to have a son but to be able to dedicate a child to God's service. Her longing for a son may have been partly so that she would be able to do just that. It could be that allowing Samuel to be brought up in the temple was seen by her not as a necessary but terrible sacrifice but rather as a deep joy, in spite of the inevitable accompanying pain. Many believing mothers and fathers have prayed that their children might be used in God's service and have known the paradox of joy and pain as their prayers have been answered and those children have gone on to work in dangerous parts of the world.

Whether this was Hannah's perspective or not, there was no doubt in her mind that when she next visited Shiloh it would be to leave Samuel with Eli, or rather with the Lord. It was not appropriate to do that until after he was weaned. Weaning took place much later than is common in most parts of the world today. A child was rarely weaned before the age of three and could have been well over five before being fully weaned. Samuel would have been very young, but not necessarily a small infant when he arrived in Shiloh. The fact that he was a special child who had been dedicated to God would have been known to Samuel from his first consciousness. It is likely that he looked forward to going to Shiloh in the way that some children look forward to going to school. The final statement of the chapter, that Samuel *worshipped the Lord there* (28), may be a deliberate attempt to show that although Samuel almost certainly missed his family, it may not have been the trauma for him that a modern Western reader might fear.

Elkanah was happy for Hannah to fulfil her commitment and it must have been he who provided the animals for the special sacrifices that were made as Samuel joined the temple service. It is clear from the text, however, that in this instance it was Hannah who took the lead. The impression is often given that women played very little part in the religion of Israel, but that is certainly not the impression conveyed here. It had been Hannah who had made the vow dedicating Samuel to God's service and it was Hannah who followed it through. Her own personal relationship with God is very clear. Commitment to God always includes community involvement, but relating to God is not just a matter of being part of a believing family, or nation, or church. Individual responsibility cannot be set aside by assuming that as long as the leaders – be they national or church or family – fulfil their role, then the individual is covered. Hannah's faith was not just subsumed within the family worship nor her commitment covered by the sacrifices that her husband brought.

2. Hannah's song of exultant thanksgiving (2:1–11)

Hannah's whole life had been changed. She was no longer barren, she was the mother of a son. In confident gratitude she had dedicated her son's life to God, giving up her own rights. That gift, as revealed by the unfolding story, was going to make a real difference to the life of the people of Israel. However, at this point attention is focused not on Samuel, but on Hannah's presentation to God of her own worship through the psalm recorded in this chapter. Whether or not this was a psalm of her own composition does not really matter. It does reflect the language of other psalms, although this particular one is not found anywhere else in the Old Testament. What does matter is that it expressed what Hannah wanted to say at this moment in her own life and experience.

It was not unusual to bring a special offering of praise to God at times of particular rejoicing. Most of us have experienced that sense of bubbling over with gratitude to God because of some special experience of joy; not just big things like the birth of a child, or the first view of a magnificent waterfall, or the welcome sight of an old friend's face finally picked out in a crowd, but also everyday occurrences like the perfection of a single rose left in our room for us, or the relief that the supermarket is still open after all. There is often a thankfulness that goes far beyond the significance of the event itself. But how many times do we experience the joy and then move on, without stopping to reflect on what has been going on in the way that Hannah does here?

Reflecting on life as it happens (2:1–11)

It was not unusual for women to reflect theologically on their circumstances and to present that reflection in the form of a song. Miriam and Deborah are well-known examples of other women psalmists (Exod. 15; Judg. 5), and, later on, Mary perhaps used Hannah's song as the basis for her own reflections (Luke 1:46–55). However, the fact remains that the privilege of providing the main theological introduction to the whole account of the history of the Israelite monarchy is given to Hannah. That fact is probably not irrelevant. Many Christian believers today, both men and women, abdicate their responsibility to reflect theologically on what is happening to and around them, to ponder on the meaning of God's involvement in the world. They assume that the experts will do that. However, given the comfort and encouragement that Hannah's song can provide for those facing opposition from apparently powerful forces, maybe we should be glad that Hannah did not leave the task of theological reflection to Eli and his colleagues! Our beliefs and our experiences are not meant to be unrelated, kept in different compartments of our lives. We all have a responsibility to bring them together, to think about how what has happened to us can be understood in the light of our faith and how our understanding of God and his work can be developed in the light of our experiences.

The books of Samuel and Kings go on to describe the often rather sorry history of the power struggles within Israel as kings and potential kings battled for supremacy; sometimes taking account of God's purposes, but often not. However, the story begins here, with this reflection on power and powerlessness and on God's attitude to human views of status. It is presented via the lips of an apparently insignificant woman. Hannah tells us of the power of God and the unsupported arrogance of human beings who are essentially powerless. She was very much aware of her own weakness, but nevertheless saw herself as empowered by God; given power, not to control the lives of others, but to live in the light of strength provided by God. The message was one that future kings also needed to hear and take note of, which is almost certainly why the compilers of Samuel included Hannah's song here. It is a message that should be noted today by any person or nation, church or organization – particularly where the tendency has taken hold to overestimate our own human powers or the significance of human ruling and to underestimate the need for humble dependence on God. God is a God who turns things upside down; Hannah realized that and so should we.

It is worth examining Hannah's poem in detail.

i. Joy and security in the Rock

In verse 1, Hannah introduces her own delight as she revels in the new situation brought about by God's intervention. Her *horn*, symbolizing strength, is lifted high. In Yahweh, the Lord, she has significance and joy, and gains the right to boast. The word *horn* appears again in verse 10, forming an 'inclusio', a technique used to provide a boundary at either end of the song. However, in verse 2 we move on to the main focus of the psalm. The basis of joy, of faith and of understanding is the character and actions of Israel's holy God, who like a rock provides the strength and security needed by Hannah, and Israel, and Israel's king. This picture of God as a Rock is also found in the Song of Moses (Deut. 32), and is taken up by several of Israel's psalmists and prophets including David in the psalm recorded at the end of 2 Samuel.[4] It may be that all these writers, including Hannah, were reminded of the events described in Exodus 17 when water to refresh the thirsty and dissatisfied Israelites flowed out from the rock in the desert. Whether or not that is so, the point here is that the focus of the believer's joy should be God himself, not simply our experience of his blessing; the rock, not the water that flows from it.

ii. Strength from weakness

These verses ponder on what might be seen as the vagaries of life. Reversals of fortune may be suffered or enjoyed by the warrior and the weak, the well fed and the hungry, the fertile and the barren (4–5). We are told in 1 Samuel 2:21 that Hannah had a total of six children, but there is perhaps an implication here that even after the birth of just one, she felt as if she had already reached an ideal situation, represented by a family of seven. It is important to recognize that just as present weakness may not be the final setting, present good fortune is not necessarily anything to boast about. God knows what is going on and he does weigh actions. The result of his judgment could quite easily be, as had happened in Hannah's case, that positions in society are turned upside down. The letter of James contains similar reflections (Jas 1:2–12; 2:5; 5:1–6). Perhaps James had been studying Hannah's song at the time he was composing his letter.

iii. Status is determined by God

It is made very clear that the kind of jostling for position and wrestling for status that seems to form such a major part of human relationships is really a waste of time. It is God who *brings death and makes alive* (6), God who humbles and exalts. His actions are based on his own choices and his own judgments and cannot be either predicted or controlled by mere

---

[4] 2 Sam. 22:32, 47; cf. also Pss 18:31; 61:2; 89:26; 94:22; 95:1; Isa. 17:10; 26:4.

humans. God is able to transform lives. He can take the desperately poor, eking out an existence on the rubbish heap, and transform them into powerful princes. The earth itself belongs to God. What really counts is not position or status or power but righteousness and faith in him. He will act to protect those who show evidence of obedience and trust, that is, *his faithful servants*,[5] whereas others face only judgment. *It is not by strength that one prevails* (9), not human strength anyway. Those who pit their strength against God will meet only shattering devastation.

Hannah's desperate weeping had been turned into great joy, her *horn* had been *lifted high* (1). The same Lord who had done that for her would similarly *give strength to his king and exalt the horn of his anointed* (10). It may be that Hannah was conscious that her experience of God's action in her own life was characteristic of his action with all those he chooses to bless, including the leader of the nation. There was no king as yet in Israel, but possibly Hannah was part of a developing groundswell of opinion that the way forward might need to be via a monarchy. However, it is also possible that this final reference to Israel's king was added by a later editor to make Hannah's song an even more appropriate introduction to the history of Israel's monarchy. Certainly the reference to God's appointed king also receiving God's strength forms a very suitable link back into the narrative.

iv. Moving on

We are told that Elkanah and Hannah went back home to Ramah, but Samuel stayed behind with Eli, where he *ministered before the LORD* (11). He would continue to serve the unique, all-powerful, holy Rock in whom his mother's heart rejoiced.

3. A successor for Eli (2:12–36)

The main purpose of the books of Samuel is to describe the history of Israel and in particular God's dealings with Israel during the course of the monarchy. But the history of a nation is made up of the stories of individuals and the writer provides us with very effective pen pictures of the characters here. The fact of human responsibility – that who we are and

---

[5] 'Servants' here, as elsewhere in the Old Testament, refers to all believing Israelites who seek to be faithful to the God they serve.

what we do makes a real difference both to the developing life of the community and to the way God treats us – is taken for granted. Even at this early stage, the links between the books of Samuel and the book of Deuteronomy are evident. Deuteronomy sets out very clearly the significance of the covenant between God and Israel and the responsibilities of individuals and also the community living under that covenant. Samuel shows how the theory and the practice come together – or don't!

a. Religion without faith is dangerous nonsense (2:12–17)

Hophni and Phinehas are presented as a pair of greedy and oppressive rogues who saw their priestly role simply as a means for furthering their own ends. They had *no regard for the* Lord (12). The literal translation here is 'they did not know the Lord'. Their whole life was lived in the context of religion; it occupied their time and paid their wages; but they still had no real knowledge of God. It is not so surprising that they treated his offering *with contempt* (17). Service of God had no part in their motivation, they had no fear of his power or his judgment, and the strong implication is that they had no real belief in his existence.

Their story stands as a warning to those who would treat religion as a means for manipulating others or obtaining personal gain. The writer wants every reader to be very clear about just how significant their sin was. The actual example given in verses 12–17 could be seen as trivial and a bit obscure to modern readers. As priests they were entitled to a portion of the sacrifices,[6] and they wanted their portion to be taken out before the meat was cooked rather than after. Surely this slight rearrangement of the regulations would not be too unacceptable? The common practice described here, to plunge in a three-pronged fork and let the priest have whatever it brought up, was apparently in itself a rearrangement of the regulations anyway. There is certainly no indication of such a practice in Leviticus. It may be that we are given these details to indicate that it wasn't actually the change in the regulations that was the problem. The real sin was treating the sacrifice as if the key point was providing their share. The people's preference was violently overridden and God's strict requirement that the fat was to be burned was completely ignored.

Hophni and Phinehas were sure of their own authority as priests; what the people wanted or thought that God wanted was an irrelevance. They

---

[6] Exod. 29:27–28; Lev. 6:17–18; 7:28–36; 10:13–15.

were not just inadvertently following a different pattern, they were deliberately and aggressively going against what they knew, or ought to have known, to be right. As priests they had a responsibility to fulfil God's requirements and to help the people to serve God, but they set aside both elements of this responsibility, using their position and the people's respect for religious leaders in order to satisfy their own greed. For the reader, who still has in mind the picture of power presented in Hannah's poem, the action of Eli's sons would seem as foolish as it was wicked. God would not tolerate this kind of presumption. The misuse of power by religious leaders may take a different form today, but it is equally unacceptable. To take advantage of the deference and respect felt by believers for those in positions of authority within the church is an abhorrent practice. However, maybe there is also an indication here that such respect should be reserved for those who do God's work in a way that reflects God's character, and not just given automatically to those holding a particular office. The people may have been oppressed by the two priests, but there may also have been an element of complicity in what was going on.

b. The use and abuse of power (2:18–25)

The contrast could not be more marked between the grasping materialism of Hophni and Phinehas and the simple innocence of Samuel's family story, with the generous service of the mother sewing a little coat and the child happily serving in the temple. We are told that Eli's ministry of blessing and prayer went on alongside his sons' gross misuse of their position. At the same time as they were abusing the system, Samuel was *ministering before the LORD* (18) – presumably under Eli's tuition and in a way appropriate to his age. When we find corruption within a church or denomination it is tempting to assume that the whole system is corrupt and God has absented himself. But Samuel *grew up in the presence of the LORD* (21) as well as under the shadow of oppressive immorality. Goodness can survive in the presence of evil and it is the responsibility of the believer to seek it out and nurture it. God strongly condemned Eli's sons but continued to use Eli himself in showing his grace to Hannah and her family.

However, it is clear that Eli knew about his sons' behaviour. They not only showed contempt for the sacrificial system but were involved in cultic prostitution. Sadly, that kind of sexual abuse by religious leaders – who portray sexual activity with them as service of God – is by no means unknown today. It is as abhorrent and as alien to God's real purposes now as it was then. Eli himself did not participate in their activities. He was much disturbed by what they were doing and even rebuked them for it, although they simply ignored this. Their failure to listen was a result of their contempt for God's power, but the writer here presents it paradoxically as an expression of God's power. They did not listen, *for it was the Lord's will to put them to death* (25). They thought that they were in control, but they could not have been more wrong.

c. The importance of family discipline (2:25–26)
Eli spoke to his sons but took no direct action. Perhaps he no longer had any control over them because he was so old. However, the text seems to imply that this was just another example of Eli's well-meaning but rather ineffective character. He had the right to remove his sons from priestly service but made no attempt to do so. There are many examples in Scripture, not least in the story of David (2 Sam. 13; 1 Kgs 1), where parental failure to guide and discipline at an early stage caused major problems later on. Family loyalty and love are good, but it does no good to anyone to use them as an excuse for not taking action against family members who step over the line.

Eli may have given up on his sons, but he clearly had much more success with his *in loco parentis* role with Samuel. The sons offended God and the people, but Samuel grew *in favour with* both (26). Clearly the main factor here is Samuel's own nature, but Eli must surely take some of the credit for this.

d. The buck stops here (2:27–36)
The chapter finishes with a long prophecy from an unknown man of God. It is interesting that although the sins described so far have been mainly those of the sons, the prophecy is addressed primarily to Eli. His family had received the promise of permanent ministry (as part of the Aaronic clan he shared in the priestly commission; Exod. 29:9; Num. 25:13). However, the permanent element of the ministry was clearly conditional on the continuing faithfulness of the family members. The dishonouring of God by Eli's particular branch of Aaron's line had brought that conditionality into play. The temptation to assume that any holder of a commission from God can act in any way he or she likes and God will automatically approve those actions has been common throughout

history. This is one of many scriptural passages that show such an assumption to be quite false. God's promises can never be used to support action that is in itself ungodly.

The corruption of Eli's house had been very clear to the whole of the community and their downfall would be equally apparent. Ezekiel provides an extended discussion on the relationship between the joint and separate responsibilities of family members (Ezek. 18), but Eli's responsibility here was certainly his own and not just in association with his sons. He too had 'scorned' God's sacrifice (29). It appears that Eli, even while objecting to his sons' actions, had been unable to resist the temptation of the delightful food produced from the sacrificial meat. By eating this food, or, as the writer puts it, *fattening* himself *on the choice parts* (29), Eli had colluded in their sin. He as well as his sons had rejoiced in the material benefits of the priesthood which had been obtained fraudulently. As a result of this, the sons would die and their descendants would plead to be allowed to serve in order to eat at all.

Eli is given some hope, however, in that *good will be done to Israel* (32), a real reassurance to the old priest whose care for the nation was undoubted. However, his own family will have no share in this; an alternative line will take their place. It is unlikely that this replacement was Samuel, however, as he was probably not from the Aaronic line. It is possible that the replacement priest was actually Zadok who served under David (1 Kgs 2:35). This picture of a chosen line, whose members have betrayed their calling, being set aside in favour of another prepares us for the story which will shortly be told of Saul's family being replaced by David's. For Christians there is, of course, a further underlying meaning in this prophecy; the most *faithful priest* and the true *anointed one* (35) is understood to be Jesus himself.

4. God's call to Samuel (3:1 – 4:1)

Eli's family had been rejected, but there was no question at this stage of God ceasing to work with Israel. The priestly replacement for Eli's line may have been that of Zadok, but placing the story of Samuel's calling immediately after that of Eli's rejection shows that, in terms of national leadership at least, Samuel is seen as a replacement for Eli and his sons.

What we learn of Eli here is consistent with what we have already seen. He is somewhat unsure of himself, but genuinely wanting to serve God and more than willing to act as mentor to the gifted young Samuel. It is not always easy to hand over tasks to others and Eli's graciousness is almost certainly presented as a contrast to Saul's later attempt to do all in his power to prevent the gifted young David from taking over. Generosity towards those who are called to replace us is a real mark of grace – particularly if the replacement comes as a result of our own failures.

a. Listening leading to action (3:1–7)

Samuel's experience in the night is seen as unusual and unexpected. He was not simply growing up into the kind of spiritual experience common among older believers in his community. On the contrary, *in those days the word of the Lord was rare* (1), even among the priests. Samuel was apparently a delightful, well-adjusted boy, more than willing to run around the temple doing everything that Eli asked. There is no indication as yet that he saw himself as having any special responsibility to the people or even any personal connection with God (7). He 'ministered before the Lord' (2:11) and 'grew up in the presence of the Lord' (2:21), but at this stage he, just like Hophni and Phinehas, *did not . . . know the Lord* (7) in any personal way. The difference was that with the knowledge that he did have, he 'continued to grow in stature and in favour with the Lord and with people' (2:26). To the young boy, serving God meant serving Eli in the temple, and he was glad to do it.

The story of his first encounter with God is told in a very evocative way. It is easy to picture the young boy asleep in the inner area of the temple. If Samuel was sleeping in the actual area *where the ark of God was* (3), then it shows just how much he had become integrated into Eli's priestly family. It also shows that the regulations of the law, where there are severe restrictions on access to the ark of the covenant (Lev. 16), were not fully observed at this stage. The ark plays no part in this particular story and it is likely that the mention of the ark is simply the narrator's way of preparing us for the next series of stories where the ark plays a crucial role. Certainly these chapters are a superb example of the storyteller's art. Sometimes familiarity with the overall story prevents us from getting the full impact. This account would certainly keep first-time readers on the edge of their seats.

Sometime before dawn[7] Samuel is woken by a voice and immediately jumps up and runs to Eli. This was probably not an unusual occurrence.

---

[7] The temple lamp burned 'from evening till morning' (Exod. 27:21) and it had not yet gone out.

It is quite likely that the aged, overweight and almost blind Eli needed help every night. Perhaps he also sometimes called out in his sleep or got confused as to whether he had called or not. It speaks much for the young Samuel's character that he sprang into action three times in the middle of the night, apparently without complaint, even when his help turned out not to be needed. It may be that the reader is being led towards the thought that this young man is ready and worthy to receive the prophetic word.

b. Partnership in learning (3:8–14)

After three interruptions from the usually alert Samuel, Eli begins at last to sense that there is something going on and it dawns on him that God may be involved. God could have made himself known to Samuel without Eli's intervention, so it is not insignificant that he chose to use the ailing and failing Eli to draw Samuel into a closer understanding of God and to enable Samuel to hear God's word. Eli's work may have been drawing to a close, but it was not over yet. There is great encouragement here for those who feel that their usefulness has come to an end. Samuel may have been growing 'in favour with the LORD and with people' (2:26) but old Eli still had things to teach him. The word of God thus came at last to Israel via a boy[8] and an old man. This picks up the initial focus on the power of God and his empowering of the powerless. The inexperienced youth, the decrepit priest and the barren woman are all presented as significant tools in the outworking of God's purposes.

Samuel is not yet quite convinced about the validity of Eli's conclusion that the voice he has heard is from God. He obeys Eli by responding to the fourth call but does not actually use the name of the Lord. The difference is almost certainly deliberately noted. The tentative faith of the listener is enough. One does not need to have dispelled all doubt before God's voice can be heard. Again this is a comforting thought to those who are not always confident about the strength of their own faith. When Eli asks for an update on the night's activities, he too is unsure that his initial conviction has been correct. He asks first, 'What was it he [not referring explicitly to God] said to you?' Only after hearing the message does he conclude that 'He is the LORD' (17–18).

---

[8] We can't be sure exactly how old Samuel was at this stage; the word used in verse 1 is quite flexible. However, there does appear to be a deliberate stress on his youth.

c. God's word is not always easy to speak or to hear (3:15–18)

The message was not an easy one for Samuel to hear or to report. He almost certainly had not heard the previous denunciation of the man of God (2:27–36) and to be given this fierce condemnation of gentle old Eli must have been hard. It is not surprising that he stayed in bed as long as he could and went immediately to his regular duties, avoiding Eli for as long as possible. There was a comforting normality about opening *the doors of the house of the LORD* (15). Perhaps it helped Samuel come to terms with what he had heard. It seems strange to a modern Western reader that such a young person was chosen to hear and pass on such an adult message. We normally try to protect children and young people from what are seen as the harsh realities of life, but that does not seem to have been an issue here. It may be that we sometimes underestimate the ability of the young to understand and to cope with hard truths.

Eli can't be put off any longer. He insists on hearing what God had to say, however unpalatable the message might turn out to be. In fact, there is nothing here that he did not already know. Eli accepts without question the reality and the justice of the coming judgment. Such acceptance at this stage is positive but it is also consistent with Eli's character. He has been portrayed as rather drifting through life without making too much effort to change things. He had known about his sons' behaviour but 'he failed to restrain them' (13). An accepting attitude towards situations that arise in life can be good, but sometimes it is essential to be rather more proactive. Eli stands as a warning against drifting through life with a well-meaning attitude but without taking up the responsibilities that are really ours. It is not enough just to avoid wrong actions; we must follow through and actually make the effort to do what is right.

d. Knowing leads to growing (3:19 – 4:1)

For Samuel, this first hearing from God proved to be a turning point. From this time on his relationship with God was close and constant. After a while there was no doubt in anybody's mind that Samuel was *a prophet of the LORD* (20). 'The word of the LORD' was no longer 'rare' (3:1) but was, through Samuel, freely available throughout the land – from Dan in the north right down to Beersheba in the south. It really was *all Israel* (4:1) who were ready to hear God's word through Samuel. The challenge of hearing and responding to God's word was there both for Samuel, to whom God spoke directly, and for the people, to whom he spoke through Samuel.

The text does not expand on the issue of how it was that the people recognized and affirmed Samuel as *a prophet of the Lord*, but the implication is that they had both the ability and the responsibility to judge when it was that God was speaking. In the New Testament era when the Spirit of the Lord is available to each believer, that ability and that responsibility is perhaps even more pronounced. Those who hear and discern God's word have a responsibility to speak out, but that does not remove the responsibility of those to whom they speak.

Questions to ponder

1. Why does the narrative begin with the story of Hannah? Is this coincidental or does the writer have a distinct purpose here?
2. Does chapter 1 affirm or criticize the practice of polygamy?
3. What is really in Hannah's mind as she prays her song?
4. How far could Eli be seen as responsible for the conduct of his sons?
5. Does 2:30–33 have anything to teach us about the way that God works with families today?
6. Do we underestimate what God can do through children?
7. Recovery for Israel began with a new hearing and a new speaking out of the word of God. Will growth in the modern church also depend on a renewed emphasis on God's Word?

1 Samuel 4 – 8

2. Samuel: the reluctant kingmaker

1. The ark is lost (4:1–11)

So far the focus has been on events occurring at the Shiloh shrine and the specific interests of those who lived or visited there. We now move on to a broader canvas and learn something of the position of the nation as a whole. The timing here is a little vague. Samuel is not mentioned again until chapter 7, which describes events taking place more than twenty years after the defeat recorded in chapter 4. By the time we get to chapter 8, Samuel is already old. The national recognition of Samuel's gifts did not happen overnight and the loss of the ark clearly took place during the time before he had taken over from Eli as a national leader. Thus the gap between chapter 3 and chapter 4 could have been fairly short or as long as twenty years or more. Sometimes timing is crucial to the point the writer wants to get across, but here that is clearly not so. Samuel is not mentioned at all within the ark narratives,[1] even though there are similarities in content and style between chapters 1–3 and chapters 4–6 that suggest a common writer. This may be a deliberate ploy to make it clear that Samuel had nothing to do with the decision to use the ark as a weapon in the fight with Philistia.[2]

This pattern of describing particular incidents in great detail and then covering whole sweeps of history in a few verses is repeated throughout the books of Samuel and Kings. It stands as a challenge to readers to take

---

[1] Chapters 4–6; cf. also 2 Sam. 6.

[2] It has been suggested that the ark narratives came from a separate source that was unaware of Samuel and his significance, but that is clearly not the only way of understanding the text at this point.

careful note of what we are intended or expected to learn from these stories. It also stands as a warning not to decide too quickly the significance or otherwise of seemingly trivial incidents in the lives of individuals or of seemingly dramatic events in the life of the nation. It appears that we are being prepared in different ways for the story of kingship in Israel that is soon to be told. The book began by raising questions about Israel's current leadership in the context of a consideration of the nature of power. That underlying interest continues as we are faced with the issue of whether God's power can be tapped into or controlled by making use of the sacred ark that from the time of Moses has symbolized God's presence for Israel. It is never explicitly stated that God cannot be manipulated like this, but the story is told in a way that ensures that any careful reader will be very clear about it. The narrator expects readers to think about what they are being told and to draw out these conclusions for themselves.

a. The dangers of superstition (4:1–4)

The book of Judges describes something of the continuing conflict between Israel and the Philistines (Judg. 3:1–3; 10:6–11; 13 – 16). Here we have the story of one particular battle in which the Israelites, not unusually, suffer a defeat. Like Hannah, the Israelite elders reflect theologically on their experience of life. Like her, they are convinced of God's power and are thus sure that it is the Lord's decision and not any superior power on behalf of the enemy that has caused them to be defeated. However, there are limits to their understanding and they show little of Hannah's insight. They ask no questions about their own attitudes, behaviour or even strategies. We have much to learn from the common assumption in the Old Testament that all events in life can be traced to the influence of a sovereign God. Secondary causes exist, but they are often bypassed as the participants reflect on why it might be that God has allowed this particular situation to arise. However, this story shows very clearly that this approach to God's sovereignty can also lead to misunderstandings. In this instance, rather than questioning their own actions, they jump to the somewhat superstitious conclusion that what must be missing is the tangible symbol of God's presence, that is, the *ark of the Lord's covenant* (3).

This kind of superstition that transforms helpful, God-given symbols into quasi-magical ways of ensuring God's support was a problem not just for ancient Israel. The European Reformers reacted so strongly against the wrong use of so-called sacred objects, pictures and symbols of all kinds that for many years any possible positive use of such symbols became unthinkable. In the modern Protestant church we are recovering the positive use of symbols, but we are still not immune from such superstition. Particular bodily postures in worship (whether kneeling, standing, hand-raising), the timing or method of daily Bible reading, the instruments used to support singing, the arrangement or alternative usage of the worship space, the Lord's Supper – even sincere believers can view these things in superstitious ways as guarantees of spirituality or as a means of ensuring God's blessing.

In this case, the ark is sent for and arrives accompanied by Eli's sons Hophni and Phinehas, probably revelling in their role as guardians of the ark and expecting a handsome remuneration.

b. God can't be controlled by our actions (4:5–11)

The Israelite army was ecstatic. There was no doubt in their minds that their victory was now assured. The Philistine army was horrified. What chance could they have against such powerful magic? The result was that one army apparently became complacent and the other fought with desperation. The phrasing may be deliberate, *the Philistines fought, and the Israelites were defeated* (10), with no mention of any Israelite effort. In spite of the presence of the ark, the Israelites were comprehensively beaten and many lives, including those of Eli's two sons, were lost.

The relationship between the ark and the covenant is mentioned in verses 3, 4 and 5 and may be intended to remind the reader that what God really wanted from Israel was a life lived in accordance with the principles of the covenant (although the Septuagint, the Greek version of the Old Testament, omits the word 'covenant' so this may not be a key point). However, there does seem to be an implication that the root cause of this particular defeat was Israel's assumption that God himself could be controlled by their actions; their trust was in the presence of the ark rather than in God himself. It is a continuing temptation for believers to think that if an end result seems good to them, it must, therefore, be God's will and that they can automatically expect, if not demand, that God will take action to bring about this end result. The ark narratives, both this one and that found later in 2 Samuel 6, provide a strong warning of the dangers of such an attitude. Isaiah 55:8 reminds us of God's perspective:

'For my thoughts are not your thoughts,
neither are your ways my ways,'
declares the LORD.

2. Eli's death: the end of an era (4:12–22)

a. Eli's inglorious end (4:12–18)

The scene changes sharply back to Shiloh. The writer's brilliance as a
storyteller is again apparent. One can almost smell the tension in the air,
feel the exhaustion of the fleeing Benjaminite, sense Eli's anguish as he
waited there by the side of the road, and hear the noise of the people's
despairing response to the news. It could be that Eli had been told of the
removal of the ark only after it had happened. He could no longer stand
easily, but had insisted that his chair be taken to a place where he could
watch the road through his virtually sightless eyes. He probably hoped
against hope, but *his heart feared for the ark of God* (13). In spite of his
indecisive ways, he did have spiritual discernment. He knew that the ark,
over which he had watched for so long, should never have been used in
this way and perhaps suspected that God would deal decisively with the
Israelites' wrong attitude. He clearly did not share the conviction of
the Israelite army that the coming of the ark to the battlefield would
ensure victory for them. As he waits, he hears a desolate cry go up in the
town. The difference between this cry and the shout of triumph that went
up when the ark had arrived in the army camp is probably a deliberate
emphasis on the author's part. Eli is desperate for news. He hears about
and accepts Israel's defeat and the death of both his sons, but, in spite of
his fearful premonitions, the shock of the news of the ark's capture is just
too much. His forty years as priest and leader of Israel come to a somewhat
inglorious end as he falls off his chair and breaks his neck. His excess
weight, perhaps emphasized here because it resulted from over-indulgence
in the 'choice parts of every offering' (2:29), is brought out as a factor in
his death.

b. God's power is not dependent on any individual symbol or circumstance (4:19–22)

The death of Eli's daughter-in-law, sent into premature labour by the
shock of the day's events, heightens the sense of tragedy. In her dying
moments, she too reflects theologically as she names her newborn son

Ichabod, meaning 'no glory'. Her statement that, because of the capture of the ark, *the Glory has departed from Israel* (21–22) reflects an understanding that God himself, who was Israel's glory, had left them. The Philistines' conviction that they had captured Israel's god was almost certainly shared by many Israelites. One can perhaps imagine the desolation that such a thought would bring. If God had indeed gone, there was no hope at all. This understanding would very soon be proved wrong; God had by no means been captured, but nevertheless, life for Israel did change. Eli's family did not in fact die out (1 Sam. 14:3; 1 Kgs 2:27), but they were removed from significant leadership. Shiloh lost its significance as a religious and a political centre[3] and the ark never returned there. It certainly was the end of an era.

Throughout history people have commonly drawn the conclusion that a particular tragic event must mean that God is no longer powerful or probably has disappeared from the scene. How many people have refused to believe in God any longer because of some specific tragedy in their own lives? The basis on which such an understanding is built is shown in this instance, and on many other occasions, to be fallacious. When Israel was taken into exile in Babylon, the sense that God was not powerful enough to protect his own people was very strong. However, Ezekiel made it very clear that the exile, far from being a sign of God's powerlessness, was actually an indication that he was very much in control, and was a direct result of God's judgment on the people (Ezek. 6; 20; 36). He would not allow his name to be dishonoured by other people thinking that he approved of or would tolerate the injustice, immorality and idolatry that had come to be characteristic of Judah. We, as much as the Israelites of Eli's time or of Ezekiel's time, must beware of thinking that God's power and presence can be demonstrated only in ways that we believe to be appropriate.

3. God is in control (5:1 – 6:12)

The storytelling skill of the writer continues to be evident and a note of humour appears. One can imagine the guffaws of laughter as this story was later recounted around Israelite army campfires. 'How could we ever have thought that a Philistine god would be any kind of match for the Lord

---

[3] Jeremiah (7:12–14; 26:6) tells us of the destruction of Shiloh. We don't know exactly when that took place, but it is possible that it happened at this point.

Almighty? Can you imagine the faces of the Philistine priests when they found the statue of Dagon on the floor the first time, and then his hands and his head fell off? I only wish I had been there!' But whatever the humour, we must not miss the underlying insistence that it really mattered what other nations thought of God.

a. God must be seen to be God, by believer and unbeliever alike (5:1–10)

It was important for Israel to understand that their God was not under their control and could not be manipulated into doing what they wanted simply by moving the ark. It seems to have been equally important that the Philistines understood something of God's power. God-given symbols like the ark are not to be treated superstitiously in the way that the Israelites did, but equally they are not to be treated disrespectfully in the way that the Philistines did. The Philistines were very much the enemy of Israel; nevertheless the Israelites had a responsibility towards them. God's covenant with Israel had been instituted so that they could live in such a way as to indicate to the world who God was and what he was like. On many occasions when they failed so dismally to do this, God, as here, acted on his own behalf. The challenge remains today for God's people to represent God's character adequately before those who do not follow or believe in him.

The triumphant rejoicing of the people of Ashdod very quickly turned into fear and pain. Their god Dagon had been utterly humiliated in his own territory and Israel's God shown to be powerful in an area well outside what might have been seen as his territory. It is often suggested that monotheistic thinking developed very late in Israel's history and was not really understood until the time of Amos or even Isaiah. However, one cannot avoid the monotheistic implications here.[4] Dagon was a lifeless statue which could be broken in pieces like Humpty Dumpty.[5] In no way was he comparable with Israel's mighty and transcendent Lord. But it was not only Dagon that suffered. The sudden outbreak of very painful tumorous boils was assumed also to be a result of the presence of *the ark of the god of Israel* (7). This understanding remained, even though they

---

[4] Of course, the final editing of Samuel and Kings probably took place after the lifetime of Isaiah, but this story must have been handed down over generations and the implication remains.

[5] Gordon (1986), p. 92.

were clearly also aware of the link between the boils and the appearance of rats.[6] The Philistines were in no doubt that they needed to find some way to deal with this situation.

The black humour of the lively eyewitness-style narrative continues as the ark is moved around Philistia from Ashdod to Gath to Ekron and each city suffers from an outbreak of tumours. If the Septuagint is right and these boils were in the groin, they would have been particularly painful. No wonder the people wanted to pass on the problem to some other city. It took seven months before the Philistine authorities could come to terms with the fact that their problems would be solved only by returning the ark to Israel. Their hesitation is understandable. The return of the ark would undoubtedly be seen as an acknowledgment of the power of Israel's God – as indeed it was. It could also be seen as an admission of weakness and even as an encouragement to the Israelite army to attack – a consequence which would be disastrous for Philistia as they recovered from the plague epidemic. Their problem was how to appease the Israelite God without inciting the Israelite army. Their solution was a triumph of diplomacy and strategic thinking. The political leaders decided the policy – the ark was to be returned – and the religious leaders were consulted as to the best way to do this.

b. There is sometimes much to learn from unbelievers (5:11 – 6:12)

The Philistine priests were clear that they must admit their guilt and pay compensation for the mistakes they had made in their dealings with the ark. By placing gold rats and tumours in the ark they provided a tribute, symbolically removed the problems from the five areas of their territory and at the same time acknowledged that God was at the root of their troubles. Their desire to learn from history is interesting. They had heard the story of Israel's escape from Egypt – although the earlier mention of this story in 4:8 which confused the Egyptian plagues and the desert wanderings indicates that it had lost something in the telling! The provision of a *new cart* to carry the ark was a recognition of the holiness of God. Sending no human attendants and using cows that were unused to the yoke and whose recently born calves had been penned up was a master stroke. On the one hand, it could be seen as a recognition that God

---

[6] The Septuagint mentions a plague of rats in 5:6 and the connection between the tumorous boils and the rats is confirmed in 6:4.

was so powerful that he did not need any human help in returning to Israel and could even overrule the natural desire of the cows to return to their calves. On the other hand, without causing any further offence it allowed for the possibility that the God of Israel was not the cause of their troubles. As an added bonus, it avoided the need for any direct contact with the Israelites that might have proved humiliating. Even though the cows' continuous lowing indicated their distress at the absence of their calves, when they moved *straight up towards Beth Shemesh* (12) all doubts about God's sovereignty were removed from the watching Philistine leaders.

The people of Israel could have learned much from the Philistines, as indeed could modern readers. They were able and willing to recognize that God was at work and that they needed to take action. They were able to think intelligently about what that action could be, taking into account the knowledge that they had of Israel's God. They were able to identify and allow for the possible consequences of their action and they were able to cooperate together in taking that action. There are echoes of the image of the creator God that can be seen in all humanity and it would be foolish to think that even those who can be seen as the enemies of God and his people have nothing to teach us.

4. The ark regained (6:13 – 7:2)

The reaction of the people of Beth Shemesh, a border town which may have been one of those assigned for Levites to live in,[7] showed their immediate recognition of the significance of what had happened. Their first thought was to worship God and, even though in that border territory to leave wheat too long in the fields was to risk its loss, they left their work to sacrifice. The cart was clearly new and the cows were young and healthy, but it would be inappropriate for these things to be used for anything except sacrifice. Placing the ark on *a large rock* enabled the watching Philistines to see that their gesture had been accepted. At the same time it stood as a symbol of victory for the Israelites: neither Philistine nor Israelite could be left with any doubts about the greatness of the power of Israel's God.

---

[7] Cf. Josh. 21:16. It seems less likely that the Levites mentioned in verse 15 were specially appointed to deal with the ark as it arrived, although this too is a possibility.

a. Our God is an awesome God! (6:13–20)

At this point, the reader, as much as the local citizens, expects that all will now be well and great blessing will follow for Israel. We, as much as they did, take God's reaction for granted. So the next section comes as something of a shock to us as well as to them. A large number of people in Beth Shemesh died.[8] The coming of the ark had the same disastrous effects on their town as it had on the Philistine cities. What was going on? David's reaction of anger and fear (2 Sam. 6:8–9) when Uzzah died in similar circumstances must have been repeated here in many of the mourning households. Was God after all just an arbitrary tyrant who killed at random? Surely not? The writer is only too aware that sometimes things happen in life which appear incomprehensible and even unfair. The books of Job and Habakkuk and several of the psalms (e.g. Pss 22; 38; 44; 89) remind us that sometimes the incomprehension remains and the believer has to learn to trust in spite of not understanding. However, we are encouraged to examine the context and the circumstances a little more closely.

In spite of their sacrifices, the people of Beth Shemesh had still not understood what was going on. The theme of the right and wrong uses of and attitudes to God-given symbols continues. Rather than treating the ark with proper respect and recognizing the power and sovereignty of God, they seem to have seen it as a kind of trophy signifying the defeat of the Philistines and victory for Israel. They ignored all the regulations about the way in which the ark was to be treated because it was a symbol of God's holiness (Exod. 40; Lev. 16:2; Num. 4:5; Deut. 10:8). They had no qualms about looking inside to see what goodies the Philistines might have placed there. There had been no change in attitude from the time that God had allowed the ark to be captured. There was still no real recognition that it was neither Israel nor the Philistines who had ultimate power but God who was sovereign over both.[9] Perhaps Paul had incidents like this in mind when in 1 Corinthians 11:27–30 he spoke about the seriousness of misusing the Lord's Supper. The deaths of the inhabitants of Beth Shemesh were a terrible punishment, but the consequences for Israel of

---

[8] Although the figure in the Hebrew text is 50,070 there is an unusual construction and the NIV's *seventy*, which would be a marked loss in a small town, is probably correct (cf. D. M. Fouts, *VT* 42 [1992], p. 394).

[9] Joshua had needed to learn this lesson too; cf. Josh. 5:13–14: 'Now when Joshua was near Jericho, he looked up and saw a man standing in front of him with a drawn sword in his hand. Joshua went up to him and asked, "Are you for us or for our enemies?" "Neither," he replied, "but as commander of the army of the LORD I have now come."'

failing to understand the significance of the holiness of God could be even more tragic. We do no favours to anybody by representing God as a kind old gentleman who can always be pacified by the right present. Our God really is an awesome God and, as the residents of Beth Shemesh discovered, we fail to acknowledge that fact at our peril. He will bless and protect his people but not at the expense of justice or of holiness.

b. Learning from the past (6:21 – 7:2)

Just like the Philistines, their reaction to the tragedy was to move the ark on so that it might become someone else's problem. Indeed it seems that the Philistines had learned more from events than had the Israelite inhabitants of Beth Shemesh. The Philistines at least recognized that their problems originated from their own attitudes and behaviour towards the God of Israel. It is not clear whether the residents of Kiriath Jearim were aware of what had taken place at Beth Shemesh, although it is hard to envisage that such news, both the good and the bad, would not have spread very quickly. It certainly appears that they received the ark gladly, sending their own people to collect it. Beth Shemesh had rejoiced too at the coming of the ark, but they had brought great sadness on themselves by assuming it meant God was going to do great things for them. They didn't take God's holiness seriously. However, the people of Kiriath Jearim appear to have understood that it was a different matter to welcome the ark because of the opportunity it gave for them to serve the Lord, recognizing him as the Holy One of Israel.[10] Modern believers would do well to note the difference.

The ark was placed in a specially chosen house with a specially chosen guardian to look after it. We are not told whether Abinadab's family had any choice in the matter or not, although the consecration of Eleazar seems to imply that they did. One of Aaron's sons was named Eleazar and it is possible that this family too was from the priestly line. In any event, the ark remained safely in their care for many years[11] and it appears from 7:2 that Israel had finally heard something of the message that events had been shouting out at them. At last they realized that rather than trying to make God do what they wanted, they should mourn their own sinful

---

[10] In fact this precise phrase is not used until the time of Isaiah, but the truth it expresses was relevant throughout Israel's history.

[11] The twenty years of verse 2 is sometimes seen as the time between the return of the ark and David's taking it to Jerusalem, but as Saul's reign appears to have been substantially longer than that we cannot be certain. It is probably better to see the twenty years as referring to the time before the battle of Mizpah.

behaviour and seek to do what God wanted. Sadly this was a lesson that Israel needed to learn time and time again and forms the heart of the message of many of the prophets.

5. Samuel's ministry (7:3–17)

In chapter 7 Samuel comes back into the picture, now presented as a mature and influential adult. He has noted the resurgence in religious commitment but is aware that sincerity is evidenced by action and not just by words of mourning. Like us, they had to understand that allegiance to the Lord Almighty, however sincere they might feel it was, was completely meaningless while they were also paying any kind of tribute to other gods. In the modern world, a government will not act to help one of its citizens if that person also holds citizenship of the country in which he or she has got into trouble. Similarly, God would not deliver the Israelites from the Philistines while they served Philistine gods. More than that, the concept of dual citizenship was completely unacceptable in this context. It was vital that they recognized God's total uniqueness and sovereignty; it was impossible for them to serve God unless they served him only. Citizenship in God's kingdom cannot ever be held by those who want to keep a passport that allows them to hold on to 'worldly' values. Service of God is never to be seen as a supplement, a back-up to other means of security, whether these are Canaanite idols, the god of money (Matt. 6:24; Luke 16:13) or conformity to any other of the values of the modern world. Our reluctance to speak out against ungodly values for fear of becoming unacceptable to our peers or losing our chance of promotion or wealth may lead to us becoming unacceptable to God himself. For us, as much as for the people of Samuel's day, that is not a risk worth taking. Jesus makes just this point when he uses Deuteronomy 6:13 ('Fear the LORD your God, serve him only') to resist Satan's temptation to become ruler of this world (Matt. 4:10; Luke 4:8).

a. Repentance → confession → recommitment → blessing (7:3–12)

Once Israel had signified the reality of their commitment to the Lord by getting rid of all their Baals and Ashtoreths, then it was possible for Samuel to lead them in a ceremony of repentance and reaffirmation of their allegiance to God. Their original mourning was probably as much related to their failure to remove the Philistine threat as it was to any awareness of their own sin, but now Samuel accepted the confession that they had *sinned against the LORD* (6) as genuine. They had finally realized that it was their own unconfessed sin that was the real problem, and had finally accepted responsibility for their own attitudes and actions. We do well to learn from them the damage that unrecognized and unconfessed sin can do and the benefits of actually beginning to behave as God's people. One might have expected a sin offering or a guilt offering in this context rather than a burnt offering (10), which was more often associated with praise and worship than with repentance. However, burnt offerings are also seen as effective to bring atonement and in any case the system seems to have been applied fairly flexibly in the early years of Israel's history (Lev. 1:4).

Israel had come genuinely to recognize that their only hope was in God's power, but their convictions remained fairly tentative. The Philistines, who not surprisingly were rather worried when their local enemies held a national assembly, staged what was probably a pre-emptive attack and the Israelites were petrified. In this instance, God dealt not only with the Philistines' presumption in trying to take advantage of the Israelites' preoccupation with worship, but also with the Israelites' fears. The Israelite army completed the destruction of the routed Philistines, but it was God alone who brought about their defeat. The power of the God of Israel was once more demonstrated to Israel and Philistia alike. It seems that Samuel carried on with the ceremony even as the Philistines approached. Perhaps there is a lesson there for us also of the importance of getting our priorities right. As Matthew 6:33 puts it, 'seek first his kingdom and his righteousness, and all these things will be given to you as well'. The great stone, set up as a memorial and named *Ebenezer*, or 'stone of help', would commemorate the victory and maybe also help to ease the painful memories of their earlier ignominious defeat.[12] It provided a reminder that God's help was a much more reliable support for Israel than any human effort or ingenuity. The writer almost certainly notes the irony that the description of Israel being saved from defeat by God alone is almost immediately followed by their request for a king to be their helper. Finding the right balance between exercising their responsibility to use the minds and strength that God had given them and trusting in God alone to guide and help was a continuing dilemma for Israel, as it is for God's people today.

---

[12] In the battle where the ark was taken, the Israelite army had camped at Ebenezer (4:1) and this might have been in Samuel's mind as he named the memorial stone. In spite of their foolishness and wrong attitude towards the ark, God had continued to help them.

b. Continuing service – in relative peace as well as in crisis (7:13–17)

The statement that *the Philistines were subdued and they stopped invading Israel's territory* (13) is a somewhat optimistic assessment in that the Philistines remained a problem for Israel right up until the early years of David's reign. However, there is no doubt that from this point on, in spite of some resurgences, their influence was lessened considerably. The last verses of chapter 7 mark the passage of time and set the scene for the next stage in Israel's history. A number of border towns were removed from Philistine control, apparently including those in the territory of other surrounding peoples as well as Israel. Improving relations with the Amorites – the native Canaanites who still occupied parts of the land – was a side effect of this and probably left Israel more free to deal with the remains of the Philistine threat. We gain further insight into Samuel's long ministry from his 'retirement' speech in chapter 12. At this point we are told simply of his role as a circuit judge,[13] combining religious and political leadership. His faithful service, year on year, travelling round bringing justice and encouraging worship must have had a stabilizing effect on the community. He does not seem to have been thought of primarily as a priest, although we know that he did carry out sacrifices. He also built an altar at his home base in Ramah although, perhaps because it was not the place where the ark of God was kept, this is never portrayed as a worship centre in the way that Shiloh was. It is interesting that Samuel saw Ramah as his home rather than Shiloh. Perhaps after Eli's death he thought it better to dissociate himself from the corruption of Eli's sons which must have been related in some people's minds to the shrine there.[14]

6. Sons and successors (8:1–5)

a. The use and abuse of power – again! (8:1–3)

Samuel was a stronger and more gifted character than Eli, and his ministry was much wider. He had learned a lot from Eli and shared Eli's desire

---

[13] Bethel and Mizpah are fairly close together and at least one of the several Gilgals in Israel is not far away. This has led some to assume that Samuel was more of a local judge than a national leader and that the conclusion of 3:20 that 'all Israel from Dan to Beersheba' recognized him as a prophet is an exaggeration. However, Ramah itself is at some distance from the other towns, as is Shiloh, and it is inconceivable that Samuel did not visit the ark at Kiriath Jearim. That he should later visit Bethlehem to make a sacrifice seems not to have been thought of as out of the ordinary, so perhaps we should not play down Samuel's influence too much.

[14] Or perhaps Shiloh was already destroyed (cf. ch. 2 n. 3). Later on, the central worship place seems to have been at Nob (1 Sam. 21:1) but we have no information as to when or why it moved there.

to serve God, to heed God's word himself and to seek to enable others and, indeed, Israel as a whole to do the same. However, it appears that Samuel had not learned from Eli's failures as a father. The similarities between Hophni and Phinehas and Samuel's two sons, Joel and Abijah, are striking and again are almost certainly accentuated by the writer. The particular kind of corruption may have been different, but the pattern is exactly the same: *They turned aside after dishonest gain and accepted bribes and perverted justice* (3). In other words, they abused their position and misused their power in exactly the same way as Eli's sons had done – even if their particular crimes were different. They showed the same contempt for God, the law and the people. They were clearly totally unsuitable for public service of any kind, let alone as leaders of God's people. And yet their doting father, in spite of his own undoubted integrity and insight, was apparently unable to see them in their true colours and actually appointed them as judges. Nepotism and other kinds of favouritism have arisen in virtually every society since the creation of humanity. Many unsuitable leaders have been appointed as a result. God's people, present as well as past, have not been exempt from this.

These adjacent accounts of the failure of the next generation in two families raise the question of whether any situation of inherited power is bound to lead to corruption and the abuse of power. This question remains in the air throughout the story of the monarchy, although no clear-cut direction is provided and, to a large extent, readers are left to draw their own conclusion on the matter. What is very clear is the need for taking particular care in discerning the gifts or otherwise of those in whom we have a vested interest, be they family members, friends or those we have mentored. It is no more acceptable to allow people to have power or status or even respect for this kind of reason than it is because of their wealth or perceived importance. James 2 shows this kind of favouritism to be completely inappropriate.

b. Beware of vested interests! (8:4–5)

It may be that the mention of Joel and Abijah serving at Beersheba, presumably the city in the far south of the country[15] well away from Samuel's usual circuit, is intended to provide some kind of excuse for

---

[15] Those who argue for the limited range of Samuel's influence assume this must have been another Beersheba situated nearby.

Samuel's lack of awareness of his sons' corrupt behaviour. But the elders of Israel, the tribal leaders, were very much aware of what was going on! Therefore, it is reasonable to assume that if Samuel was not aware of the problems, then such blindness was to some extent deliberate and certainly blameworthy. There was no question of Samuel colluding in his sons' actions or benefiting from their corruption in the way that the weak, food-loving Eli did, but there is also no indication that he made any attempt to stop them, not even with the kind of ineffectual remonstrances that Eli tried.

In a sense, the elders' action can be seen as a credit to Samuel's ministry. They ask the right questions and their main motivation seems to be to find a way forward for Israel that will enable them to live rightly as God's covenant people. Given the lack of perception of past leaders, one can see Samuel's beneficial influence in this. In spite of Samuel's personal desire that it should be so, continuing national leadership from Samuel's family was not going to solve Israel's problems any more than the replacement of Eli by his sons would have done. This was very clear to the well-taught elders and indeed to everyone except Samuel himself! The elders were seeking to find another way forward. They seem to have recognized that Samuel's style of leadership was good, but his sons did not *follow* his *ways*. Perhaps the appointment of a king would provide a good replacement for Samuel and enable his kind of ministry to continue.

c. There are implications, positive and negative, when leadership structures are changed (8:5)

At this stage there was no formally agreed method for a change of government; in fact, there was not really any formally recognized national government at all. The nearest they got to it was the gathering of the tribal elders and the sporadic leadership of judges and prophets. Samuel could be seen simply as the latest and perhaps the best of these judges. It is likely that the recognition for a strategic, structured and systematic response to the Philistines and other aggressors stimulated the desire for a king, but that point is not stressed here. Maybe there really was a spiritual motivation also, a desire for the kind of government that would better enable the nation to live in the way that God intended.

Certainly it was to Samuel that the elders came, asking him to appoint a king as an alternative to the leadership of his own sons. They were not seeking to bypass the current system. Samuel was recognized as 'a prophet of the LORD' (3:20), as one who was able to discern God's will and speak God's words. That they came to God's representative to ask for a king suggests they were not primarily, at least at a conscious level, seeking to replace God as their true national King. The concern that the elders expressed about the inadequacy of Samuel's sons and the fact that they were looking for a king to 'judge'[16] them seems to confirm this. However, the end of their request does introduce an element of ambiguity. They want a king *such as all the other nations have* (5). This could simply be a way of describing what they meant by a king, but the Lord's words in the next section strongly suggest that it did include the desire to imitate the other nations who seem to be more successful than them. We can't avoid the implication that they thought that trust in God was not quite enough.

The attitude towards kingship seen throughout the somewhat inglorious history of the monarchy is one of unresolved tension, and that tension is reflected in the ambiguity here. On the one hand, particularly in the Psalms (e.g. Pss 2; 45; 72; 89), the monarchy is viewed very positively; it was a God-given gift. The king was God's representative on earth, able to lead the people in their service of God and reflect God to them, helping them to understand his character and purposes. On the other hand, Samuel and certain of the prophets[17] saw the monarchy as a rejection of God and his kingly rule; the king stood between the people and God, drawing their allegiance to himself and away from God. In this view, the monarchy was neither necessary nor useful for the life of God's covenant people. Nowhere is this tension really brought out into the open. We are simply presented with the two different approaches. The monarchy can be seen as good and it can be seen as bad.

In some ways the description of the attitudes to the ark of the covenant has prepared us for this dilemma. The ark can be seen as a sacred symbol reminding Israel of God's presence and God's holiness. It can also be seen as an object of superstition, embodying a power in its own right which can be directed as desired by human 'owners'. It seems as if what actually counts is not the object or, in the case of the monarchy, the institution. What counts is the attitude towards it and the health or otherwise of the underlying relationship with God. If this point had been understood,

---

[16] The NIV's *to lead us* here translates a term associated with the leadership style that had existed in Israel since the time of Moses. The more traditional translation 'to judge us' is reflected in the title of the book of Judges, which describes the work of the men and women who had functioned as leaders during that time.

[17] E.g. Hos. 3:4–5; 7:3; 10:3–15; 13:10–11; Amos 5:26; Mic. 4:9.

many of the debates, both past and present, about which form of church government or worship style is acceptable to God might have been avoided or at least been less acrimonious.

7. Kingship: the dangers and the choice (8:6–22)

a. Does embracing the future mean rejecting the past? (8:6–7)

Samuel was *displeased* by the elders' request. It seems clear that the main source of Samuel's displeasure was his own feeling of rejection. He felt, indeed was sure, that he had done a good job (compare his farewell speech in chapter 12), but he saw this request for a king as a rejection of everything that had gone before. If the elders wanted a change, that must mean they had not appreciated what he had done. In fact, there is no suggestion of this in the elders' request. Their problem was not with what had gone before but with what might come next. Those who have spent their working lives in a particular field that new technology has made redundant find it hard not to feel that all they have done has been a waste of time. In reality, the fact that the part they played has come to an end in no sense lessens its value in its own time or in the overall progress of society. Those who have dedicated their lives and ministries to a particular youth organization or a certain musical instrument and have seen God blessing their work can feel that their whole ministry is being rejected when a church decides it is time to close down that group or cease using that instrument. Those of us who face such situations need to heed God's words to Samuel: *Listen to all that the people are saying to you* (7). We must not jump to the conclusion that desire for change implies personal rejection.

In this case, although not of course in every case where change is sought, the elders' request did involve an element of rejection, not of Samuel, but of God himself. At no point is there any suggestion that the facts they brought to Samuel were wrong. He was old and his sons did not 'follow [his] ways'. There is no doubt that some kind of change from the present position was necessary. The problem was that the people had come to Samuel, not in order to seek God's help in finding a new way forward, which Deuteronomy 17 indicates may indeed have been kingship,[18] but to ask him to set

---

[18] Deut. 17:14–20 provides instruction for the kind of kingship that Israel is to have. That there will be a monarchy at some stage is taken for granted. There is debate as to whether Deuteronomy serves as an introduction or a conclusion to the Deuteronomic history of Samuel and Kings (cf. Introduction, p. 5), but in any case Abraham and Sarah were promised right at the beginning that there would be kings among their descendants (Gen. 17:6, 16).

in motion their own predetermined solution. They were of the opinion that if they were to survive as a nation they needed to have a recognized leader with the military abilities and the international status that they thought a king would bring. The victory recorded in chapter 7 had not convinced them that God's power was sufficient.

b. Where does our security lie? (8:8)

Their motivation may not have been entirely wrong, but verse 8 makes it abundantly clear that they were still following their ancestors in forsaking the Lord and serving other gods. They were, as God had pointed out to Samuel, still seeking security in something other than following God's path. In this case their dependence was on kingship as a system of government which they perceived to have been at the heart of the success of other nations. They may not have been intending to turn away from God but they had failed to understand who God was, or the extent of his sovereignty and power. In the modern world it is often such things as education, a sizeable bank balance, insurance policy or pension fund, the armed forces or perhaps market forces, or public or private health care that are seen as essential supplements to our trust in God alone. Like the monarchy for Israel, these things are not in themselves wrong, and can often be part of the means that God uses in his care for us. Nevertheless, our dependence on them can become in reality a rejection of the lordship of God in our lives and indicate a failure to understand God and his sovereignty.

c. Accepting the consequences of our decisions (8:9–22)

God's response to their request is noteworthy. He first instructed Samuel to make sure that the people understood exactly what their request involved. In appointing a king they would be opening themselves up to tyranny. As we have already been told of the corruption of both Eli's sons and Samuel's sons, it could be that the reader, like the Israelites, is being asked to consider the possibility that all power corrupts. Perhaps the writers are deliberately emphasizing the irony of what was happening. The elders knew that the hereditary principle for appointing leaders had failed, but the best they could come up with as a replacement was an even more intractable system! To grant even more power to an individual by creating a monarchy was to risk even more corruption and oppression. In the event of such consequences arising from a decision that they had freely and knowingly made, they would not be entitled to ask God to bring them relief (18). In the same way, if we choose to participate in dangerous sports, it is not reasonable to expect God to preserve us from injury; if we choose to join the rat race, it is not reasonable to expect God to prevent us being affected by its stresses. Once Samuel had made certain that the people had heard the possible consequences of kingship, even if they had *refused to listen* (19), then God assented to their request. He instructed Samuel to *give them a king*. It is made very clear that the introduction of kingship was in no way an actual threat to God's sovereignty. God was still in control and, in spite of his personal reservations, Samuel as God's representative was the one who would take charge of the process of appointing and installing the king. In this way the institution of kingship can be seen as a rejection of God by his people and yet at the same time also as a gift from God to his people.

Samuel's instruction to the Israelites, *Everyone go back to your own town* (22), was not a dismissal of their request, but an indication that it was likely to take time if he was to deal with that request in a fitting way, making sure that the man of God's choice was appointed. Human responsibility within these narratives has great significance. The portrayal of God's response here is consistent with the picture presented throughout the Old Testament. Human beings are created with the ability and the responsibility to make choices and in general God will not overrule those choices – even if their choices could be seen as contrary to his will for them, or not in their long-term interests. Likewise, in general God will allow the consequences of those choices to stand; human responsibility is real and will be taken seriously. There seems to be a discernible pattern here; God starts from where people are at, accepting their choices, and then moving on to provide them with new choices that could lead them forward in a way that is consistent with his ultimate purposes. In this instance, the appointment of a king at precisely this juncture may not have been God's preference for Israel. He knew it would have consequences for them and, as history shows, he would not step in to prevent them from happening. Nevertheless he did not simply leave the people of Israel to their own devices. If they were to have a king, he wanted them to have the best king possible and he continued to be involved in the process. There is both a daunting challenge and a reassuring encouragement in all this.

d. Great leaders don't sulk!

Interestingly, Samuel was not as ready as Eli had been to accept that his sons were not to succeed him. But Samuel does stand as a wonderful example in terms of his continuing behaviour. He took his sense of hurt and rejection to God in prayer. He went back to the elders and warned them of all the difficulties that could or would stem from the choice they wanted to make. However, once that choice was ratified by God, Samuel accepted it and, as we shall see, gave his backing to the new procedures and his full support to the new king. This is in spite of the fact of his own continued displeasure at the situation (10:19; 12:17).

Questions to ponder

1. What relevance, if any, does Eli's weight problem have for us?
2. Are there modern equivalents to using the ark to try to manipulate God?
3. Why are three whole chapters dedicated to the ark story?
4. What is the link between symbol and reality? How useful are such symbols?
5. Are there parallels between the ark and the sacraments of the Christian church?
6. Is Samuel's ministry best seen in the isolated incidents recorded or in the continuing activity represented by the gaps?
7. Does inherited leadership or status always involve the abuse of power?
8. Was instituting kingship as the pattern of government good, bad or neutral? Is there such a thing as an ideal pattern of leadership in a given situation?
9. Should an awareness of the possible negative consequences of a choice always prevent us from making that choice?

1 Samuel 9 – 15

3. Saul: majesty and mania

1. Saul is introduced (9:1–14)

a. There is no aristocracy in God's kingdom (9:1–3)

At this point Samuel moves away from centre stage and, although he retains an important role, Saul now comes into focus as the central character. There is some irony in our first introduction to Saul. On the one hand, we learn that his father was *a man of standing*, with a lineage to be proud of,[1] and that Saul himself was an impressive young man, in terms of both gifting and appearance. There is no doubt that we are being led to understand that Saul, *as handsome a young man as could be found anywhere in Israel*, was a man fit to be king. On the other hand, Saul does not stride confidently into the picture exhibiting great wisdom or great courage or facing some great challenge with triumphant ease. Rather he emerges onto the scene as a very ordinary young man, somewhat indecisive and lacking in confidence, on the lookout for his father's lost donkeys. He presents his own background (21) as notably insignificant. The theme of God's empowering of the powerless thus continues into this next section.

The high-flown statements of verses 1–2 may have been added to match the pattern of introductions to later regnal accounts, but their addition

---

[1] *Son of Abiel, the son of Zeror, the son of Bekorath, the son of Aphiah of Benjamin* (1). In 1 Chronicles (9:35–36, 39) Saul's father Kish is described as the son of Ner, the son of Jeiel. There is also another Kish who was Ner's brother (Saul's great-uncle). This slight discrepancy with 1 Sam. 9 is easily explained if Abiel and Jeiel are seen as the same person. The omission of a generation is not seen as significant in a genealogy as long as the line is direct. However, 1 Sam. 14:51 also speaks of two brothers Ner and Kish, but in this instance Ner is Saul's uncle, the father of Abner who became Saul's general. There may be some slight confusion over two men of the same name, but it would not be unusual to have both a Ner and a Kish in two generations of the same family, so that Saul has a father and a great-uncle called Kish and an uncle and a grandfather called Ner.

reinforces the irony of the whole situation. We are not sure how many donkeys were lost, but the possession of donkeys in the first place indicates some wealth. However, the extraordinary attention to detail with which this story is told emphasizes the very ordinary nature of what was going on. Saul may have been destined for kingship but he was nevertheless an ordinary man with ordinary concerns. He was first of all one of the people, as indeed the kingship regulations of Deuteronomy 17 suggested that he should be. The concept of an aristocracy easily distinguishable from those of a more plebeian background and from whom the king should be chosen is incompatible with the theology of the covenant. A king may have a special role, but he remains a brother to all other Israelites. Like them he is a member of God's chosen people. The concern of the prophets[2] that both king and people should realize this is apparently shared by the historian. Saul had to seek for donkeys, David had to look after sheep. Leaders who see themselves as in a class apart, having special status, and people who place leaders on a pedestal all need to be reminded that even kings once had to look for donkeys!

b. In God's kingdom, minor characters matter (9:4–11)

Saul and his unnamed servant travelled many miles through the tribal areas of both Benjamin and Ephraim in their fruitless search for the precious donkeys. It is not clear why we are told so much about the journey, but by the time they reached the area where Samuel's family clan, the Zuphites, lived (1:1), Saul had certainly had enough. However, the servant, who appears, at this stage, to have had rather more initiative than Saul, suggested that while they were there they might as well look up the *man of God* (6) who lived locally and who had a reputation for discovering and speaking truth. Saul seems to have viewed Samuel as a kind of fortune teller who would take payment in return for information on such matters as lost donkeys. This probably reflects the opinion of those who had not actually come within Samuel's sphere and is not to be seen as a genuine picture of Samuel's normal activities as judge and prophet. It is possible that the editorial comment in verse 9 explaining the relationship between a seer and a prophet is meant to clear up any mistaken impression that Samuel was simply some kind of soothsayer. The servant's willingness to

---

[2] When Huldah sends a message to Josiah (2 Kgs 22:15) she seems to be making a point when she refers to him first of all as 'the man who sent you to me' and only later as 'the king of Judah' (cf. Hos. 10:3; 13:10).

contribute what appears to have been his own money to aid their search indicates a close relationship to Saul and his family. The lack of rigid separation between employer and employee and Saul's willingness to listen to his servant's advice could be seen as a further indication of Saul's potential for kingship. At least the potential was there for avoiding many of the problems of the abuse of power that Samuel had outlined. The spiritual awareness of both Saul and the servant seems somewhat vague and their seeking out of Samuel was certainly self-interested. Nevertheless, it was as a *man of God* that they sought him out, and again the potential for listening to God's word is indicated. The pattern of God responding to those who seek him, however limited their initial knowledge, and leading them on to a deeper understanding, is repeated many times throughout Scripture.[3] It is also seen in the experience of his people throughout history.

The relevance of the two young women who met Saul and his companion on their way into town is unclear. It seems to add little to Saul's story that two women who were clearly not invited to the sacrifice should tell him that it was about to happen. Perhaps, like the donkeys, the incident is recorded to emphasize the everyday reality of what was going on: Saul was about to be made king but young women still needed *to draw water*. Perhaps it is there to remind the reader that the central characters in the continuing story are not the only ones who count: the unnamed women, like the unnamed servant, have their place in the history of God's people and indeed in Scripture itself. That the women were so helpful in explaining how Saul could get hold of Samuel may simply tell us that they were good-natured people. However, it could also be an indication of the personable character of Saul and his friend and the way in which they inspired confidence and confidences. If so, this could be a further pointer to Saul's suitability for kingship. We learn of Saul's military prowess later, but it may be that the narrative here is the writer's way of pointing out that God looks for many things besides obvious gifts and abilities in his chosen leaders.

c. Worship is an important part of community life (9:12–14)

We do not have a full understanding of how public worship was conducted in the period before the temple was built. However, the picture here of

---

[3] We have already seen something of this in the way God chose to speak to the willing, serving Samuel when his personal knowledge of God was still very limited (1 Sam. 3:7).

locally held area sacrifices as well as the personal or family sacrifices such as those brought by Elkanah and Hannah ties in with what we do know. In this instance, the mention of specially invited guests indicates that this was a sacrifice brought for a special purpose. However, we have no information as to what that purpose was. The excitement of the young women indicates that the whole town was aware of what was going on. We are assured that this was a sacrifice, not just an ordinary party. The feast could not begin without Samuel, acting as priest, to *bless the sacrifice*. What we have here is a fellowship offering (Lev. 7:11–34) where part of the animal is burned as a sacrifice to God and part is given to the priest. The rest is eaten in a sacramental meal celebrating the covenant relationship between God and his people. Later writers in Kings and Chronicles had grave reservations about worship in centres built in 'high places' away from the temple, but before the introduction of the temple these were the accepted places of worship and there is no underlying implication of negativity here. Samuel was in the habit of offering sacrifices in the towns he visited, perhaps as a result of special requests or as a normal part of his visits around the circuit acting as judge.

2. Saul is anointed (9:15 – 10:8)

a. God's choice and our choices (9:15–20)

It is not clear how much time had elapsed since Samuel had originally agreed to set about appointing a king, or how seriously he had been looking. This particular feast, unknown to Saul and to the other participants, served as a celebration to mark the finding of God's appointed leader, but although 9:24 indicates that Samuel had sensed that there would be something special about this feast, it is likely that it had been arranged with some other purpose in mind. It could be seen as a coincidence that there happened to be a feast arranged just at the time when Saul arrived. Most of us have experience of the way in which different agendas so often seem 'coincidentally' to fit together. The balance between our purposes and God's purposes is an interesting one to observe! What is very clear in this instance is that the choice of Saul was entirely God's. Just the day before, Samuel had been told to expect a Benjaminite who was to be anointed as leader of Israel, and, as Saul arrived, God again confirmed that *this is the man* . . . [who] *will govern my people*. There is no room here for misunderstanding. Saul was God's appointed man.

The language of kingship is missing from this chapter. The word used in verse 16 is *nāgîd* ('leader'), which has military connotations and could have been applied to any of the earlier judges. The word *melek* (meaning 'king') is not used here and Saul is primarily anointed as a *nāgîd*. The thought remains in the air that God had had Saul in mind as the future *nāgîd* of Israel from the beginning and that if Samuel had not jumped the gun by appointing his own sons as judges, then history might have progressed in a different way. However, we have already seen that God takes human responsibility and human decision-making seriously and moves on from the reality of the present circumstances. Speculation about the 'might-have-been' or the 'what-if' is always unprofitable. Similarly, the suggestion that the appointment of Saul was a mistake and it was David who should really have been the next leader is strongly refuted by the wording here. Saul was indeed God's response to the cry of the people (16).

A note of humour creeps in as we are told that the first person Saul and his servant meet as they come into the town and request directions to *the seer's house* is Samuel himself. Saul's failure to recognize Samuel is contrasted with Samuel's immediate and God-inspired recognition of Saul. The servant's awareness of Samuel as a respected seer is immediately, and no doubt for them somewhat dauntingly, confirmed, not only by the way he greets Saul, but by his reference to the donkeys which apparently have been found. It was obvious, however, that Samuel's greeting held more significance than the reference to donkeys. His words are a mixture of clarity and obscurity. They are to eat with Samuel at the high place – a surprising statement perhaps from someone they have only just met, but quite clear none the less. Then Samuel says that next morning he will send them on their way and tell Saul *all that is in* his *heart*. This is obviously not a reference to the donkeys because that information, also very clear, is given immediately. We have the first real hint here that Saul himself may have had secret ambitions for leadership. Perhaps he was aware of a deep desire for Israel to be freed at last from the Philistine threat and dreamed of his own part in obtaining that freedom. The final statement that Israel's deep desire was for Saul and his family is also obscure, but, in the light of Hannah's song (1 Sam. 2:10), may be a further indication that there was a growing sense (perhaps even a God-given awareness?) within Israel that the future lay with an organized national leadership. Israel might not know it yet, but Saul was the answer to their prayers.

b. Prepared for calling (9:21–27)

Saul's response, which may indicate a genuine lack of self-importance but equally could simply be a normal part of formal manners, shows that he understood that Samuel was suggesting he was to play a significant role in Israel's future. That he drew this conclusion from such an obscure statement might confirm that he heard it in the context of his own sense of calling to leadership. The relationship between the thoughts of our own heart and the challenge brought by others often forms part of the confirmation of God's calling and perhaps that is what was happening for Saul here. And perhaps Saul's immediate grasp of his meaning brought encouragement to Samuel as well, confirming that he really was hearing God's word correctly.

Even though nothing explicit had yet been said, the pride of place given to Saul at the special feast would have confirmed to him that his hopes and possible fears concerning his future leadership were correct. The fact that Saul's servant was placed with him shows that his position as guest of honour was not just a matter of identifying status within the community – after all, Saul's father was 'a man of standing' (1). It was common practice to honour special guests by giving them special portions of the meat.[4] The thirty or so guests must have wondered why Saul and his servant were being singled out in this way, but their curiosity was not satisfied at this stage. One can imagine their reaction when Saul was eventually appointed king at the Mizpah gathering: 'We knew something was going on back in the Zuph area.' 'We were there when Samuel first met Saul, you know!' In any event, Saul's place at the table would have enabled Samuel to spend time getting to know him. The emphasis in the text that *Saul dined with Samuel* and later on that *Samuel talked with Saul on the roof* before they went to bed shows that Samuel thought it was important to take time to develop a relationship with Saul. There is no sign that Samuel doubted that Saul was God's choice. It could be that Samuel wanted to ensure that when Saul became king he would know Samuel well enough to listen to his advice. On the other hand, it could be that he was testing Saul to make sure he really was suitable kingship material. If it was the latter, then it appears that Saul passed the test.

When the brief anointing ceremony took place next morning, no-one else, not even the servant, was allowed to be present. It was apparently

---

[4] Elkanah's giving of a special portion to Hannah (1:5) reflects this practice.

important that the people saw from the beginning that Saul was God's choice. As his role was to lead the whole nation and not just his own tribe, it was vital that his appointment be ratified in a national gathering, open to all. This preliminary anointing was for Saul alone, preparing him for what was to come. Apart from a passing reference in 10:14 the servant now disappears from the scene. It is possible that the instruction to Saul to *tell the servant to go on ahead* was meant to symbolize the fact that from this point on Saul must make his own decisions and take responsibility for them. He should no longer rely on others, not even his faithful companion, to take the lead.

c. Building confidence in God and his calling (9:27 – 10:7)

The *message from God* that Samuel brought to Saul had two parts. First came the statement making explicit that the anointing was God's commissioning of Saul to serve him in a leadership capacity.[5] Second, there was a description of three events that would take place to confirm the reality of all that had been said. The first two events, meeting two men who would confirm that the donkeys had been found and meeting three pilgrims who would share their food with him, are unremarkable in themselves. Their significance probably lies in the fact that Samuel had predicted them, although the first could indicate that Saul and his family's business were already widely known, and the second that Saul had the kind of presence that led people to want to support or honour him. For Saul they provided evidence that Samuel's word could be trusted, that his action in anointing Saul really was carried out on God's behalf and at God's instruction. If Saul was to lead God's people in God's way, it was vital that his own faith in God was firmly based. The third sign was that Saul would meet a group of ecstatic prophets and, in an experience that would change his life, be given the spiritual power to join them for a while and prophesy with them. This personal encounter with God would transform Saul. His awkwardness and lack of confidence would become a thing of the past and his potential for leadership would become a reality. Once this has happened, then Saul can be confident of God's presence with him and in this context he is to *do whatever* his *hand finds to do*. The implication here is that as he lives in the light of God's presence and expects God to work

---

[5] In the Septuagint this statement comes in an extended form, but the extra detail adds little to what is said here.

within his life, then Saul can be trusted, and can trust himself, to make good decisions and to act decisively and confidently as events unfold. There is little sign in Samuel or anywhere else in the Old Testament that we should expect direct guidance for every action that is to be taken or every decision that is to be made. The responsibilities that God trusts his people with are very real and demanding.

Samuel's instruction only applies to the Saul who has been *changed into a different person* (10:6). The following chapters make it clear that this was not an assurance of an automatic divine endorsement of Saul's every action. Sometimes we assume that, because a person has clearly been chosen by God and used by God, he or she has a continuous and permanent ability to make right decisions and to take right actions. We can even feel that to question the words or the behaviour of such a person is to question God. Saul is a living example of the fallacy of this assumption.

d. Planning for the future (10:8)

It is hard to see how the detailed information as to where and when Saul is to meet Samuel fits in here. There is a meeting at Gilgal described in 11:14 and Saul refers to these instructions in 13:8, but why instructions for an as yet unplanned meeting should be given here is not clear. It could be that this is a recognition that even a transformed character might come across problems in doing whatever his 'hand finds to do'. If Saul was ever unsure of how to proceed or needed Samuel's help, then he was to go to Gilgal and Samuel would meet him there within seven days and sacrifice to God on Saul's behalf. Saul was not to be afraid to lead, but this did not mean that he had no need of appropriate outside guidance. The challenge of finding the balance between having the confidence to make decisions and yet not acting with arrogant autonomy faces all leaders at one time or another.

3. Saul is appointed (10:9–27)

a. People can change (10:9–13)

Saul had met Samuel with a vague notion that a man of God might be able to help find lost donkeys. He went away having had his heart changed by God. It may be that verse 9 simply summarizes the results of the whole day, but the implication is that Saul went away with a heart that was ready to accept the implications of the signs that he would encounter. It was

God, not the signs themselves, that changed Saul's heart, although the third sign, which is the only one where the fulfilment is described in any detail, played its part in transforming his character. Groups of prophets were often found at shrines around the country. This group, though, seem to have been a travelling band who happened to be passing through Gibeah at the time when Saul arrived. Their ecstatic prophecies, often accompanied by music, appear to have had a different function from the proclamation of the word of God which was the more usual function of the better-known prophets. Samuel is normally described as working alone, but in 19:20 he too is seen leading such a group at Ramah.

Because the prophetic encounter took place in Saul's home town (10:26), it was observed by those who knew the old Saul and were very surprised at this turn of events. He had not been known for religious observance before this time and his behaviour became a major talking point around the town. When Saul was a national figure, the saying *Is Saul also among the prophets?* (12) became a widely known proverb. At this stage there would have been puzzlement as to what was going on, but it may be that when Saul was made king, remembrance of these events helped his fellow citizens to accept his appointment. It is not easy to accept that those we have known well are capable of changing. This is one of several accounts in Scripture that challenge us to beware of pigeonholing people and not accepting that change may have occurred. Perhaps this incident helped Saul to accept the reality of the change in his own heart as described in verse 9. Sometimes allowing *ourselves* to change is the hardest part of all. It is interesting that once his prophetic experience was over, Saul's first action was to go straight to the high place (13). Presumably his main purpose was to worship God at the local shrine there, but probably he also needed time to come to terms with all that had happened and therefore sought the place where he might best expect to sense God's presence. It is important in any kind of spiritual transformation to take time to recognize God's involvement and to acknowledge that it is God himself, rather than any particular experience, who really counts.

b. Transformation does not mean perfection (10:14–16)

The meeting with Saul's uncle brought him back down to earth. It is not difficult to be a transformed person when we remain at the 'high place', but it is not so easy when we meet our uncles! Saul had been away for several days and the enquiry as to where he had been was quite natural.

The uncle clearly knew of Samuel and his request for Saul to tell more of the interview could have been natural curiosity, wanting to hear more about a meeting with a famous person. However, it could also be that he sensed the change in Saul and suspected that there had been more to his discussion with Samuel than talk about donkeys. In any event Saul's reply was evasive. This could be a sign of Saul's discernment: his awareness that the time was not yet right for his new status to be declared; or it could be a sign that he had not yet fully come to terms with what had happened and that the shadow of the old unconfident Saul was still in evidence.

Profound spiritual experiences can have profound effects on our lives, but do not change everything about us. We may be transformed, but we remain ourselves; conversion does not normally result in a changed body or temperament. The ungainly or clumsy person may find a new vitality or energy, but is unlikely to become a great athlete overnight. The converted melancholic may find new ways of dealing with his or her temperament but is likely to remain melancholic. Sometimes we put heavy burdens on ourselves or on others by expecting the effects of spiritual transformation to be greater than they are.

c. The choice of a leader involves everyone (10:17–24)

The rumour that Israel was going to get a king must have spread across the land since Samuel's original meeting with the tribal elders (8:4–22). Everybody was expecting something to happen, wondering who was going to be chosen. Maybe there were others who, like Saul, were wondering whether it might be them. We don't know how much time elapsed, but now the time was right and Samuel summoned all the people to Mizpah.[6] The draw was to be made, the announcement was imminent. Excitement must have been high. If the king was to have any chance of succeeding, then it was important that the whole nation was involved so that they could 'own' his appointment. He was to be their king, acknowledged as such by the whole people and therefore owed loyalty by the whole people.

It is not entirely clear if the whole of what Samuel says in verses 18 and 19 is a report of God's words or if he adds something of his own perspective in the last section. Once again the writer indicates that the decision to appoint a king who may or may not be able to save them (cf. verse 27)

---

[6] Mizpah was often used for national assemblies like this one (Judg. 20:1; 21:1, 5, 8; 1 Sam. 7:5). It was a central site that was reasonably accessible.

rather than putting their whole trust in *God, who saves … out of all … disasters and calamities* (19) may not have been the wisest choice. Nevertheless, the decision has been made and confirmed. It is interesting to note that God used their dubious choice as the basis for his rich messianic blessing.

Issues of transformation again come to the fore! There is no indication that in maintaining their desire for a king the people were continuing to sin. The only task that remained was to find the best man for the job, the man who could be seen by all to be God's choice. We don't know the method by which each tribe or clan was selected or rejected, but it was clearly some kind of lottery that was accepted as valid by the whole people.[7]

Only two people knew that the choice of the tribe of Benjamin, of the clan of Matri[8] and finally of the son of Kish, was inevitable. Samuel could of course have informed the people from the beginning that Saul was God's choice, but it was vital that they did not see Saul as being foisted on them by Samuel. When we are convinced that a particular person is God's choice then there is a strong temptation to manipulate the appointment and not to give the people chance to 'own' the choice. Samuel, however, resisted that temptation. Whatever method of selection is chosen, and even within Scripture several methods are used, God remains sovereign and does not need our intervention to ensure that the right person is appointed. In this instance the selection begins with every single Israelite[9] in the reckoning. There is no question of precedence being given to any particular group. The existence of an aristocracy was never acceptable within covenant thinking. All Israelites were equal. The king was appointed from among them and remained one of them. Today in the church we sometimes create an effective aristocracy by limiting the pool of potential leaders, consciously or subconsciously, to a restricted group: for example, middle-class professionals aged between thirty and fifty-five. This kind of thinking should probably also be seen as unacceptable.

---

[7] The ephod (not to be confused with the priestly garment of the same name, which was worn by the boy Samuel in 1 Sam. 2:18) and the Urim and the Thummim were used by priests to discern God's views on a matter (Exod. 28:30; Judg. 17:5; 1 Sam. 23:9; 28:6), although their exact nature is now somewhat obscure. Lots were drawn to identify offenders (Josh. 7:14–18; 1 Sam. 14:38–42) as well as to select people for more positive reasons here or by the disciples in Acts 1:26.

[8] This name is unknown elsewhere but it is clearly the larger clan to which Saul's family belonged.

[9] In spite of the awareness of the concerns of women shown by the writer and his recognition of their significance as part of God's people, there is no doubt that in this instance the choice was restricted to Israelite males.

Humour again comes to the fore when Saul is named but is nowhere to be found. He had *hidden himself among the supplies.* Saul's new character was evidently taking some time to emerge and he still lacked self-confidence. His apparent fear of what lay ahead of him is endearing as well as amusing and certainly understandable. There is no sign as yet of the arrogance of later years when he sought to cling to power by all means possible. Once he arrived, his unusual height meant that everyone could see who and where he was. It is possible that Samuel was referring to more than Saul's height when he asked the people to note that *there is no one like him among all the people,* but we can be sure that this played a part in confirming to the people that the right choice had been made. Even today, tall people generally find it easier than short people to secure senior jobs. The writer is almost certainly aware of the irony here as it is made very clear when David is chosen that the Lord is not influenced by outward appearances (1 Sam. 16:7).

d. New structures mean new systems, new safeguards and new resources (10:25–27)

It is now confirmed that Saul is recognized as *melek* or king and not just as a judge or a local leader. Such an appointment meant that protocol had to be established and national records kept. Samuel explains what kingship entails so that king and people can both be clear about what is expected. The *rights and duties of kingship* probably refers to those set out in Deuteronomy 17. Differing expectations have caused many problems between leaders and those they seek to lead, and it was as important then as it is now to minimize such problems, perhaps by the use of a proper job description. In this case, it was a God-sanctioned appointment in a country where God was still to be acknowledged as the leader of the people and therefore the documentation was kept *before the LORD* (25). Presumably at this stage that meant at the place where the ark of God was kept. Israel was to be quite clear that, whatever their initial motivation, the appointment of the king was made by God but was never meant as a replacement for God. On occasion the king was to act as God's representative or on God's behalf, but he was not God.

In the new era that began once this ceremony was over, nobody was quite sure what ought to happen next. So Saul followed Samuel's general instruction to all the people and went home himself. Large-scale celebrations of this kind are often inspiring to those who attend. Many go home on a 'high' that more often than not fades when they hit the reality of everyday life. Others have been moved and challenged to such an extent that they take life-changing action as a result. That is what happened here. An indeterminate number of *valiant men* accompanied Saul back home, presumably to form the basis of a standing army, ready and only too willing to help Saul defeat the Philistines. These men supported Saul because God had touched their hearts. Whatever the original objections to the monarchy, it was now in place and God was at work within that context. Saul was God's chosen king and those who helped him did so at God's inspiration. If we refuse to support a new system just because we believe that it is not the system that should have been instituted, or even that its institution stemmed from a rejection of God's sovereignty, we risk missing out on where God is working now. Those who opposed Saul here are described as *scoundrels* or sons of Belial. In this new situation those who refused to accept Saul because they doubted his ability to save them, presumably from Philistine oppression, were in effect seen as rejecting God, of doubting his ability to save through Saul. That they brought no gifts emphasizes the fact that the majority had paid tribute to Saul. If Saul was to be able to do anything he needed resources, and the only way they could be provided was through the gifts of God's people. It must have been an encouragement to Saul that so many were willing to give financial support in this way even though no system of compulsory taxation had yet been installed. His silence in the face of the troublemakers' mockery reflects a wise realization that actions speak louder than words. Sometimes it is appropriate to refute the arguments and criticisms of those who oppose us, but it is rarely best to respond to mockery and doubt with anything other than silence. Time will prove the mockers to be right or wrong. By keeping silent and making his first action as king an inaction, Saul provides an excellent example to other leaders who might face the same kind of doubt of their abilities.

4. The new king proves his worth (11:1–15)

This chapter is the high point in the account of Saul's career. From this time on problems begin to arise, but there is no sign yet of the erratic and tortured character that Saul was to become in later life. Here we have Saul proving his worth, illustrating to himself and his people that a king could, with God's help, bring deliverance to the people and that Saul was a well-chosen king. Ironically, Saul's opportunity to demonstrate his qualifications was provided not by the Philistines and not in his own home territory but by the Ammonites to the north and on the eastern side of the river Jordan up at Jabesh Gilead.

a. No enemy is more powerful than Israel's God (11:1–3)

It is a common experience for Christians to feel that they are in a hostile world surrounded by enemies. Paul, in 2 Corinthians 4:8, felt the same way. His response to this, 'We are hard pressed on every side, but not crushed; perplexed, but not in despair', was much the same as Saul's response here when the enemies were the nations literally surrounding Israel. The Ammonites were a thorn in the eastern side of the nation of Israel for many years, just as the Philistines were to the south-west, the Arameans to the north and Moab and Edom to the south-east. As with most of these groups, Israel was sometimes in the ascendancy, sometimes under threat and sometimes even made alliances. Years later, Nahash the Ammonite king had a positive relationship with David (2 Sam. 10:2), but here the picture was not at all positive. The people of Jabesh Gilead sought a negotiated surrender to bring an end to the siege that the Ammonites had laid, but the conditions imposed were cruel and unacceptable. A strong tradition that the Ammonites did indeed gouge out the right eyes of defeated foes provides authentication for this story.[10] For Nahash, surrender was acceptable only in so far as the people of Jabesh accepted the conditions of total defeat. His motivation was to *bring disgrace on all Israel*, that is, to demonstrate the total domination of Ammon and the total uselessness of Israel and, by implication, of Israel's God. His son Hanun appears to have inherited his father's ambition to bring shame to Israel (2 Sam. 10). Nahash clearly believed that his position was unassailable and that there was no possibility of Jabesh Gilead finding a champion within seven days. His arrogant confidence led to a refusal to consider any kind of compromise. Both Nahash and Hanun suffered greatly and caused their people to suffer greatly because of their arrogance. Similar refusals to come to any agreed settlement have left many such arrogant negotiators in a situation of great loss.

That surrender seems to have remained an option for the people of Jabesh and that the reaction of the people of Gibeah on hearing the news

---

[10] Cf. Klein, pp. 102–103.

was to weep showed that they shared Nahash's conviction that defeat was really inevitable. Israel was in a state of total disarray, they had no credible national army and they could see no way in which the city could be rescued. Saul had other ideas. Israel's God, who is also Paul's God and our God, is not to be set aside so lightly.

b. Positive anger and its positive effects (11:4–7)

Kingship was a very new concept for Israel and it does not seem to have occurred to anyone that this was just the sort of situation for which Saul had been appointed; but it certainly occurred to Saul. At this stage no royal court had been set up and we have the rather attractive picture of the new king Saul hearing the news as he came back from a day in the fields like any other Israelite farmer. Maybe it was this kind of rootedness in the ordinary life of the people that enabled Saul to understand the issues and to take appropriate action. Certainly the loss of that sense of identification caused Saul and his successors on many occasions to lose touch with the people and God's intentions for them. On this occasion Saul's reaction was raging anger, though whether at the presumption of the Ammonites or at the capitulation of the Israelites is not clear. His anger was not the kind that boils but paralyses; it was the kind that provokes determined action. Both the anger and the action are seen as inspired by the Spirit of God. Anger is not always a healthy emotion and we must be careful not to let it get out of hand. However, it is not always wrong and sometimes it is exactly the right response.[11]

Saul's major achievement here was to bring the people together. We get the impression that if Israel stands together, working in unison to serve a common and righteous purpose with unselfish motivation and in dependence on God, then they will be unbeatable. That thought provides a real challenge for the church today! Saul's tactics are magnificent. He assures the people that he and Samuel are working in concert, reassuring those who trusted in Samuel's ability to discern God's will but are not yet ready to trust in Saul's power to carry it out that what they are about to do has God's backing. He deliberately imitates the tactics of the Levite in Judges 19 – 20, though in a rather less gruesome fashion, to call the people to

---

[11] The Old Testament speaks often of God's anger (Deut. 4:21; Josh. 23:16; 2 Sam. 6:7; 2 Chr. 24:18; Pss 78:31; 106:40; Jer. 52:3) and on occasion Jesus is also described as becoming angry (e.g. Mark 3:5), but God's anger, unlike his love, is limited (Isa. 57:16) and there are many warnings about the misuse of human anger (Eph. 4:26, 31; Col. 3:8; Jas 1:20).

united action.[12] Sometimes it is fear alone that will stimulate action and in this instance even the people's fear is seen as being inspired by God. It speaks well for Saul that his threat is not that those who do not respond to the national challenge will be killed but that they will lose their livelihood. This punishment reflects the consequences for the people of the east bank if the nation does not respond. Bezek, on the west bank of the Jordan, far enough away to remain unnoticed by the Ammonites but within striking distance, is chosen as a mustering point.

c. The value of unity and community (11:8–15)

Community cooperation always serves to build up confidence and three hundred and thirty thousand people responded to Saul's challenge. The separation between the forces of Israel and Judah shows that the north–south divide, which later degenerated into separation and enmity, had its roots in the very beginnings of national life. David and Solomon managed to hold the tribes together, but it was not surprising that the arrogant and foolish young Rehoboam who ignored the legitimate demands of one part of the people did not (1 Kgs 12). Saul here stands as an example and Rehoboam as a warning to leaders of churches that different interest groups can be held together to form an effective army in God's service or can be driven apart. It may be that splitting up is sometimes the right thing to do, but we should be very sure that it is not frivolous selfishness that breaks apart a fragile unity which in spite of its weakness is serving God's purposes. Saul was absolutely sure of victory; his confidence, passed on to the people of Jabesh, stemmed from the assurance of God's Spirit but was now also based on the forces available to him. The Israelite army was largely untrained and untried, but verse 11 demonstrates Saul's strategic ability. Perhaps he and the 'men whose hearts God had touched' (10:26) had spent the time since his appointment in planning for such an attack.

In national terms this was a fairly small skirmish, easily dealt with once a united front had been achieved. However, it served to establish Saul's credentials with the community. He further demonstrated his statesmanship by declining to take revenge on those who had refused to acknowledge him as king. The rationale for sparing the rebels was that the victory was really God's. God's graciousness to Israel should result in grace

---

[12] It is possible that both the Levite and Saul were following a known practice of calling people to help. Gen. 15:9–17 and Jer. 34:18 do not exactly reflect what is going on here, but both mention a ceremony which involves passing between the split parts of an animal.

and forgiveness shown within Israel. This approach, also seen in David's attitude to Shimei in 2 Samuel 19:22–23, is a precursor of Jesus' teaching in the Lord's Prayer and elsewhere. Those who seek God's grace and forgiveness for themselves must learn to demonstrate it to others. In any case, it would have been very foolish indeed for Saul to do anything to disturb the fragile national unity that was only just beginning to emerge.

It was appropriate to follow a national victory and consolidate national unity with a national celebration. Gilgal stands as a symbol of new beginnings. It was the place where Joshua first camped on entering the Promised Land and it was fitting that the nation should come together there and sacrifice *fellowship offerings before the* Lord. The fellowship offering, where the communal meal symbolized the communion not only between all the people participating but also between God and people, had an atmosphere of celebration and enjoyment and was an ideal occasion to reaffirm Saul's kingship. Saul's initial anointing at Ramah indicated to Saul himself that God had chosen him. The ceremony at Mizpah indicated to the people that Saul was God's choice. At Gilgal the people, after having seen Saul in action, were able to affirm that he was their choice too. Kingship in Israel could never be effective unless both public recognition and divine sanction were in place. To seek to lead God's people without their consent and support does not take seriously the fact that they are God's people, themselves in relationship with God. To seek to lead without being called by God is also a denial of the reality of God's relationship to his people.

5. Samuel's speech (12:1–25)

The writers of the books of Samuel and Kings often use speeches to summarize teaching and to make major points. Hannah's prayer could be seen as fitting into that category and Samuel's speech here certainly does. Some commentators take this to imply that the speech was composed at a later time and placed in the mouth of Samuel. However, the passion and the compassion, the pleading and the slight hint of petulance, the commitment and the challenge, certainly reflect what we know of Samuel at this stage of his life.

a. Moving on gracefully

Now that Saul's appointment has been fully ratified and recognized, Samuel realizes that his own role has changed. It does not mean the end of his own ministry. He has not lost the capacity to hear God speaking and he will remain in a consultancy role acting as spiritual advisor and guide. However, his function as judge and leader of the people has now been superseded by the appointment of a king. It is an appropriate time for him to bow out – as gracefully as he can manage. Retirement comes hard to some and stepping down from leadership can be very difficult, particularly for those who have led God's people. The concept that those who are in the service of God never retire can be used sometimes as an excuse to avoid acknowledging a necessary change of role. For Samuel it is made harder because of his unhappiness with the new system, but he does not shirk the task. Marking such a change with a speech of this nature can help both the individual concerned and those more indirectly affected to come to terms with the situation. Samuel therefore takes what may be his final opportunity to address the gathered nation. He wants to justify and clarify his own position and to rebuke, warn and encourage the people. It is probably significant that after this point Samuel seems to spend very little time at court. His consultancy role does not involve constantly looking over Saul's shoulder. The task of many a new minister or new leader of a Christian organization has been made more difficult by the doubtless well-meaning intervention of the previous holder of the post who still wants to be involved. It is easy for what was intended as support to become interference, and we must take care when moving on that we really do leave the pitch clear for our successors. At the heart of a consultancy role is the concept that advice has been asked for!

Samuel's speech deserves the same kind of detailed examination as Hannah's prayer.

b. Looking back on a lifetime of service (12:1–5)
i. Retired, not sacked!
As he began his speech, Samuel made it clear that he had not been deposed. It was he who, as their leader, had listened to their request and appointed a king for them. The reference to his age and to his length of service may be seen as providing justification, to himself as much as to the people, for why a change was thought necessary. The reference to his sons is ambiguous, perhaps deliberately so. It is not clear whether we should see it as a tacit admission of the role that his sons had played in the change of system, or an indication that he still did not acknowledge that there was a problem with his sons, or simply a reference emphasizing Samuel's age.

ii. An unsullied testimonial

Second, Samuel wanted to ensure that his integrity was not in question. The fact that he was stepping down was in no way to be seen as a judgment or a punishment from God. The memory of the night when he had had to bring God's message of judgment to Eli must have remained with him throughout his life. He had taken every care to avoid ever having to be the recipient of such a message. He had never taken advantage of his position or the power that went with it. He had not sought to obtain large gifts from the people; he had never altered his messages in the light of the hearers' wealth or status; he had never knowingly acted in an oppressive or deceitful way. If he had done so unknowingly he wanted to put it right before he stepped down.

iii. An example to emulate

Samuel's record is impressive and stands as a model for any leader. The questions he asks of himself could well be used as tests and targets for our ministry. Have we taken advantage of our position in any way? Have we been oppressive or deceitful or demanding? Have we adjusted the message because of financial pressures? The fear of sounding boastful (a powerful force at least in modern British culture) should not prevent us from honestly assessing the achievements of a lifetime. In this instance it was clear that Samuel's analysis was accurate. The people were more than happy to agree and even to swear that he had *not cheated or oppressed* them in any way whatsoever. Any problems that they might have had with Samuel's sons had not raised doubts in anyone's mind about Samuel's own personal integrity. There may be an underlying intention here, either from Samuel himself or from the editor, to point out that the actions that Samuel had suggested might result from the appointment of a king (8:11–18) had not been the characteristics of his own term of service. Samuel had nothing to put right, but his desire to make sure that the decks had been completely cleared before he left his position was a good one; as much worth imitating as his exemplary record.

c. Looking back over God's past dealings with Israel (12:6–11)

i. Providing a necessary perspective

Once the issue of his own integrity has been settled, Samuel moves on to provide a historical overview, putting their request for a king in perspective. The inclusion of historical reviews like this is common throughout the Old Testament and is seen also in the New Testament.[13] A sense of unity with those who had gone before and an awareness of strong and clear links with the past was very important to the Israelites. Samuel wanted to remind them that they were simply one frame in the film of God's continuing relationship with his people. To reflect on what God had done for them in the past could enable them to live more effectively in the present and to prepare with faith for future action. Again, such reflection is an approach certainly worth imitating.

ii. Knowing God

Samuel has already defended his own integrity; now he provides evidence of God's continuing support and help for his people. The evidence is given *before the Lord* (7). This history is not Samuel's own invention, to be accepted or rejected at their pleasure. He reminds them that the God he is talking about is the one who used Moses and Aaron to bring their ancestors out of Egypt (Exod. 3 – 15). It was as important for them as it continues to be for us to understand and acknowledge what their and our God is like. He is not like the gods of the surrounding peoples whose power was expected to apply only over a small area. He is the universally powerful God able to redeem his people.

iii. Failure and forgetfulness, despair and deliverance

At this point Samuel's intention to provide them with *evidence . . . as to all the righteous acts performed by the Lord for you and your ancestors* (7) appears to have been overtaken by his desire for them to realize how sinful they and their ancestors were. We know that even the Philistines had been significantly affected by their knowledge of God's redemption of Israel from Egypt (1 Sam. 4:8; 6:6), but the Israelite ancestors *forgot the Lord their God* (9): forgot who he was and forgot what he had done for them. In verses 9–11 Samuel provides a precis of the story of Judges.[14] Almost as soon as they arrived in the Promised Land the Israelites began to act as if God was no longer relevant to them. A familiar pattern emerges: they were overrun by a whole series of enemy powers; in their despair they

---

[13] Stephen's speech (Acts 7) and Heb. 11 are examples of this.

[14] These verses recall the language as well as the content of Judges (for example, *sold them into the hands of* comes in Judg. 3:8; 4:2; 10:7, and *cried out to the Lord* is found in 3:9; 4:3; 10:10). We can't be certain when the stories were brought together into a book, but it seems very likely that the book of Judges and not just the stories it contains had been reflected on in the composition of this speech.

turned to God, promising undying service; God responded by sending a whole series of deliverers (11).[15] Each deliverer brought relief and renewed stability, but the people on each occasion forgot that God played an essential part in their continuing stability, and the pattern would be repeated. We can't be sure whether the reference to Samuel in verse 11, when one would have expected to read of Samson, is a copyist's error or a deliberate ploy. It is quite possible that Samuel was drawing their attention to the fact that the God who delivered in the past was still delivering today and the victory at Mizpah which was recorded in chapter 7 was evidence of that. Saul's victory at Jabesh Gilead (ch. 11) was wonderful, but in fact God did not need a king to be able to deliver his people. It is also possible that Samuel again needed them to realize that he really had been sent by God and used by God on their behalf. Even heroes of the faith need reassurance sometimes!

d. Looking around at the current situation (12:12–21)

i. Problems that arise from attitudes won't be solved by new systems

On all the occasions when the Israelites got into trouble and needed to cry out to God, the problem was not that the system of leadership was wrong but that they had turned away from God in the first place. Their renewed security came precisely because they did cry out to God and he sent them the necessary help. Kingship might have been the right way forward for Israel at that particular time – although Samuel was very reluctant to acknowledge any possibility of that – but there was no doubt that unless their whole approach changed, it would never provide a permanent answer to their past problems. When they faced a new problem in the form of *Nahash king of the Ammonites* (12), turning to the king instead of turning to God would do them no good. Even if it was not the recent trouble with Nahash that led to the original request for a king, his aggression would have been uppermost in people's minds at the present time and the principle remained the same. Even though it had been proved time and time again that turning to God for help had been successful, the people now wanted to find a new method. Samuel is in a quandary here. On the one hand, he is totally opposed to the decision that has been made and he wants the people to know what he thinks of it. On the other hand, he

---

[15] Jerub-Baal is the alternative name for Gideon. Barak, as military leader, is mentioned in preference to Deborah, although Judges presents Deborah as the more significant figure. In fact, the Hebrew text has *Bedan* here, a name unknown elsewhere, and it is almost certainly Barak who is meant.

realizes that the decision has been made and he is very concerned that their action and attitudes from here on are the right ones. One can almost hear him taking a deep breath and getting back to the point.

ii. Leader and led must both serve God

Here in front of the people was Saul, the king they had chosen and also the king that the Lord had set over them. It was vital for them to realize that God was still in ultimate charge. As long as they saw the king as God's representative, ruling them as God's people, then it would be all right. The situation was the same as it always had been. Both king and people owe allegiance to God and as long as both *fear the* Lord ∴ . *serve and obey him and do not rebel* (14) then all will be well; but if they turn away, then, king or no king, they will receive at God's hand the same punishment as their ancestors. At this point Samuel's frustration appears to get the better of him and he asks God to send down an electric storm, not apparently to demonstrate God's power but to convince the people of their own sinfulness and in particular that they had made a mistake in asking for a king. Extreme weather conditions have always had a strong impact on those who experience them and Samuel's listeners were no exception. They were completely convinced that not only was God powerful but that asking for a king had been a bad move. We are told that they were *in awe of the* Lord *and of Samuel* (18). There may be an implication here that Samuel's motives also included the desire to remind the people that he himself was not without influence.

iii. Disagreements can be pushed too far

The people's response seems to have evoked a change of mood in Samuel. Perhaps their request for him to pray to *the* Lord *your God* made him realize that he was in danger of separating himself from the people and causing them to forget that the Lord was indeed their God and not just his. Perhaps he thought he might push them so far that they would ask him to set aside the monarchy after all, whereas he knew in his heart that whatever the rights and wrongs of their original request, God had now chosen to work through kingship. He hastens to reassure his hearers. God has made them *his own* people and, in spite of their sin, is not about to reject them. The important thing is that they put all their energy into serving him.

Turning to *useless idols* (21) – and Samuel again stresses their uselessness – is completely incompatible with their status as the people of

God. It is as if Samuel can't quite bring himself to say it, but the corollary of his words is that serving idols will separate them from God but serving a king will not. Indeed, if the right king leads them in the right way, then they may be better enabled to live as God's people. It is sometimes right that we criticize methodologies and structures, but we must never give the impression that disagreements in these areas come in the same category as those over moral or doctrinal issues. Introducing a different method of leadership or a different kind of music or anything else of similar vein will not in itself either bring us closer to God or separate us from him. We must always be very careful not to make it appear that our preferences are the same thing as God's requirements.

e. Looking forward to continuing life as God's people (12:20–25)
i. God's continuing support and power
Idols may be useless, but Israel's God most certainly is not. Idols can do them *no good*; Israel's God is the one, the only one, who can rescue them. They may have made a mess of things, but God's continuing care for them should never be doubted. They belong to God and whatever they have done in the past, if now they are willing to *fear the Lord and serve him faithfully with all* [their] *heart*, then the future is bright.

ii. Samuel's continuing commitment
As for their request that Samuel pray that they 'will not die', he commits himself not only to pray for them, but also to teach them the right way to live. His stepping aside from leadership does not involve any lessening of his commitment to them and their welfare. If the people and their king are *swept away* by God, which remains a possibility if they do *persist in doing evil*, then it will not be because they have not been taught *the way that is good and right*.

iii. Continuing responsibilities of the people
This must have been a powerful speech to listen to. The equivocal nature of Samuel's position and the frustration, perhaps even angst, that he experienced can be seen clearly, but it doesn't really distract from the underlying message. The insight we are given into Samuel's struggle can be a great encouragement to those who are wrestling with similar dilemmas, wanting to make it clear that the place where they are standing is not the place where they want to be, but at the same time wanting to move on from

that point. It is particularly encouraging that in the end, Samuel's faith, his integrity, his understanding of God's word and his pastoral heart win through. Samuel may have been an old man who struggled with the changes in the world around him, but he was indeed a 'man of God' (9.6) who served his Lord well to the end. There would have been no doubt in the minds of his listeners that it was God's support, God's requirements and God's judgments that really counted. Samuel may have been able to teach them the right way, but it would all be a waste of time unless the people themselves took up the challenge of the responsibilities that were theirs because they were God's people. Then as now it was not the ability to deliver great speeches, call up electric storms or even pray great prayers that made a great leader. It was the ability to enable people to take up their own responsibilities and to grow in their own relationship with God.

6. Saul exceeds his authority (13:1–22)

a. God chooses imperfect people

Chapter 13 begins a new and extended section summarizing the key events of Saul's reign in a way parallel to the accounts of the reigns of later monarchs found in the books of Kings, if more extended than most of these. It is not absolutely clear how this section relates to the previous chapters. The following chapters in general present Saul in a fairly negative light, perhaps using sources which were compiled in the southern Davidic kingdom where anything to do with Saul's family came to be viewed with suspicion. However, by prefacing these chapters with the positive depiction of Saul in chapters 10 and 11 the writer makes clear that Saul's reign must not be seen as a mistake.[16] We have already seen that Saul was God's choice and that he was a good choice. Any failures in Saul's reign came not because he was the wrong person in the wrong place, or because there was never any possibility that he would succeed, but because he failed to keep *the command the* LORD *his God gave* him (13).

We can sometimes jump too quickly to the conclusion that because a particular appointment has not worked out it must have been wrong in the first place. In doing this we fail to take seriously the continuing responsibility of the one doing the job. Of course, it is possible that the

---

[16] David Payne suggests that the desire to defend God from the charge of making wrong choices is a clear motif in the books of Samuel ('Apologetic Motifs in the Books of Samuel', *VE* 23 [1993], pp. 57–66).

responsibility for failure lies with those who made the appointment, but it is clear that in this instance that is not the case. Neither God himself nor Samuel is to be blamed for Saul's sin. Saul had the potential to 'fear the LORD and serve him faithfully with all [his] heart' (12:24), but he did not do so. It was for that reason and no other that he 'perished' (12:25). God must have known that Saul would fail but he still gave him a chance. Indeed, if God were to choose only those who he knew would not fail him, then the Bible would have been a very short book! Similarly, if God had been as selective as some of those in the church today who take responsibility for making appointments, then perhaps the appointers themselves might have been excluded! We do not know why so much time, including so many mistakes from so many people, was allowed to pass before God sent his Messiah, but we do know that both before and after the coming of Christ God entrusts fallible people with the responsibility to carry out his purposes in his world.

b. The everyday reality of the new system (13:1–2)

At some stage in the transmission of the text the figures from verse 1 were omitted. The numbers given in the NIV are traditional (cf. Acts 13:21) rather than textual, but are probably about right. Certainly Saul's reign was longer than the two years that the current Hebrew text states. It is just possible that this refers to two years having passed since the reaffirmation of Saul's reign at Gilgal (11:14–15), but that is not really the impression given. Time certainly has passed since the events at Gilgal. Saul has developed a standing army of three thousand trained men and the system is in place for a national call-up to be arranged should circumstances make that necessary (cf. verse 4). It may be that Saul has even set up the beginnings of a royal court in the region of Bethel (2). Two-thirds of the regular army were based with him there and the rest were stationed near the family home at Gibeah under the supervision of Saul's son Jonathan, who was still quite a young man.

c. Problems and opportunities (13:3–4)

The writer's ability to take the reader right into the situation and to provide real insight into the characters is as clear in this account of military activity as it was in the story of Hannah's family. We see Jonathan, youthful, full of confidence and enthusiasm, very definitely an activist rather than a strategist. He attacks a small Philistine base near his home, the *outpost at Geba*, without fear or thought for any consequences. There is no sign of the carefully worked-out strategy seen in Saul's campaign at Jabesh Gilead (1 Sam. 11). This was a clearly achievable undertaking, so Jonathan undertook. There is no evaluation, positive or negative, of Jonathan's action, just the recording of the fact. *The Philistines heard about it* is a somewhat ironic way of describing their angry reaction. Saul heard about it too and, like the experienced campaigner he was becoming, had no doubts at all that the Philistine response would be fierce and furious. Jonathan had solved one problem, but in doing so had he simply created another, greater one?

Saul immediately recalled the national army. In this instance they would need as many troops as they could get. Jonathan's action may be seen as foolhardy, but it could also be seen as at last providing the Israelite forces with a real opportunity to triumph over the full might of the Philistines. The relationship between problems and opportunities is always an interesting one to explore. Saul named Gilgal as the rallying point for the called-up soldiers. The reminder of the victory celebration and coronation held there would be a confidence-booster for those who gathered. It was far enough away from Philistine territory to allow them to gather in safety while the regular troops were left to hold the front line. It also gave the opportunity for Saul to send for Samuel to come and offer sacrifices in the way that he had promised (10:8).

d. So far, so good (13:5–8)

Thus far Saul had apparently done everything right. He took responsibility for Jonathan's action – verse 4 informs us that the Israelites were told it was Saul who had organized the attack; he planned wisely and meticulously; he sought to ensure the Lord's blessing before he took action; and, while others not unnaturally were panicking, he waited patiently and apparently confidently for seven days for Samuel to arrive, as promised, and carry out the sacrifices. As the news arrived from Michmash he perhaps began to worry but he continued, apparently faithfully, to wait.

The account of the unfolding events is a little confusing, perhaps reflecting the confusion involved in this kind of battlefield encounter. The Philistine onslaught was huge; not only were there vast numbers of troops involved, but thousands of chariots as well. In fact, chariots would have provided little if any advantage in a battle conducted in the hill country, but their presence could well have daunted the less-well-equipped

Israelites. The portion of the army standing guard at Michmash knew they had no hope, so they retreated into the surrounding hills. This could be seen as a good tactic. They would have more success with smaller guerrilla attacks than they would in a one-sided major battle. However, it is quite clear that at least some of the troops were in fact running away (7). Saul knew and had presumably told his men that Samuel was due to arrive on the seventh day. But surely this was an emergency and he would come a few days early? He did not. It is not surprising that those troops who were waiting with Saul were petrified, nor that as the wait for Samuel became extended, many of them began to drift quietly away.

e. Jumping the gun (13:9–12)

Saul, hearing of the advance of the Philistine army, seeing his own troops scattering and desperately needing to seek the Lord's favour, could see only one solution. When the seventh day dawned and Samuel had still not arrived, he *felt compelled* to offer the sacrifices himself. If only he could have waited a few more hours, how different the story of his life might have been. Samuel arrived, exactly on schedule, just as Saul was completing the sacrifice.

Saul's argument, told from his own perspective, is convincing and the first response of the reader is to feel sympathy and even to agree that there was surely nothing else that Saul could have done. The implication in Saul's words is that it was Samuel, not he, who was at fault. If only Samuel had arrived on time, then the problem could have been avoided. However, as verse 10 explains, Samuel did arrive on the day stated, just not at the beginning of it. An unwillingness to take responsibility for our own actions is often one of the early signs of an unfitness to lead. It is made abundantly clear in any case that Saul's chosen course of action, to offer the sacrifices himself, was completely unacceptable. The way forward for any leader who is struggling to exercise the power he or she has been given is not to seek to exercise a power he or she has not been given. Saul had disobeyed God's command through Samuel by failing to wait the full seven days. His offence was compounded by his attempting to exercise a priestly role that he had not been given.

f. Actions do have consequences (13:13–14)

Saul does not seem to have realized the implications of his action. He has no apparent qualms about telling Samuel what he has done, having convinced himself perhaps that he really had no choice and that it was all Samuel's fault anyway. But we are left in no doubt that this behaviour, described simply as his being *foolish* and as not keeping *the LORD's command*, would have serious consequences.

From one perspective, the consequences of Saul's actions don't seem particularly severe. There is no suggestion that his role as king is being removed from him. The only actual consequence is that the monarchy will not become hereditary; Saul is not to be the founder of a royal dynasty. Like Eli, and like Samuel himself, he is not to be succeeded by his sons. It may be that Samuel speaks sadly here, from his own experience, knowing that Saul would have had hopes and fears for his sons, even though the possibility of a dynasty so far has not been raised. Eli and Samuel had both been able to accept the situation, however reluctantly, and to support and mentor their successors. But for Saul, the thought of an unknown successor existing somewhere in the background took root and began to eat away at him, in the end preventing him from completing the task that was still his to do.

g. The job remains to be done (13:15–22)

We are not told whether Samuel did carry out sacrifices before he left, but he did leave. Perhaps his action was intended to symbolize that the task of combatting the Philistines remained Saul's responsibility and had still to be carried out. The confident national army that had gathered at Gilgal had been reduced to a paltry six hundred. Those who have ambitions for leadership, wanting to enjoy the status and the power, sometimes come down to earth with a bump when they are faced with a huge task, a lack of resources and the realization that the buck really does stop here. However, on leaving Gilgal Samuel went to Gibeah, Saul's home, where Saul, Jonathan and the remaining army had based themselves, so perhaps Saul and Samuel, in spite of the latter's rebuke of Saul, were still working together.

Apparently, in spite of the huge show of force from the Philistines, the full-scale battle never took place. The Philistine forces did take over sections of previously held Israelite territory, including the area of Saul's camp at Michmash, but raiding parties were prevented from reaching the area where Saul's depleted army remained. Israel was not forced into total surrender but was able to engage the Philistine forces in constant minor skirmishes, in spite of their lack of weapons. This shows that Saul and his troops were not lacking in courage or ability and indicates that Saul was indeed doing his best to fulfil his commission. Verses 19–20 describe how the Philistines had developed a monopoly on what might be seen as up-to-date technology and used their technological expertise to manipulate the economies of surrounding nations as well as to ensure military supremacy. This short passage makes interesting reading for those who have observed similar tendencies in the modern world. There is a touch of realism about this description of the lack of ironsmiths in Israel and the shortage of metal weapons and armour. It was not unusual for only a few leaders to be able to afford weapons, but it had not prevented the Israelite victory of chapter 11 and wouldn't prevent the same thing happening in chapter 14.

7. Jonathan takes action (13:23 – 14:23)

The following incidents are recorded in a dramatic style, possibly indicating that they were originally oral stories, with occasional editorial comments added. One can imagine the excitement of young Israelites sitting around the campfire, as they heard of Jonathan's daring courage. The stories are exciting and worth telling in their own right, but within the overall context behind the stories there is an underlying discussion about what God really requires of his people and how God's will can be discovered. Jonathan's understanding appears to be very different from Saul's!

a. If an enemy is to be defeated, someone has to take the initiative (13:23 – 14:2)

The problems resulting from Jonathan's previous attack on the Philistines do not seem to have dampened his enthusiasm. Perhaps from his perspective, the situation had not changed. They were still faced with a range of Philistine outposts, presumably left to guard certain routes after raiding parties had passed by. As far as Jonathan was concerned, these outposts still had to be dealt with one by one if the Philistines were ever to be driven back into their own territory. The picture we have of Jonathan, as of so many of the characters presented to us, is consistent throughout the accounts. He was brave and daring, an impatient activist with a great capacity for commitment to God, to Israel and to people. He inspired great loyalty in his troops and his own armour-bearer was willing to follow him anywhere. Once he had a particular course of action in mind,

Jonathan set about carrying it through immediately. The thought of following protocol and seeking his father's approval never occurred to him. The emphasis placed on the fact that Saul was not told provides a hint that this will have repercussions in the ensuing events.

Saul at this time was staying with his faithful band of six hundred men near Gibeah *under a pomegranate tree* (2). Why we are given this information is not clear unless it is meant to contrast Saul's inactivity with Jonathan's action. The pomegranate bush is quite small and indicates that Saul was sitting alone resting, or maybe thinking.[17] Taking time to rest and reflect is often an essential prelude to action, but there is no indication that Saul was formulating plans to deal with the Philistines. Samuel's pronouncement that Saul would eventually be replaced by someone other than his son seems to have led to such a loss of heart that he was becoming incapable of carrying out his responsibilities. Jonathan apparently decided that unless he got on with it then nothing much would happen. It is not always appropriate for junior leaders to act on their own initiative, but when their superior seems to have lost the ability to take difficult decisions perhaps that is the only way to make things happen.

b. Functioning under judgment (14:3)

One of those with Saul was Ahijah, Eli's great-grandson, clearly now acting as a priest.[18] The introduction to Ahijah is detailed, drawing attention to the fact that he was Eli's descendant and he was a priest, perhaps deliberately stressing that the judgment on Eli's family described in chapters 2 and 3 had not, as might have been supposed, meant complete destruction. Sometimes our assumptions about the kind of punishment that God intends go way beyond what God has actually stated. Eli's family had suffered much loss but there was nothing in the prophecy (2:31–36; 3:13–14) that prevented any living descendants from having an effective ministry. Saul's reaction to the judgment pronounced on himself and his family (13:14) might well have been different if he had grasped the significance of Ahijah's presence in his entourage. Note that we are told again that no-one had noticed Jonathan's departure. Perhaps the writer is making the point that no effective guard had been placed on the camp – if

---

[17] Trees were often significant places, used as meeting points or even as courtrooms (Judg. 4:5), but something as unimposing as a pomegranate tree would not normally be in that category.

[18] He wore the priestly ephod and in verse 18 Saul asks him to act in a priestly capacity.

a departure went unnoticed, so might an arrival – but it is more likely that the writer is again preparing the reader for what is to come.

c. When God's purposes are clear, obedience means action (14:4–14)

The cliffs on either side of Jonathan's path were obviously well known. Everyone would have been aware that this was a very difficult and dangerous undertaking. Anyone who happened to be looking would have been able to observe the two men from above and lay a trap for them. The implication is that the Philistines were too sure of themselves and the Israelites too fearful to bother looking. It is clear that Jonathan's action was inspired by a total conviction of God's power. He couldn't be completely sure that God would use him to save Israel, but he was sure that God could and would save and if Jonathan didn't try, he would never know whether it might have been through him (6). The contrast with Saul is marked. There was no room in Jonathan's mind for long and anguished debates as to what might be God's precise will in this situation, nor for holding back until he was completely sure that his action would be successful. That the task needed doing was already abundantly clear. As far as he was concerned, Saul had already been commissioned and equipped by God to do it. What possible reason could there be for further delay? Sometimes the apparently spiritual decision to seek further guidance can simply be an excuse to procrastinate. Jonathan's active faith has much to teach us in this regard.

Jonathan's intention was to fight, therefore there was no point in hiding from the Philistines, and he and his equally brave armour-bearer deliberately drew attention to their presence. They decided to take the Philistines' reaction as a sign; not as to whether they should fight or not, but whether the fight should be at the bottom or the top of the cliff! The Philistines, perhaps just a small handful of guards bored with the lack of any Israelite opposition, were amused by the sight of the two men and mockingly called them to come on up, arrogantly confident of their ability to defeat them. Jonathan was equally confident, not only in his own ability but in God's power and desire to save Israel. The cliff climb required both hands and feet, so while they were climbing no weapon could be used. Defeat at the hands of those waiting above would have seemed inevitable. No wonder that Jonathan took the Philistines' self-confident boasting as a sign from God. It removed any chance of an ambush before the fight could take place and was to prove the Philistines' undoing. Jonathan's faith was repaid in abundance. He and his armour-bearer made short work of the cliff-top boasters and then with the advantage of surprise were able to kill about twenty others in the surrounding area.

d. One small act of obedience + a great God = dramatic results (14:15–23)

The two men's actions had astounding repercussions. It was as if God was able to take their faith and their courage and multiply its effects. Those in the Philistine outposts realized how insecure their position was and withdrew back to the main camp in panic. An earthquake of some kind apparently accompanied their retreat, adding to the spreading panic and probably convincing all sides, as the author here was certainly convinced, that God was involved. It was the turn of the Philistine army to melt *away in all directions* (16). The news that something significant was occurring quickly spread to the Israelite camp. Saul's reaction was immediate but surprising. Where one might have expected prompt action to take advantage of the new situation, he ordered a full parade of his soldiers to work out who was not there. This must have taken some time, and he also asked Ahijah[19] the priest to carry out some kind of ritual, presumably once more seeking assurance of God's will. What a contrast with Jonathan who took it for granted that, as there had been no indications that God had changed his mind, the task remained the same! The precise nature of the ritual that Saul wanted is not clear. There is no other evidence that the ark ever left Kiriath Jearim during the time it was housed there, and no known ritual that involved placing a hand on the ark. The language here parallels that of 1 Samuel 23:9 and 30:7 where it is the ephod[20] that is used to determine the next step. It seems likely that the Septuagint, which speaks of the ephod rather than the ark in this verse, is correct. This would make sense of the request for Ahijah to withdraw his hand, or cease after all from the required manipulation of the ephod.

It was only when chaos in the Philistine camp became extreme that Saul decided he needed no further confirmation before he could move. He interrupted Ahijah's ritual and at last allowed his troops to join the battle. Success is a great recruiting campaign; they were quickly joined by

---

[19] It is not clear whether Saul used Ahijah because he happened to be there or whether he had made a deliberate decision not to use Samuel.

[20] Cf. n. 7, p. 60.

Hebrews[21] from the Philistine camp and by those who had been hiding out fearfully in the hills. Once again, when the Israelite army were fighting together and with confidence in God they emerged triumphant. God had given them the victory. The statement that *the LORD saved Israel* (23) may simply be a recognition of God's power, but it may have the deliberate implication that it was not any action on Saul's part, or even on Jonathan's, that ensured victory. The Philistines were not yet destroyed – the battle simply moved on – but Jonathan's action had, with God's help, resulted in a significant amount of Israelite territory being removed from Philistine control.

8. Saul and Jonathan: alternative approaches (14:24–52)

a. To fast or not to fast? Ritual practice versus active service (14:24–30)

The reflection on how God's will should be discovered and how one should interpret God's actions continues in the account of two possible offences against what was thought to be required by God. The link between these offences and their precise timing in relation to the events already described is not easy to determine. The first incident is introduced with the information that the Israelites were in distress. At the time when they were about to fight the Philistines and needed all the energy they could get, Saul bound them by oath not to eat until the fight was over. The writer, as usual, records the facts without any explicit critique or comment, but there is no doubt that the reader is intended to question the wisdom of Saul's actions. Fasting was a well-known way of indicating commitment to God, and Saul may have felt that surely this would be something that God would see and honour. However, fasting was normally appropriate for times of reflective retreat, not during a battle, and it was certainly never meant to be used as a means of ensuring God's support.

The lessons stemming from his predecessors' misuse of the ark had clearly not been learned. Saul's lack of confidence in his own ability to know and to do God's will comes to the fore again. What is interesting is

---

[21] The distinction between Israelites and Hebrews, the latter term not usually used within Israel itself but only by outsiders or when speaking to outsiders, may indicate that those in the Philistine camp were in fact outsiders who had switched their allegiance from Israel to the Philistines and now were switching back.

that not one of his soldiers went against Saul's oath. Whether this is a sign that they were afraid of the results of his curse or an indication of a continuing respect for Saul himself is not clear. There are a number of indications that the portrait of the dithering and somewhat erratic Saul seen in this chapter is not the whole picture. The brief report of Saul's successes given in verses 47–48 is perhaps included to redress the balance and to provide a background to the continuing loyalty that was felt towards Saul by his men. He was clearly a gifted leader. It is a shame that his inability to recognize and make use of his own potential caused such damage.

The description of the scene is vivid. One can see the honey *oozing out* of the comb, the men with their tongues hanging out watching with a mixture of envy and dismay as Jonathan comes along and immediately feasts on the delicious and nourishing honey. Saul was presumably seeing the fasting as a means of persuading God to give them victory. Jonathan sees the honey as God's provision enabling him to fight more effectively. He has not heard about the oath, but when he does he shows no signs of guilt or fear concerning the results of his father's foolish curse. As far as he was concerned, giving the men food would have been a far better way of ensuring God's help. They would have been stronger and able to drive the Philistines back even further. Jonathan's dependence on God is unquestioned, but he had a clear understanding that God works through his people and expects them to play their full part in carrying out his will. For him, religion is not something that can be separated from the realities of everyday life. The writer here strongly implies that it is Jonathan rather than Saul who has a better understanding of what God requires and, by implication, a better knowledge of God himself. Jonathan is emerging as a brave and godly soldier with many other qualities that might be expected in an ideal king. It appears that the question of whether Saul's son will succeed him is at least being opened up for debate. Surely God would see Jonathan as 'a man after his own heart' (13:14)?

b. Dealing with offences: which is best, following procedures or extravagant religiosity? (14:31–44)

The discussion of Saul's oath and its results is interrupted by an account in verses 31–35 of a further incident where God's command not to eat blood is broken. There is no reference to Saul's oath, but it is possible that it was the men's hunger and exhaustion as a result of the oath that led to this breach of the regulations. The procedure for dealing with sins of this nature is quite clear. Sacrifice must be offered. Saul therefore sets up an altar on the battlefield, sacrifice is made and apparently that is the end of the matter. There does not seem to be a criticism of Saul at this point, so it is probable that it was a priest, perhaps Ahijah, rather than Saul himself who carried out the sacrifices.[22] It is not clear whether we are to see significance in this being the first time Saul had built a field altar (the altar at Gilgal in chapter 13 was already in existence). It may be that Saul developed the habit of building field altars and the writer is simply noting that this was the first. In the overall context, however, it may be emphasizing that this is the first time Saul followed the procedures for offences against God. The implication is that Saul was capable of following laid-down procedures and it was this, rather than extravagant curses, that God really required. If this is so, then it explains why the writer placed this incident in this context.

Verse 36 appears to follow on from verse 30. Saul's procrastination has now been replaced by great fervour. Saul even wanted to take the unusual step of initiating a night fight. The army was willing but the priest, perhaps Ahijah again, sounded a note of caution and felt that perhaps this was a good time to enquire of God. There is no comment made as to whether this was wise caution or another unnecessary delay, and we are not told whether the enquiry was ever answered, but verse 46 tells us that the campaign was in fact called off.

There were a number of means used to make enquiries of God when specific prophetic pronouncements were not available.[23] In most instances these enquiries resulted in a simple 'yes' or 'no' answer or distinguished between two possible results – as with the identifying of Saul and Jonathan and then between them in verses 41–42. There are no details of methods that could provide more complex information or that left room for no answer; nevertheless, that is clearly what happened here. The writer records without comment Saul's conclusion that the lack of response must be because of sin. Lots were cast and Jonathan's 'offence' of honey-eating was brought to light.

---

[22] Until the building of the temple there was no prohibition of building altars in different places (cf. Gen. 12:8; 13:18; 35:3; Exod. 17:15; Judg. 6:24). There was some flexibility in the procedure relating to sacrifices at this time but Saul was strongly rebuked in chapter 13 when he took over the priestly role himself and it is unlikely that that occurred here.

[23] Cf. n. 7, p. 60.

c. Common sense and godly living are not mutually exclusive! (14:45–52)

Jonathan is understandably incredulous that he should face the death penalty, not because of any real sin on his part but simply because his father has made an unconsidered oath. The men, loyal to Jonathan and convinced that far from being cursed he actually has been blessed by God, intervene with their own oath and Jonathan is spared. There appear to have been no consequences. Saul's oaths were set aside, yet nothing happened to Jonathan. We are left with a strong impression that this was not the way to determine God's will. The writer undoubtedly is convinced that God does have plans, makes those plans known and is capable of ensuring that they are carried out. However, it is equally clear that God cannot be forced to act in a particular way simply because someone has made a foolish oath or curse. David obviously understood this for, later on, when he was cursed, he showed an utter lack of fear, recognizing that God will act in the way he wills, not in the way that any curse-maker decides (2 Sam. 16:5–12). The nations surrounding Israel lived in constant fear of curses, assuming that once spoken the curse itself had power, and could be revoked only by the carrying out of powerful anti-curse rituals. That was not how it was meant to be for Israel, however, where anti-curse rituals are never found. The only curse they are to be afraid of is the judgment of God on sinful behaviour. God will not allow himself to be manipulated. He is sovereign over all curses, even those supposedly made in his name.[24] The superstition involved in Saul's approach to life is clear and stands as a warning to those today who are governed by essentially superstitious fears, even when as here they are couched in spiritual terminology. Similarly we can be tempted to assume that praying at night is automatically more spiritual and more effective than praying in the daytime, or that 'living by faith' (interpreted as depending on the resources of fellow believers for survival) is automatically more spiritual and effective than earning one's own support. Neither of those things is wrong and they can both be part of our service of God, but the lesson from Saul is that it is attitude, obedience and godly living that count, not any particular act of supposed devotion.

The positive summary of Saul's reign in verses 47–52 does not mention the Philistines, but makes it very clear that Saul achieved a lot in the time

---

[24] For further discussion of the way that curses are understood within Scripture see M. J. Evans, '"A Plague on Both Your Houses": Cursing and Blessing Reviewed', *VE* 24 (1994), pp. 77–89.

he was king and his reign was by no means a disaster. The notes on Saul's family[25] serve to introduce characters who will play a part in the narratives to come: Merab (e.g. 1 Sam. 18:17–19), Michal (e.g. 1 Sam. 18:20–28; 19:11–17) and Abner (e.g. 1 Sam. 17:55–57; 26:5–14; 2 Sam. 2 – 3) will all be seen again.

9. Saul is rejected (15:1–35)

a. Our God is beyond understanding (15:1–3)

The description of the rejection of Saul is prefaced by a reminder of his commissioning and comes in the context of his carrying out his royal responsibilities. The stress in Samuel's statement *I am the one the LORD sent to anoint you . . . so listen now* (1) is on the 'I', emphasizing that in spite of the worsening relationship between the two, Samuel had played a part in Saul's life and Saul still needed to listen to him. However, the important thing for Saul to remember is that *the message* is *from the LORD*. It was God who had chosen Saul and God who now had a further task for him to do. The Amalekites had been placed under a *ḥērem* and Saul was given the responsibility of carrying it out. This was to be no ordinary raiding party. The *ḥērem* was a complete dedication to God of a person or a group who had offended against him. It usually involved total destruction[26] and, unlike in ordinary raids, no plunder or hostages were allowed to be taken. There could be no possibility of misunderstanding about that. In this case, the reason for such severe action was the way in which the Amalekites had attacked the Israelites during their wilderness wanderings.[27]

In today's world the concept of the *ḥērem* is hard to grasp or accept, but the cultures surrounding Israel would have had no problem with it, and we have already seen that God begins to work with people in the context of their own understanding. Of course it remains important that the holiness of God is taken very seriously, but the coming of Jesus into the world has made a difference. New Testament passages such as John 3 and Hebrews 10 make it clear that because of Jesus' death and resurrection, holiness can be attained not through the destruction of those who offend

---

[25] On the divergence between this verse and 1 Chr. 9:35–36, 39 see n. 1, p. 50.

[26] In practice, the destruction was not always total, as is seen by the fact that the Amalekites remained a problem for David several years later.

[27] Exod. 17:8; Num. 14:43; Deut. 25:17–18. There is a close link between Deut. 25:17–18 and the language used here, emphasizing the influence of Deuteronomic thinking in the books of Samuel (cf. Introduction, p. 5).

against God but through trust in Jesus. God's purpose in sending Jesus was not to condemn but to save. It would be quite wrong to use chapters like 1 Samuel 15 to justify any kind of 'ethnic cleansing' exercise today. On the other hand, Hebrews 10.31 reminds us that 'It is a dreadful thing to fall into the hands of the living God', and Hebrews 12:29 reinforces the Old Testament teaching that our 'God is a consuming fire' (Deut. 4:24; cf. 2 Sam. 22:9; Isa. 30:27, 30; 33:14). The call for destruction is an expression of his holiness. Our inability to cope with this fact maybe indicates that we have not grasped the awesomeness of the sovereign God who will call people to account for their actions. We must resist the temptation of our generation to ignore the serious consequences of offending God.

b. Obedience to God can't be 'pick and mix' (15:4–9)

Saul's actions at the start of this attack are reminiscent of the early campaign against the Ammonites at Jabesh Gilead. He takes his responsibility seriously, gathering the whole army together and working out an effective strategy. As this was a *hērem* directed specifically against the Amalekites, Saul warned the Kenites, allowing them to escape. The Kenites were allies of the Amalekites but as they had helped the Israelites in the wilderness instead of attacking them, they were not under the same judgment. The attack was carried out successfully and many Amalekites died. Thus far, Saul's conduct had been exemplary. However, at this point both Saul and the army lost sight of the concept of a God-ordained punishment mission. They destroyed only people and things that were not seen as useful and kept everything that could be of use to them, including the Amalekite king Agag and the best of all the animals. This was not simply an act of disobedience, although of course it was that; it was a direct affront to God, a refusal to take seriously the concept of his holiness and the complete dedication of the Amalekite people and goods to him. Saul and his army kept for themselves what was God's. Achan committed a similar offence which was seen as deserving of the death penalty (Josh. 7).

c. The cost of failure is not borne solely by the one who fails (15:10–11)

Saul's action brought grief to God and also to Samuel. The anthropopathism[28] here helps to bring out the reality of God's involvement with

---

[28] That is, the speaking in human terms of God's emotions. In a similar way, anthropomorphism, which the Old Testament uses regularly, speaks of God as having a human form, for example of his hands or his face.

humanity and the cost to him of that involvement. God is never portrayed as separate from his creation or his people, dispassionately observing what is going on. Saul's failure brought God great pain. For Samuel, apparently learning of Saul's disobedience directly from God, the news brought a troubled and sleepless night. His extended, broken-hearted praying only confirmed what he already knew: that Saul was going to come under the judgment of God. He probably remembered another sleepless night when as a young child he had to bring the message of judgment to Israel's leader. Now as an old man he was faced with the same task and again he was filled with grief. Samuel had not wanted the monarchy to be instituted and his relationship with Saul had had its ups and downs. However, he had a great affection for Saul. He had poured his heart into Saul, believing in his ability to do well and delighting in the times when he did. It is possible that even here Saul's first reaction to this commission had filled Samuel with great hope. He was certainly devastated by Saul's failure. Samuel's feelings at this point will be familiar to all who have been involved in teaching or mentoring others, putting something of themselves into the one mentored and then seeing that person turn away from faith. There is no room for an 'I told you so' reaction. Samuel continues to serve God in his old age and he stands as an example to us all of how to react to disappointment, frustration and the failure of people we love.

d. Whose honour are we serving? (15:12–21)

There is something of the surreal in what happens next. Saul moves on to Gilgal, stopping at Carmel[29] to build a memorial to himself. When Samuel eventually arrives Saul greets him and gives no hint of grief or trouble, just the assurance that Saul's mission has been completed successfully. It is not clear whether this is deliberate dissimulation on Saul's part or whether the mental problems that plagued him in later life began at this point, causing him to lose touch with reality. In either case, it is clear that he is held fully accountable for his actions. Although we are given the information without comment, there is a great irony in Saul building a *monument in his own honour* (12), presumably to remind the people of Israel of the benefits they have gained from his kingship, just at the point where he seems to have lost all sight of God's honour. In the past, despite

---

[29] The Carmel mentioned here is not the northern mountain but a town in the centre of Judah. It lay on the route to the Amalekite territory in the south.

his mistakes and misunderstandings, he appears to have had a genuine desire to serve God and to do what God required of him. From this point on, Saul's concern for his own reputation and status takes priority. The building of the monument[30] points the people to Saul rather than to God as the one who has rescued them from their enemies.

Saul seems to have had no intention to deceive Samuel; it would be hard to do that with the sheep bleating in the background. Instead he shifts the responsibility in a way that we have not seen him do before, explaining that the soldiers had saved the best animals to sacrifice them. This is not the way that the events have been recorded so far, but perhaps Saul genuinely convinced himself that sacrifice was always intended and that he really had done what God had asked him to do.

Samuel's impatient interruption is completely understandable. It was hard enough for Samuel to bring the message of judgment without having to listen to what he clearly perceived as nonsense. Saul had been appointed king by God; he had been and remained nothing apart from his role as God's agent. God had given him a task to do, yet he had acted as if his own material gain was more important than obeying God. Samuel had ignored Saul's statement that the saved animals were for sacrifice, so Saul reiterated the point. He had retained *the best of what was devoted to God* (21) for sacrifice to God. Surely that was better than destroying it? Samuel's reply came in the form of an oracle rather than an argument – perhaps he had recognized that Saul was no longer able to respond rationally and the prophetic form might get through to him more easily.

e. God must be served on his terms, not ours (15:22–23)

The oracle reflects on the relationship between ritual practice and righteous behaviour, and forms the background to a number of other Old Testament oracles (e.g. Prov. 21:3; Hos. 6:6; Mic. 6:6–8). The sacrificial system was there to enable the people of God to express in symbolic form their desire to love and to serve him and to cover any lapses in the life of obedience. It was not a magic formula to ensure God's cooperation or a nice present to distract God from his original demands. In effect Saul was treating God as if he were a child, or an idol. The dedication to God of all Amalekite property required it to be destroyed: to keep it, even for such a

---

[30] Absalom built a similar monument as a memorial because he had no sons to carry on his name (2 Sam. 18:18). There is no indication that Saul had any motivation other than self-aggrandizement.

noble purpose as sacrifice, was not an acceptable alternative. Sacrifice can never be an alternative to obedience and without obedience is an irrelevant abomination.[31] In modern terms, attendance at services or dedication to other forms of religious observance can never be used as a way of offsetting behaviour or attitudes in the rest of life which are offensive to God.

Saul had taken a stand against occult practices like divination (cf. 1 Sam. 28:9), recognizing such practices as horrific and completely unacceptable for God's people. However, his disobedience came into the same category and was equally horrific. Saul's arrogance, thinking that he could himself make the decision as to how and when God's commands should be kept, was as much an abomination to God as idolatry. James 2:1–11 tells us that showing favouritism is just as bad as murder or adultery. Again in modern terms, ignoring the command to love our neighbour, or even some minor disobedience that we may think unimportant, is as unacceptable to God as if we were taking part in pagan worship. Seen in those terms, Saul's action had taken him beyond the point of no return. He had, therefore, become the cause of his own downfall. He had *rejected the word of the LORD* (23), and as a direct result, he himself had been *rejected . . . as king.* No amount of sacrificing was going to change that. After Saul's disobedience in chapter 13 when he failed to wait for Samuel to arrive at Gilgal, he was told that he would not be the founder of a dynasty, but there was no question of his own responsibilities being taken away from him. After this second offence it was made clear that any possibility of him being the kind of king that Israel really needed had now disappeared. His role within the system might remain, but there was now no way that he could function as a king who represented God to the people.

f. The consequences of passing the point of no return (15:24–35)

Whether or not Saul's previous attitude of uncomprehending self-justification had been conscious or unconscious, he now comes back to reality with a bump. The possibility that he might really lose the kingship does not seem to have occurred to him previously. He now accepts that he has sinned, and admits that it was in fact deliberate and that he had paid more attention to what the people might think of him than to what God

---

[31] Passages like Amos 5:21–24 and Isa. 1:10–17 make the same point. Neither Samuel nor the prophets are implying that sacrifice itself is wrong; rather that sacrifice with the wrong motivation or without obedient service is far worse than no sacrifice at all.

had required of him. He then pleads for another chance. But that was not how it could be. The responsibility that God gives to all human beings and particularly to leaders is a real one and the consequences of failing in that responsibility will normally be allowed to stand. This time there can be no going back for Saul. At first Samuel refuses even to stay and conduct a worship service for fear it would look as if he were condoning Saul's actions. Eventually, however, after reminding Saul that God, *the Glory of Israel* (29), was transcendent and could not be manipulated in the way that Saul had tried to do, Samuel did agree to hold the service. Perhaps, in reminding Saul that God is transcendent and vastly different from human beings, Samuel was himself reminded that God is merciful. The decision to take away the kingship from Saul may have been irrevocable, but that did not mean there was no possibility of forgiveness or further worship for Saul. It will never be possible to sidestep the consequences of sin, but it will always be possible for the genuinely repentant to find a different way forward in service of God. It remained to be seen whether in this instance Saul's desire to worship God was genuine or simply a wish not to lose face in the sight of the elders.

The relationship between obedience and disobedience and in particular the reason why some sins, such as David's adultery with Bathsheba, can apparently be atoned for and others apparently cannot is one of the continuing interests of the books of Samuel.[32] Only God knows when in a series of disobedient actions we will reach the point of no return. As Christians, we know that for all who remain capable of repentance, Christ's redemptive work remains effective, but this should not blind us to the fact that sin is serious and sometimes has irreversible consequences. The treasurer who steals from the funds will not be able to function as treasurer again; the children's worker who accesses Internet porn will never again be able to work with children. It is not a light thing to ignore the word of God.

In this instance it is possible that Saul's actions reflected not just disobedience but a denial of God's power. Giving in to pressure from the people, rather than helping them to understand and follow God's path, was itself an abdication of the responsibilities of kingship. The kingship was taken from him because in one sense he had already given it up.

---

[32] D. Gunn picks up this concept and discusses it extensively in his book *The Fate of King Saul: An Analysis of a Biblical Story*, JSOTSup 14 (Sheffield: Sheffield Academic Press, 1980), pp. 44–56, 123–131.

The execution of the Amalekite king was a final reminder to both Saul and the people that God's will cannot be set aside. The information that Agag, having been reprieved once, was not now expecting death shows that Saul's action had led not only the Israelites but also Agag himself to underestimate the significance of God's sovereignty.

This rather sad section comes to an end with a final description, paralleling that in verse 11, of the grief of both Samuel and God. Samuel accepted the need for judgment and, from then on, perhaps because of his continuing role as God's prophet, he kept away from Saul. But he did so sadly, continuing to mourn for the lost possibilities of Saul's life. It should be noted that God's grief was not that he instituted kingship but that he made Saul king. The question of how the God who *does not lie or change his mind* (29) could nevertheless feel grief at having made Saul king is left in the air for the reader to continue to consider.

Questions to ponder

1. How does looking for lost donkeys prepare one for kingship?
2. Saul was God's choice and full of potential. What went wrong?
3. What does Samuel's speech reveal about his own strengths and weaknesses? Was his complete openness about his unhappiness with the new system a good thing or not?
4. How far was the desire to hold on to power the root of Saul's problems?
5. Was Saul's instability the cause or the result of his disobedience? Can he be held accountable for his increasingly erratic behaviour?
6. Does this section clarify our understanding of whether or when the consequences of actions can be set aside, or of whether and when God can change his mind, or at least appear to?

1 Samuel 16 – 24

4. David: the young 'pretender'

1. The anointing of the shepherd musician (16:1–23)

The interest of the writer remains focused primarily on characters rather than on events or even on the institution of kingship as such. The writer is well aware that God always relates to the people themselves and not the jobs they hold. The story of David's anointing reinforces this point, already clearly made in accounts of the appointments of both Samuel and Saul. Saul himself does not disappear from the scene until chapter 1 of 2 Samuel, and there is a continuing interest in many more minor figures. However, from this point on it is clear that the central character is David. Our first introduction to him is as the absent youngest son. In many ways this is parallel to the young Saul's search for the lost donkeys. Like Saul, David was chosen for his potential, rather than for his current achievements or status. From the beginning of his story, therefore, the question lies before us as to whether his potential, unlike Saul's, will be realized. We have learned from Saul that obedience to God's word is more important for the Lord's anointed than anything else he may or may not do. It remains to be seen whether David will provide a better picture than Saul did. Will David be a clearer reflection of the real 'Anointed One', that is, of the Messiah who we eventually learn will be one of his descendants (Isa. 9:1–8; 11:1–16), and who is revealed in the New Testament as Jesus, 'the Son of the living God' (Matt. 16:16)?

a. Letting go of the past (16:1)

The mention of Samuel's continued mourning provides a link with the previous section. Mourning for the loss of the 'might have been' is understandable, but eventually present realities must be accepted and action taken to influence future events. God had another task for the now very elderly Samuel to undertake. He was to anoint the next king. Samuel's speech in chapter 12 indicated that he had expected to take a back seat, with his leadership role handed on to another. In some ways the calling of Samuel to initiate the process by which David would become king makes the reign of Saul appear as something of a 'blip' in the continuing history of Israel. It is Samuel, not Saul, who hands the leadership over to David. It is a measure of the writer's skill that he manages to portray Saul's reign as a diversion, a detour taken before the proper path is found, while making it clear that if Saul had fulfilled his potential, his reign could have been the key first section of the new road ahead. It is a challenge for all leaders to consider whether their time in office will be seen as a diversion or a section, however small, of the route of the particular organization involved. The call to Samuel also makes plain that God's decision to give Israel a king has not been revoked. The failure of one person in any new situation or system does not necessarily mean that the system was at fault.

b. Dealing with fear (16:2–5a)

Samuel's fearful response seems at odds with his previous confidence in dealing with Saul. We do not know how long has passed since his final meeting with Saul and thus his reaction may be a sign of his own increasing frailty or Saul's increasingly erratic and even violent behaviour. It seems likely that Saul had already begun to set up a network of spies who would make sure that no-one was acting against him without his knowledge. If so, this would be evidence that he had begun to view as the enemy the people he had been called to serve and protect. God takes Samuel's natural fear seriously, as he does in other instances where those he has called are fearful or reluctant, and provides a way forward to deal with the problem without changing the task.[1] So Samuel heads off obediently to Bethlehem to carry out a sacrifice in the town and to anoint Jesse's son. The omission of any genealogy for Jesse is probably a deliberate technique to emphasize the ordinariness of David's background, although we are aware that Jesse would not have been considered a poor man (16:20;

---

[1] The calls of Moses (Exod. 3) and Jeremiah (Jer. 1), for example, are among those that follow a similar pattern. When they became aware of God's call on their lives, both these men expressed fear about what might lie ahead and their ability to cope with it. In both instances God reassures them of his constant presence and that he will provide any requisite help.

17:17–18).[2] There is a touch of rather bleak humour in the story as the fearful Samuel is met by even more fearful town elders – perhaps aware of the split between Samuel and Saul and unwilling themselves to risk Saul's wrath. However, they also are reassured and the preparations for the sacrifice go ahead.

c. God's surprising choices (16:5b–13)

It appears that Jesse and his sons meet with Samuel separately before or after the town meeting takes place. This would explain both Samuel's haste – he wants to complete all the sacrifices quickly and return to his home – and the fact that the anointing of David takes place *in the presence of his brothers* (13) but without it becoming common knowledge or in particular becoming known to Saul. The description of Samuel's meeting with Jesse and his sons is again told in the vivid, evocative style that brings the reader right into the situation. Eliab is introduced and Samuel is impressed. This man had the look of a king; the mention of his height may indicate that he reminded Samuel of the younger Saul. God's gentle reminder to Samuel that it is not appearance but attitude that really counts stands as a continuing lesson to all who are involved in making appointments of any kind. For Samuel it also renewed his sense that the choice of Israel's king was to be God's, not his. It is a real endorsement of Samuel's ministry that throughout his life he was able to discern and respond to God's word even when he did not particularly like what he was hearing. In this case, he was aware that although he had been told clearly that he was to anoint one of Jesse's sons, none of the seven he was introduced to was chosen by God. There had to be another brother.

It is usually assumed that David was too young or too insignificant to attend the sacrifice, or that, being the youngest, he was left to mind the sheep so that all the others could go. However, if all seven of his brothers were able to attend, it seems likely that there would have been servants who could have taken David's place. Perhaps David, although his own spirituality is undoubted, was impatient with ceremony and chose to avoid the official sacrifice, or perhaps he spent so much time *tending the sheep* (11) out of choice and, as is often the way with teenagers, no-one had been able to find him when they received the news of the hastily arranged sacrifice. Whatever the reason, he was absent and Samuel refused to begin the

---

[2] Jesse's genealogy is recorded in detail in 1 Chr. 2 and, as the writer of Samuel normally includes genealogical information, it appears that the omission here is deliberate.

ceremony until he had arrived. God had already stressed that his choice was not made on the basis of appearance, but we are told nevertheless that David, like his brothers, was an exceptionally good-looking boy. The failure to mention height may simply be an indication of his youth. God made it clear to Samuel that this boy was in fact his choice; so Samuel anointed David before leaving for Ramah. Although the readers have been told that one of Jesse's sons was chosen to be king, there is no indication as to whether this information was conveyed to David or any of his family. The long conversations that Samuel had had with Saul before his anointing certainly have no parallel here. There is no further reference to David's anointing until 2 Samuel 2 where he is anointed by the people of Judah to be their king. However, anyone anointed by Samuel would know that this was God's call to serve him in a special way, and this was confirmed for David when *the Spirit of the Lord came powerfully upon* him (13). We are not told if this empowerment could be observed by others, but there is no doubt that David himself had a strong sense of God's presence. In any case, whether those present at David's anointing were aware of it or not, there was now no doubt that the young shepherd boy would one day be king of Israel. David himself may not have had pretensions to kingship, but he was now the 'young pretender' to the throne of Israel.

Verses 14–23 apparently record the first meeting between Saul and David, but the style is much less vivid than that found in the surrounding narratives and it is hard to know how this section fits in with chapter 17. It seems likely that the editor included this account from a different source as it contained a message that was appropriate at this point. It does indeed extend our knowledge of both Saul and David, and helps to explain later events.

d. Living with – and without – a sense of God's presence (16:14–23)

Immediately following the statement that 'the Spirit of the Lord came powerfully upon David' (13) we are told that *the Spirit of the Lord had departed from Saul* (14). The New Testament concept of permanent in-dwelling by the Holy Spirit was unknown at this stage and all spiritual endowment was seen as intermittent and temporary. Perhaps for Saul it meant that there were no longer any signs of the charismatic power that had been noticeable earlier. What is plain, however, is that Saul, although still known as king, could no longer be regarded as the agent of God. In fact, Saul was now tormented by episodes of bleak depression which prevented him from functioning normally. These episodes are presented as stemming from *an evil spirit from the* LORD (14). Everything that happened, good or bad, was seen as coming from God, and in this context *evil* can simply mean 'harmful'. Saul suffered from these terrible moods and therefore God must in some way be seen as responsible for them. Some modern believers find it helpful to make a distinction between things which God allows and things which God commands. Both can be seen as coming from God. There is no evidence that the servants saw anything that could be described as demonic in what was happening to Saul. It would be understandable, however, given the uncontrolled nature of his behaviour during later fits, if these were seen as reflecting demon possession. Although this kind of depression can have many causes, by no means all having their roots in past behaviour, it is possible that in Saul's case his own guilt, and the lack of any sense of God's presence which resulted from his disobedience, at times proved too much for him to cope with. It is noteworthy that neither here nor anywhere else is there any sign that this *evil spirit* can be blamed for Saul's actions. Saul himself is always held fully responsible.

Throughout the ages, music therapy has been used to calm troubled souls, and Saul's loyal servants thought that this might be of help to him as well. One of them had knowledge of a young Bethlehemite who was an excellent musician and might be able to help. So David was sent for. The description of David on the one hand as *a brave man and a warrior*, and on the other hand as *with the sheep*, is a little confusing and may reflect the influence of later descriptions of David. But there is no reason to suppose that good farmers cannot also be good soldiers and we have already been told that David was a well-built young man. In any case, David's music did prove helpful for Saul, and David entered into service as an armour-bearer, a kind of junior officer required to help Saul dress for battle,[3] and was also used as a music therapist when necessary. We are told that Saul *liked him very much* and was *pleased with him*. This emphasis makes it clear that the two got on really well and any future tensions are, therefore, to be seen as the result of jealousy rather than any long-term personality clash.

e. Learning the job from the bottom up

The irony of the situation was probably not unnoticed by the author; Saul, unknowingly, was being used to introduce his successor to the requirements

---

[3] Jonathan's armour-bearer was clearly a close friend and colleague (14:1–14).

of kingship. David was able to exercise his natural gifts and to take full advantage of the opportunities that life presented to train for the future that had been laid out for him. There is no evidence here of the false dichotomy sometimes made between natural and spiritual gifts, and there is no sign in David of that tendency, which can tempt those with a strong sense of calling, to avoid all tasks that seem unrelated to that ultimate calling.

2. The giant killer (17:1 – 18:5)

Chapter 17 is a complete story told so dramatically one can easily imagine it – like the stories of Jonathan's exploits – being related over and over again by young soldiers as they passed time in the evening around the campfire. In fact, there are remarkable parallels between Jonathan's actions described in chapter 14 and David's actions here. Both are portrayed as activists, courageously standing out from the crowd and ignoring any personal danger. Both are convinced of the reality of God's power and his willingness to intervene on behalf of his people. In both cases the action led to a major defeat of the Philistines. The picture of the battle scene given here is realistic: two opposing forces lined up on two facing hillsides with the valley between preventing either side from instituting an ambush or initiating an unexpected attack. The towns named here are well south of the area mentioned in previous battles with the Philistines, and on the edge of Philistia itself. Saul and Jonathan had by no means eliminated the Philistine threat but there had clearly been success in driving them back. On this occasion there appears to have been an impasse between the two forces, with neither side willing to take precipitous action. In situations like this it was not unknown for each side to send out a champion to fight on their behalf. The side whose champion was defeated would then withdraw their claim to whatever territory was at that time being disputed. There was no obligation to take up the challenge, but to refuse was humiliating and gave a clear psychological advantage to the other side.

a. An unlikely hero – with God on his side – faces an incredible opponent (17:1–40)

The Philistine champion was a huge man from Gath[4] named Goliath. Whether the measurement of his height was an accurate one or a

---

[4] Gath was one of the five major Philistine towns. At a later stage, a large group of Gittites gave their support to David (2 Sam. 15:18) but in general they stood as the enemy of Israel.

description of how tall he appeared from across the valley is irrelevant. He was an exceptional figure,[5] apparently substantially taller even than Saul who stood head and shoulders above his compatriots (9:2). The extent and weight of Goliath's armour, given the scarcity of such resources, may indicate that his appearance was intended to frighten the Israelites and there was no real expectation that he might have to fight. The Israelite army certainly were overawed and although they did not actually surrender or withdraw, neither Saul nor anyone else had any idea what to do next. Into this situation steps the young David, apparently not old enough to join the army but certainly old enough to travel independently, carrying supplies to his brothers and a gift for their commander. For the first time readers actually encounter David as an individual: an enthusiastic, patriotic youngster, overconfident perhaps, but with complete faith in the power of Israel's God. He introduces the concept, forgotten or ignored by Saul and his troops, that they were *the armies of the living God* (26). A failure to acknowledge the reality of this living God has brought similar disheartenment to many of God's people throughout the centuries.

The embarrassed and annoyed reaction of David's brothers to the interfering criticism of an arrogant boy brings an earthy reality to the account. When David's persistence did eventually bring him into Saul's presence, it is a sign of Saul's desperation that he would listen even to the views of a boy like David. In spite of Saul's initial incredulity, he accepted David's offer to act as the Israelite champion. He was unlikely to have been convinced by David's stories of victory over lions and bears, but perhaps David's absolute confidence in God made Saul remember his own experience of the empowering of God's Spirit, long since lost sight of, and caused him to believe that this youth might actually have a chance. The incident with the armour sheds light on the characters of both men. Saul is unable to trust that God will be able to work without the help of the best and most up-to-date resources. David is impatient of pretence and unwilling to use anything other than the resources which he is competent to use and through which he has known God's help on previous occasions.

---

[5] 2 Sam. 21:15–21 mentions other exceptionally tall men coming from Gath, one with six fingers and six toes. Possibly there was a genetic defect that caused the giantism that was prevalent in Gath. If so, this could also have resulted in bone deficiency, which, if shared by Goliath, would explain the ease with which David's stone penetrated his skull.

b. God's help proves to be sufficient – again! (17:41–58)

The two contrasting champions draw near, each for different reasons despising the other, both speaking of their own gods. It was perhaps the improbability of David as an attacker that made it easier for him to defeat Goliath. The message to Samuel that 'the Lᴏʀᴅ does not look at the things people look at' (16:7) certainly has relevance in this context. Goliath saw an inexperienced young man and confidently allowed him to approach. However, David's words make it clear that he was fighting in God's name and with God's help. As far as David was concerned, his action was a sign, not of his own greatness, but of God's power. It would indicate to everybody, Philistine and Israelite alike, the extent of God's sovereignty and that he did not need army, armour or armaments to defend his cause. God's honour had been offended by the Israelite army's inaction, but would be restored and proclaimed by God's own action through David. There is no implication here that God would not usually work through the ordinary means, in this sort of situation by the use of armies with normal weapons. David himself fought with the troops many times. What was important was the recognition of their dependence on God and of God's dependability.

It appears that the Philistines' whole dependence had been on their massive champion, and they were unready or unwilling to fight further. The Israelite army – fear and dismay now forgotten – follow up David's success and drive the Philistines further back into their own territory. David, in an extravagant action that reminds us of his youth, cuts off Goliath's head and brings it back into the camp.[6]

At this point (17:55) Saul sends Abner, his cousin and general, to find out who this young man is. The text makes no attempt to reconcile Saul's lack of knowledge of David with the events of chapter 16. The editor must have been aware of a possible discrepancy but does not seem to consider it significant. If David's activity as a music therapist was intermittent and his services were called upon at times when Saul was not fully aware of all that went on, it is not surprising that he did not recognize David. People who are conscious of their own high status often pay little heed to those seen as of lesser significance. Also, those who mix with many people do not always recognize even those who have served them. It is certainly possible

---

[6] The mention of Jerusalem in verse 54 is unusual as at this time Jerusalem still belonged to the Jebusites and was not part of Israelite territory. Perhaps a tradition that Goliath's head was eventually kept as a trophy at Jerusalem had come into the text here.

to speak at a conference for a week with the same sound engineer working with you every day and yet forget his name and face by the time the next year comes round – even if you really did appreciate the work he did!

It may of course be significant that Saul's question refers specifically to the identity of David's father. Perhaps he knew David as a court musician, but now wanted to investigate his background. Such a gifted young man must surely have had a special kind of upbringing, and it is even possible that rumours of some form of anointing ceremony had reached Saul and he was beginning to be suspicious that David might be connected with this. However, the description of Saul's first contact with David in chapter 16 clearly states that David was Jesse's son, so the potential discrepancy remains.

c. Generosity: another form of heroism? (18:1–5)

David's life now changes dramatically. His many hours spent caring for or communing with his beloved sheep are over. Now he has a full-time role at court and his presence and his services are appreciated by all. He is befriended by Saul's son Jonathan, their relationship cemented by a common confidence in God's support for Israel and a common desire to be in the thick of whatever action is going on. Jonathan's generous-hearted acceptance of David fits well with what we read of him elsewhere. There is never any question of jealousy or pettiness. Jonathan apparently recognized that the Spirit of God was with David and rejoiced in that fact. Whether Jonathan knew that Saul had been told that his dynasty would not endure, or of Saul's rejection by God, is never made clear. But that Jonathan would have handed over his potential inheritance as generously as he handed over other gifts is not in question. Jonathan is consistently presented as a great man, the equal of David in faith and in courage and perhaps his superior in generosity. The question remains why Jonathan was not the one chosen to be king. It may or may not be significant that all the giving and the loving in the relationship is depicted as coming from Jonathan's side. It was Jonathan who initiated the covenant, or committed friendship, between them. This may be simply because at this stage he was the higher in status of the two, but there may also be a hint here that in personal relationships of all kinds David was better at receiving than he was at giving.

David's success with Goliath is shown to have been much more than a fluke. He became a warrior to be reckoned with and his rapid promotion within the army was welcomed warmly by all. Discord between Saul and David is about to be introduced but it is made very clear that at this stage there was complete harmony between Saul's family, David and the people.

3. A soured relationship (18:6 – 19:24)

a. The destructive power of jealousy (18:6–16)

The timing here is again uncertain. Precision in relation to the timing of events is often more of a concern to us than it was to the writers of Old Testament narratives! Certainly enough time had passed for David's reputation to have grown and spread around the country, so it is probably quite a while after David's encounter with Goliath. Up until this point Saul has seen David as his protégé and taken a happy pride in his achievements. However, all that is about to change. The exuberant singing in the welcome parade praised both Saul and David. Saul in general had been a popular monarch and was used to receiving this kind of acclamation. The women may or may not have meant the differentiation between the two to have had any significance, but Saul took it personally. For Saul, having lost the assurance of God's support for his kingship, the only thing that gave him security in his role as king was the popular acclaim. If that was taken from him nothing was left. We have a real demonstration here of the power of jealousy to destroy good relationships. David had been a constant support and joy to Saul, but Saul now became consumed by jealousy and began to see David as a source of danger and a threat. He appears to have transferred his own obsessive desire for status and recognition onto David and was unable to believe that David did not desire to take the throne away from him. The knowledge that somewhere God's chosen successor, 'a man after his own heart' (1 Sam. 13:14), was waiting to replace Saul appears to have eaten away at him and turned his jealousy into an obsession. Perhaps David, who was so clearly aware of God's presence and so clearly trusted in God's power, was that man. If Saul could have accepted the judgment on his behaviour and moved on from that point, the situation could have been so very different. Eli was able to accept the judgment on himself and his family and to welcome and mentor Samuel as his replacement. Samuel had accepted Saul and taken time to mentor him. If Saul, having recognized David as a potential replacement, had acknowledged him and mentored him, then he might have found something of the peace that he sought so desperately. But this was not to be, and in many ways it was Saul, rather than David, who eventually suffered the most because of his animosity.

Saul allowed his jealousy to ferment overnight and it fuelled one of his black moods. The description of an *evil spirit from God* (10) coming on Saul, in this case *forcefully*, is again[7] used to describe the bleak depression that thus far had been alleviated by David's music. The statement that Saul was prophesying seems in this instance to have had no religious significance but perhaps indicates that Saul's fit involved some kind of ecstatic activity or convulsions. The *forcefully* marks out this episode as particularly violent. In this instance David's harp-playing inflamed rather than settled Saul's spirit. However much Saul's complaint caused him to lose control, the text is quite clear that he knew what he was doing and that his repeated attack on David was a deliberate attempt to destroy him.

We are not told of David's reaction to Saul's first attack. Perhaps as he dodged Saul's spear the first time he saw it as an involuntary result of Saul's 'prophetic' episode, but the second attack, again successfully avoided, might have caused him to wonder – even though at this stage he had no reason to doubt that Saul viewed him as anything other than a favoured adopted son. It may be that David's ability to dodge Saul's spear confirmed to Saul the impression that God was with David and not with Saul. It's not clear if Saul sent David away for fear of what David might do to him or whether with returning lucidity came the fear of what he might do to David. The amazing success of David's campaigns was a great consolidation of the position of Israel as a nation and could have been seen by Saul as promoting his own position. But for Saul in his tortured state, increasingly aware that *the LORD was with David* and not with himself (10, 12, 14), David's victories, and the loving support they brought for him, not only in his own tribe of Judah but throughout Israel, served to increase Saul's own fear.

b. Using people as pawns – not a recommended leadership style (18:17–30)

The way in which Saul uses his daughters to further his own ends is noted without comment and certainly without approval. First he offers David his elder daughter Merab as a bride. That this would involve finally keeping the somewhat reckless promise made to any Israelite champion

---

[7] Cf. the comments on 16:14.

who could remove the threat of Goliath (1 Sam. 17:25) is not commented on here and may be an ironic side effect that had not occurred to Saul. His desire is for David to be killed in battle, but it is not clear how marriage to Saul's daughter would precipitate that result. Perhaps he thought it would be more difficult for David to act in opposition to Saul if he was his son-in-law. David's self-deprecating statement is unlikely to have been a refusal of Saul's suggestion but rather a polite way of beginning the process of negotiating a bride price. Saul's motivation in then changing his mind and marrying Merab elsewhere is hard to fathom and may not have had a basis in logic, although it may have been an attempt to humiliate David.

Saul's younger daughter Michal now appears in the text as a character in her own right and we are presented with a picture of someone who loves David, not as other grateful fellow citizens did, but as a woman. Michal is in fact the only woman in the Old Testament narratives who is actually described as loving a man, and although no explicit comment is made, the impression given is that Saul's manipulative abuse of her love is completely unacceptable. As far as Saul is concerned, Michal and her love for David are simply tools that he can use to further his own ends. For David, too, Michal seems simply to be part of the power games that he is beginning to play with Saul – not in any sense wishing Saul's destruction but not wanting to give in to Saul's jealous enmity. It is probably significant that here, as indeed when Jonathan's friendship with David was introduced in verse 1, there is no mention of David reciprocating Michal's love. Saul hoped that Michal would be *a snare* (21) to David and increase the possibility that he would be killed by the Philistines, a possibility made more likely by David's bravado in agreeing to and doubling Saul's grotesque bride price which would involve killing two hundred Philistines in close combat. The writer clearly conveys Saul's growing fear and frustration as he sees David's increasing success and realizes that, far from Michal becoming a snare to David, she has joined Jonathan, the people and the Lord himself in supporting him. In Saul's mind it was now impossible to understand love for David as anything other than political support and hence opposition to himself. He could not see David as anything other than a permanent enemy.

c. The value of friendship (19:1–7)

Saul was becoming increasingly isolated in his fear and dislike of David, but this did not stop him trying to recruit *Jonathan and all the attendants to kill David* (1). It seems that Saul's obsessive hatred had caused him to lose all sense of reality, as is so often the way with such obsessions. He could not believe that others did not share his knowledge of the danger that he perceived David to be. Surely Jonathan would know. But, as we have already been told, Jonathan loved David. The word used here is exactly the same as the one used in 18:22 to describe Saul's attitude to David. Some have suggested that the relationship between Jonathan and David was homosexual in nature, but this cannot be justified from the text and implies a failure to understand that good friendship can exist that is not sexually based. The same failure today can make it difficult to form that kind of good friendship. It is important for God's people to resist the pressures stemming from the assumption of current world-views that all relationships are sexually based. Rather we must find ways of nurturing friendships and not allowing them to be destroyed by false assumptions. David and Jonathan's relationship was founded on their shared commitment to God and to the future of God's people as well as on mutual interests and attitudes – an excellent basis for any friendship.

Jonathan's response to Saul's suggestion again brings out his practical wisdom and general good-naturedness. He warns David to stay out of the way and at the same time seeks to persuade his father that, far from being a threat, David has been a support both to Saul and to the nation of Israel. Saul had previously been really glad (5) to see what God had achieved through David, and so to kill such a man would be foolish as well as wrong. Jonathan must have been aware of Saul's fear that David would replace him, but he himself appears to have accepted the implications of David's many victories with serenity – he could not be other than happy to rejoice in the good fortune of another. In any case, he was convinced that it was not David's intention to damage Saul. His calm good sense appears to get through to Saul, although the swearing of an oath to reinforce his intention not to kill David might be seen as a further indication of his mood swings and instability. In any case, David is able to return to court for a further period. Part of Jonathan's concern was for David, but it is likely that he was also doing his best for his father, trying to prevent him from damaging himself further as a result of his obsessive fear. His ability to defuse the situation without taking sides provides a wonderful example of pastoral diplomacy and deserves to be studied by all who are faced with conflict between those they care for.

d. The dangers of obsession (19:8–17)

We cannot be sure how long the lull continued, but when the next military campaign took place and David was again successful, the cycle resumed.[8] Once more David was able to dodge Saul's spear, but this time when he made his escape it led to a permanent departure from Saul's court. Saul's oath had not been strong enough to prevent his animosity returning. Once the obsession took over again, Saul lost all power to control it. His intention to kill David now dominated his life. The next attempt was formulated not in the midst of a violent fit but as a premeditated plot. This time it was Saul's daughter rather than his son who helped David to escape. She *let David down through a window* (12) and then used a ruse to give him enough time to get well away. Michal's use of an idol to deceive Saul's men brings to mind Rachel's use of household gods (Gen. 31:34). There has been a previous parallel in chapter 18, when the offering of both Merab and Michal in marriage to David is reminiscent of the offering of both Rachel and her sister Leah to Jacob. In that instance we were clearly told that Jacob loved Rachel (Gen. 29:18, 30) and there is perhaps an expectation here too that we will learn of David's love for Michal, but it is not to be.[9] In spite of the fact that she risked her life to help him, David appears to have left Michal behind without a second thought. He certainly makes no effort to visit her and does not see her again until, for what appear to be political reasons, he insists that she be taken from her second husband Paltiel, who did love her (2 Sam. 3:13–16). Using people to suit his own purposes was not the sole prerogative of Saul.

Michal's last glimpse of David on this occasion was as she watched him disappear. Perhaps in 2 Samuel 6:16, when she again watches 'from a window' in a much more critical way, her attitude is understandable. David was undoubtedly a brave warrior, a gifted musician and a faithful follower of the Lord, but he does not seem to have been a great husband. The biblical account is always realistic and knows nothing of the assumption found in some of its readers that a great person must be great in every area. Hero worship, even of great biblical characters, is not recommended.

---

[8] The similarity between this incident and that in chapter 18 has led to the suggestion that they are parallel accounts of the same event, but given Saul's unstable nature there is no reason to suppose that the same behaviour pattern could not have been repeated.

[9] Cf. R. B. Lawton, '1 Samuel 18: David, Merab and Michal', *CBQ* 51 (1989), pp. 423–425; R. G. Bowman, 'The Fortune of King David / The Fate of Queen Michal', in Clines and Eskenazi, pp. 97–120.

e. God's sovereignty and human responsibility (19:18–24)

There is no discussion in the text as to the rightness or otherwise of David's decision to leave the court. In the chapters to come we will learn of God's support and care for David during the dangers of his life as a fugitive. Although it is fruitless to speculate about events that did not happen, there is no reason to suppose that God would not have supported and cared for David if he had continued in the court. It is worth noting that there is no mention of any attempt to seek God's involvement in the decision to leave. At other times David does not show a great concern for his own safety and it is possible that part of his motivation for leaving could have been frustration with the formality of the court system and a desire to do his own thing again out in the countryside. There is an indication here of the extent to which God takes human decision-making seriously. Whether David's decision to leave was right or not, it was the decision he made and God honoured it, allowing him then to move on from that point.

David fled to Samuel, probably seeking spiritual reassurance as well as physical safety. But Saul's manic animosity was not lessened by David's absence and not even fear of rebuke from Samuel prevented him from repeatedly sending troops to capture David. These troops were unable to carry out their commission, not because of David's military prowess but because they were caught up in an ecstatic experience that prevented them from proceeding further. Saul himself finally went to search out David, but he too was overtaken by the prophetic experience. Saul and David were both made aware that God himself would not permit Saul to harm David – whether through the spears thrown within the court or in the place of escape. Significantly, in incapacitating Saul and his men, this *Spirit of God* also prevented David from having to harm fellow Israelites in order to defend himself. God's actions are often seen to have more than one effect or purpose, and we see here God's continuing concern for both David and Saul and his protection, in different ways, of both.

Stripping naked was sometimes part of the ritual for ecstatic prophets; in this case Saul stripping off his royal robes could be seen as a further symbol that it was Saul's own action that was causing royalty to be stripped from him. In 1 Samuel 10:11 the saying 'Is Saul also among the prophets?' had resulted from a very positive if rather surprised conclusion that God's hand was on Saul. Over the years and in the light of Saul's periodic ecstatic excesses the attitude had been modified, and the same statement now appears to reflect a much more critical assessment, perhaps even questioning Saul's sanity.[10] Samuel was present when Saul prophesied, but there is no sign that the two men communicated in any way (cf. 1 Sam. 15:35). The action of the *Spirit of God* had in the past transformed Saul's life. On this occasion it would seem there were no lasting effects at all. It had temporarily removed his ability to harm David but it had not altered his desire to do so.

4. Jonathan: the son without jealousy (20:1–42)

a. Taking sides: a difficult decision to make (20:1–7)

Apparently David had not yet made any final decisions about his own future and wanted to consult with Jonathan before he took any further action. There was still a possibility that Saul might calm down and David could take up his place at court again. He has clearly not set aside the possibility of attending the approaching New Moon celebrations. Jonathan, unaware of his father's latest action, finds it hard to accept that Saul has reneged on his earlier oath. However, he accepts David's account of the facts and agrees to take any action necessary to help David avoid Saul's wrath. At this stage Jonathan does not want to take sides, but perhaps in the process he is acknowledging implicitly that the time may come when that is exactly what he will have to do. It is always good to seek to listen to all participants in a dispute, to seek to mediate and to avoid direct involvement if possible. But sometimes it is necessary to use critical judgment and acknowledge that one side or the other really is wrong. To hide under the cloak of impartiality and avoid facing reality is quite the opposite of good leadership. Jonathan's example is again worth noting and following.

The events of this chapter are simple. David and Jonathan meet and discuss how they can determine Saul's attitude and how they can convey that information if it is impossible for them to meet. The plan is carried out. Saul's extreme hostility is proved to be implacable. David is informed of this and, rightly or wrongly (the reader is left to make his or her own judgment on this point), he leaves town to ensure his safety. However, the understanding of relationships that is conveyed in the several conversations and the clear characterization of the three men provide a remarkable

---

[10] In 2 Kgs 9:11 the prophet Elisha is described as a 'maniac' or mad fellow. Ecstatic prophecy was not always understood, even in Old Testament times.

demonstration of the writer's skill. David has assessed Saul well. If he has calmed down, then he will accept David's absence from the feast with equanimity; if not, he will fly into the kind of uncontrolled rage that they have seen so many times before. It would be necessary to wait for two days because Saul would know that anybody could miss one day through inadvertently becoming ceremonially unclean.[11]

b. It is a strong friendship that survives mistrust (20:8–17)

It appears, however, that in spite of their friendship, David has less insight into Jonathan's character. He appeals (8) to the covenant that Jonathan has initiated between the two of them as if that was necessary in order to solicit his support. He also hints at a possibility that Jonathan might be colluding with Saul to kill him. Jonathan strongly denies any suggestion of such a thing and a potential dispute is avoided by a change of scene and a return to the question of the means for conveying news to David. It is impossible to tell whether this was a deliberate ploy or a subconscious response, but many tense situations can be defused by temporarily setting aside a disagreement and starting again in a different context.

Jonathan may have been hurt by David's suggestion of disloyalty, but he knows David, understands his need for reassurance and shows great pastoral wisdom in his response. He assures David that not only will he provide the necessary information but he will also guarantee David's safe departure if Saul does react adversely. He backs up his assurance with an oath, intended to be taken rather more seriously than an oath from Saul might have been. He then makes explicit the so far unspoken understanding of both men that Saul's suspicion that he will be succeeded by David and not by Jonathan is correct. Jonathan prays that God will bless and be with David in that situation, *as he* had *been with* his *father.* He asks only that David will take care of him and his family and not follow the custom of surrounding countries where any relatives or close supporters of previous regimes are put to death. He prays also that the Lord will *call David's enemies to account* (16). Given the context, it seems impossible to understand this as anything other than Jonathan recognizing and accepting that if Saul remains David's enemy, then he will surely stand under God's judgment. Finally, after outlining the arrangements for giving

---

[11] Nobody who had become ceremonially unclean, for example by coming into contact with an unclean animal, was allowed to take part in the ceremonial meal which played a major part in some sacrifices (cf. Lev. 7:20).

news, Jonathan reconfirms his commitment to David's cause by calling on the Lord as witness. It is not surprising that the editor felt it necessary to make further comment about Jonathan's love for David (17). Only a very remarkable person could exhibit this kind of gracious unselfishness. Jonathan's physical valour is strongly affirmed in earlier chapters and here it is recognized that it is not only as a warrior that Jonathan stands as a hero.

c. Taking a stand: even the most patient characters sometimes need to react (20:18–42)

At the feast, the friends' worst fears about Saul's reaction were confirmed. Saul's *anger flared up* (30)[12] not just at David but *at Jonathan*. Jonathan's defence of David brought down Saul's wrath, first verbal and then physical. Logic was not exactly Saul's strong point, as is shown ironically in the record of his intemperate raving: *You son of a perverse and rebellious woman! . . . you have sided with the son of Jesse . . . to the shame of the mother who bore you* (30). This contradiction – a genuinely perverse mother would hardly feel shame – was most likely picked up by at least one of Saul's hearers and, like the precise account of the seating arrangements given in verse 25, suggests again that we have here an eyewitness account. Interestingly, Saul was provoked into hurling his spear at Jonathan by Jonathan's refusal to accept Saul's words *neither you nor your kingdom will be established* (31) as a reason for killing David. Perhaps even in his irrational state it dawned on Saul that all his passionate hostility towards David, which somewhere in his mind had been on Jonathan's behalf, was from Jonathan's perspective both unnecessary and wrong. The normally even-tempered Jonathan was at last provoked into losing his cool. His anger was apparently not related to the attack on himself but to the treatment of David, which in his view was so patently unfair. The reference to Saul's behaviour as *shameful* is probably deliberate irony in the light of Saul's own comments. One wonders whether Jonathan's withdrawal from the feast was to give himself time to calm down and to stop himself taking any precipitate action against his father. If so, then perhaps his earlier initiation of a change of scene was indeed deliberate.

The news of Saul's reaction was sent to David, and the two friends had a brief and emotional farewell. That *David wept the most* (41) may show

---

[12] There is no way of determining whether Saul's attacks of depression, his obsessions and his inability to control his temper were symptoms of some psychological disorder or whether the latter two at least were simply the result of jealousy being deliberately allowed to fester.

that his affection for Jonathan was really genuine, but it probably also reflected his awareness that an era had ended and he was now a fugitive, a declared enemy of the state. Up to this point Saul's attempts to destroy David had been underhand and secret, but now the death sentence had been proclaimed in the presence of all the army leaders, including Abner. Rather than fighting for Israel and her king, which he had done so gladly and so successfully, David would be forced, in some measure at least, to fight against them.

When *David left . . . Jonathan went back to the town.* He must have been tempted to accompany David, but that could be done only by launching a full-scale rebellion against Saul, and neither of them wanted to do that. Jonathan, in spite of his loyalty to David and in spite of his father's irrationality, returned to give what support he could in the continuing running of the kingdom. There is just a slight hint here that if Jonathan could stay with Saul, even at risk of his life, David might also have been able to do so. It is never easy for those who work in situations where physical danger might arise to decide if they should move away from the situation or stay and trust in God's protection. We should continue to pray for those who find themselves in such situations, whichever choice they eventually make.

d. The forerunner of Christ?

The presentation of Jonathan's character in this chapter again raises the question of why such a man – unselfish, loving, brave, loyal, committed and wise – was not destined to be king. Unlike the accounts of Eli and Samuel there is never any suggestion that it was due to the behaviour of his son that Saul's dynasty would not continue. The portrayal of Jonathan is uniformly positive; he was surely, as much as any human being could be, a man after God's own heart. The books of Samuel resonate with the truth that God is sovereign and transcendent. There is no doubt that he has the right to make choices, nor that those choices may be unfathomable to the human mind. However, it is possible that we are being asked here to consider other matters from a different perspective. The debate on the nature of power with which the book begins and which is so clearly set out in Hannah's psalm is relevant here also. The assumption that the position of greatest power is bound to be the highest or greatest calling is common but perhaps false. Jonathan apparently had no real ambition to be king and certainly felt no jealousy when he came to understand that David had been called to that position. His desire was to serve God and his country in the best way he could. Indeed, one could say that Jonathan, though he was born royal, did not consider royalty a thing to be grasped, but was happy to humble himself and to take the role of a servant (cf. Phil. 2:6–8). David as king was called to be a forerunner of Christ and is known as such. Perhaps Jonathan too has the right to be seen as a forerunner of Christ in his self-emptying and humble service. Jonathan was not chosen to be king, but he was certainly chosen for a high calling and there is no need to feel sympathy for him. The classifying of calling, or the ascribing of spiritual status in terms of the amount of power associated with a particular role, was no more appropriate under the old covenant than it was in a New Testament context (Matt. 19:30; 20:16, 26–28; Jas 1:9–10; 2:1–9). Jonathan has much to teach God's people today.

5. David's escape via Nob (21:1 – 22:23)

a. Another difficult decision, another point of no return?

David clearly felt that this time there was no going back. Saul was not going to cope with him being part of the court and, given that his military successes goaded Saul beyond bearing, he could not even be part of the army. It is to David's credit that in spite of his own popularity and abilities, the possibility of staging a coup or setting up in opposition to Saul was never an option. As far as he was concerned, Saul had been anointed and appointed by God, and in spite of his faults, would remain king until God removed him from office (1 Sam. 24:5–10; 26:9–24). Also David had entered Saul's service and in spite of Saul's unjust suspicions of him, he took that position very seriously. Whether David or indeed anyone other than Samuel had been told of Saul's rejection by God is never discussed. David must have had some awareness that Saul had lost his confidence in God's presence, but it made no difference to him. There are instances in Scripture when those understood to be called by God are removed from office because they have failed to exercise their calling properly. David's own grandson Rehoboam comes into that category (1 Kgs 12; cf. Num. 12; Acts 15:36–39). But this is not to be one of those instances. In the world and in the church today we need great wisdom and discernment when we are faced with the decision to support or remove a failing leader. The right thing to do is not always obvious! From David's perspective there was no other choice than to flee the country. Any alternative would put other people in danger or undermine Saul's position and David had no desire to do either of those things. Anyone who is convinced of having the gifts and abilities to do a better job will find it hard to sit back and watch someone else make a mess of it without trying to remove that person. Perhaps it was something of that which pushed David into going rather than staying.

b. To trust or not to trust: that is the question (21:1–9)

David's first stop was at Nob where Ahimelek the priest was working. He perhaps deliberately avoided going to Samuel's home because that was likely to be the first place that Saul would look for him. Nob was a sanctuary, similar to and perhaps replacing the one at Shiloh, and David knew that he was likely to find the necessary supplies there. Ahimelek was probably Eli's great-grandson and the brother of Saul's priest Ahijah.[13] Once again the account is vivid and realistic, and reads something like a spy story.

Ahimelek was suspicious of David at first, unused to seeing him unaccompanied. Although he would not yet have heard of David's public condemnation, he was perhaps aware of Saul's continuing hostility, although 1 Samuel 22:14 could imply that he and maybe most of the people had seen no reason to doubt David's loyalty. He was apparently reassured by the story of a secret mission and a hidden troop. David's deceit may have been because he was unsure where Ahimelek's sympathies lay or because he wanted to protect him from any suspicion that he may have deliberately helped a known rebel. The hidden-troop story gave David an excuse for obtaining a good supply of bread and he also took with him Goliath's sword, which had been kept there. The presence of *Doeg the Edomite, Saul's chief shepherd* (7) is mentioned in passing, although the alert reader may note the emphasis that this was Saul's man and rightly expect that the reference will have significance in the unfolding narrative. The reference to Doeg being *detained before the LORD* is obscure. It is possible he was suffering some kind of imprisonment – his subsequent behaviour certainly reveals him as a violent man – and that his report of this incident to Saul was an attempt to get himself back into favour.[14]

---

[13] Cf. 1 Sam. 14:3; 22:9. They were both sons of Ahitub. Although this name, like Ahimelek, was a common priestly name (2 Sam. 8:17), it is likely that in this case the same man is meant.

[14] David's immediate recognition of Doeg (22:22) could support the view that he was a known troublemaker.

c. Are rules made to be broken? (21:4–6)

Technically Ahimelek had no right to give the consecrated bread to non-priests (cf. Lev. 24:5–9) even if they were ritually clean. In Matthew 12:1–8, however, Jesus supports Ahimelek's action when he uses this incident as an example of how God's real desire is for 'mercy, not sacrifice' and that concern for those in need may override concern for the precise details of the ritual law.[15] Perhaps Ahimelek asks about whether *the men have kept themselves from women* because he wanted to confirm that they really were on duty. Possibly David was already known for his strict enforcement of the 'no sex on duty' rule[16] that was going to cause both him and Bathsheba's husband Uriah so much trouble later on. It would certainly not have been right to go against the ritual requirements for the benefit of soldiers on a weekend off! Setting aside important rules or even conventions may be possible and even right on certain occasions. To set them aside just for our own convenience is as bad, if not worse, than the inflexible legalism that refuses to see that there may be more significant principles at issue. A modern-day Ahimelek might approve the breaking of a by-law or a speed limit when to do so would save a life or bring some other parallel benefit; such a person would be very unlikely to approve of the setting aside of such rules for a lesser purpose.

d. Deceit: a necessary tool in the armoury of the exile? (21:10–15)

David's hope to find sanctuary in Gath appears to have been unrealistically optimistic. His original intention was apparently to hire himself out as a mercenary soldier, but that depended on his remaining anonymous, which was unlikely given his high profile. The impression of the king of Gath's servants, that David was actually king of Israel, may have been common. If Saul had got wind of that rumour, it certainly would have added weight to his fears about David. Once he had been recognized, David's life was in great danger, and he again used deceit to ensure his safety.

---

[15] Jesus' conclusion that 'The Sabbath was made for [people], not [people] for the Sabbath' (Mark 2:27) is also relevant in this kind of situation.

[16] There is no record of a rule like this in the Old Testament law, although Exod. 19:15 does provide a precedent for sexual abstention in the context of preparing for a special ceremonial occasion. However, it appears to be something that David was known for. Some modern sports managers enforce the same rule by insisting that members of their team leave their families behind and concentrate only on training for the couple of days before an important match. It is by no means to be seen as portraying a negative attitude towards sex and sexuality.

This time his spur-of-the-moment tactic in feigning madness proved to be a clever move. The Gittite king Achish is presented here and in chapter 27 as straightforward, even guileless and kind-hearted. Certain cultures are superstitious about insanity, believing that to harm such people is unlucky. Perhaps that is what happened here, although the impression given is simply that Achish saw David as presenting no danger and had no desire to kill anyone unnecessarily. Whether or not it was right for David to deceive the good-hearted Philistine in this way is again left for the reader to decide.

In wartime situations some Christians have decided that telling the truth is always paramount and God must be trusted to deal with the consequences. But other equally sincere believers have decided that deceiving the enemy in order to save lives is perfectly justified. It remains a challenge for us to know how to behave in such a situation, but David's action should not be seen as a rationale for treating all those who do not belong to the community of God as if they have no right to the truth!

We do not know how long David stayed in Gath or why he left. It may be that sustaining his charade became too difficult or that he was just bored by being unable to work as a soldier.

It is interesting to note that Psalm 34, which the traditional heading presents as David's reflection on these events in Gath, makes no mention of his deceit and sees not David's cleverness but the goodness of the Lord as the determining factor that kept David safe.

e. Even the discontented can make good soldiers (22:1–5)

David stayed for a time at Adullam, a town originally captured by Joshua (Josh. 12:15) about halfway between Gath and David's home town of Bethlehem. The nearby caves formed an ideal hiding place for a fugitive band. Given Saul's intemperate nature, perhaps already evidenced by the events at Nob recorded in verses 6–23, David's family were now in danger, so they joined David in the relative safety of Adullam. It seems likely that David's brothers remained with him, but their parents were taken to Moab for sanctuary. Moab in general was opposed to Israel but no battles with Moab are described in the books of Samuel and there are only two brief references to their being subdued by Saul (1 Sam. 14:47) and David (2 Sam. 8:12). David, himself now seen as an enemy of Israel, may have been able to persuade the Moabite king on those grounds and although Ruth, Jesse's Moabite grandmother, seems to have severed all links with her homeland, it is possible that the family connection there did help.

The *discontented* of various kinds who soon *gathered round* David (2) may have been others who had suffered from one of Saul's irrational antipathies or may have included criminal elements. Wherever they came from, it says much for David's skill that they soon developed into what appears to have been a disciplined and effective force. The ability to take whatever material comes to hand and mould it into a useful team is one of the signs of a great leader. Nowhere in Scripture is there any backing for the tendency of middle-class Westerners to write off as lacking in potential those who wear the wrong clothes or live 'on the wrong side of the tracks', or in particular those who have exhibited discontent with society. The location of the stronghold where David was based after leaving Moab[17] is unknown, as is the site of Hereth which was his next port of call when *the prophet Gad* urged him to move on. We are given no information about Gad's background, although he clearly advised David throughout his reign (2 Sam. 24; 1 Chr. 21:9–19; 29:29). The willingness to take advice from others who may have a different kind of spiritual perception is another sign of good leadership ability.

f. When predetermined conclusions come in the door, justice flies out of the window (22:6–17a)

Saul has now become a travesty of the gifted king he once was and there is great perception as well as sadness in the way that his next actions are recorded. He sat, *spear in hand*, apparently unwilling to be separated from it even for a moment (6; cf. 18:10; 19:9–10; 20:33; 26:7, 16, 22). The spear was a weapon, but it also stood as a symbol of kingship. For Saul it had perhaps become a superstitious talisman. If he lost sight of the spear, the kingship too would no longer be his. His paranoia had convinced him not only that David's whole aim was to win the loyalty of all Israel, especially the army, but that he must have bribed those of Saul's own tribe who remained with him. The reference to *men of Benjamin* (7) may indicate that Saul was now afraid to let any except those of his own tribe into his presence. Even Jonathan comes under suspicion – his friendship with David must mean betrayal of Saul, and there is a sad humour in the account of Saul's complaint that *no one tells me*, when he clearly has been told.

---

[17] The stronghold was not in Judah (5) and therefore could not have been Adullam.

Jonathan's continuing presence with his father at this time says much for his character, although Saul in his more lucid times was only too well aware that Jonathan was in no way a danger to him.

It seems that Saul's officials generally ignored his paranoic rantings and waited for them to pass, but this time Doeg the Edomite was present and only too willing to add flame to the fire. He reported what he had seen at Nob. The account may have been deliberately slanted; perhaps Doeg had a grudge against Ahimelek. Whether this was so or not, and whether the previously unrecorded enquiry *of the* Lord by Ahimelek on David's behalf took place or not, Saul interpreted the help given to David as a deliberate act of treason. A meeting was held but it bore no relation to the kind of trial that the law required. There was only one witness[18] and Ahimelek's own very plausible explanation that by giving help to David he thought he was actually supporting Saul's cause was completely ignored. Saul was incapable of hearing anything that conflicted with his own pre-determined conclusion. It is a common temptation to jump to conclusions about guilt and ignore evidence that conflicts with those conclusions, not only in a court of law but also in less dramatic situations within our own families and communities. Yielding to such temptation is always un-acceptable especially in those who do not have the excuse of Saul's mental instability. In a totally illegal way, not only Ahimelek but his whole family were sentenced to death.

g. The devastating consequences of temper (22:17b–23)

The unwillingness of the king's officials to act may have been for fear of reprisal from the Lord if his priests were harmed, particularly in this unjust way. However, it is probable that, as with Jonathan, their knowledge of Saul and their loyalty to him motivated them to protect him from himself. They knew that this action was completely unjust and wrong and it was possible that Saul himself would regret his outburst shortly. Doeg, with no hint of that kind of sensitivity, took Saul at and beyond his word. The danger of allowing a burst of temper to get the better of one and making unconsidered claims or demands is nowhere illustrated more clearly than here. The encouragement to 'be oneself' and 'let it all hang out', which is a feature of modern society, does have some positive elem-ents, but can only ever be valid if it is accompanied by a strong awareness

---

[18] Cf. Num. 35:30 where it is forbidden for the death sentence to be carried out if there is only one witness.

of responsibility for the consequences of our self-absorption. Not only the priests but the whole of the little town of Nob were destroyed in this devastating demonstration of violence resulting from Saul's self-indulgent display of temper. It must have reduced Saul's credibility in the nation far more drastically than anything David could have done. The use of the language of *hērem* in verse 19 (cf. 15:3) brings out the irony of the fact that Saul, who was unwilling to obey God's command to destroy the Amalekites totally, seems to have had no problem in completely disregarding God's law and permitting the total destruction described here.

Ahijah, Saul's own priest, was presumably one of those who died in the massacre. He is never referred to again. The only survivor was Ahimelek's son Abiathar, who escaped to David's camp taking the ephod with him (23:6). The ephod was used to ascertain God's way forward in a given situation. The fact that David now had access to the ephod and Saul did not reinforces the picture of Saul, as a result of his own actions, becoming increasingly separated from contact with God. The attempt to preserve his status as God's anointed king was only one in a long series of actions that destroyed Saul himself as much as the people he attacked. Disobedience and temper are both things that can separate us from God, just as much as they did Saul. We have no record of Saul's reactions when his temper died down and the full horror of Doeg's actions came to light. We do not know if he accepted the responsibility that Abiathar placed securely on his shoulders (21). Doeg may have been the actual murderer, but there is no doubt that *Saul had killed the priests of the Lord* and it is inconceivable that the weight of this thought did not bear heavily on Saul. But David, further demonstrating his own leadership qualities, did accept his own responsibility, however unwitting, for the death of Abiathar's family and for the continuing safety of Abiathar himself.

6. The continuing campaign (23:1–14)

a. Am I my brother's keeper? (23:1–6)

The interest of the writer of 1 Samuel has been centred on the power struggle within Israel and the characters involved in that, but the context of the need to protect the Israelite people from outside incursions is not forgotten. Whether David's assuming responsibility for defending the residents of Keilah indicates a lack of action on Saul's part or simply that David's camp was nearer is not stated. The situation was urgent. Keilah was a border town and must have been used to the Philistine troops claiming tribute, but *looting the threshing-floors* was different. This act would have deprived the people of the grain for the next year's crop and would have caused major hardship. For David, this kind of campaign was a new step. He was not yet the appointed leader of the land and to act in this way might have been seen as usurping Saul's role, but he couldn't bear just to sit and watch the disaster happen. He therefore *enquired of the Lord* as to whether this was the right way forward. The language used implies that the ephod brought by Abiathar was quickly brought into service, but it is possible that some other, unknown method of enquiry was used.[19] David did not make specific enquiries of God before every action or campaign. Where, as in the past, he had been fighting directly as Saul's representative or where God's will had previously been made clear, such enquiry was inappropriate. But this was a new situation and David wanted to be sure his involvement was warranted. There are times when seeking and waiting for God's clear and specific guidance is actually a sign of the disobedient shirking of responsibility, but there are times when it is a sign of faith. Identifying the difference has always been a challenge for believers!

David's enquiry received a positive answer, but the men with him were wary of leaving the relative security of the Judean hills. A leader who takes on new campaigns without the action being 'owned' by all involved is foolish indeed and David takes the unusual step of enquiring *of the Lord* a second time, presumably on this occasion in the presence of his troops. It is possible that those with David, knowing that they were considered as enemies by Saul, who was God's anointed king, were unsure of God's attitude to themselves. In a way that recurs throughout Old Testament history, their fears are taken seriously and they are given reassurance.

It is always encouraging to realize that God does take seriously the worries of his people and that this applies to us just as much as to David's men. Once the men are sure of God's support, they join David in taking action. It is, as promised, successful and the Philistines are in turn deprived of their own livelihoods. David and his men, perhaps glad of the company of supportive people and the luxury of easily available supplies, remain in Keilah for a little while.

---

[19] In verse 6 Abiathar is described as bringing the ephod to David *at Keilah*, in which case it would not yet have been available for use, but the suggestion that the place name has become misplaced does have some merit in this instance.

b. Loyalty and betrayal (23:7–14)

Keilah's willingness to betray David even though he had rescued them is perhaps a further sign of the ability of the younger Saul to inspire loyalty. But Saul's reaction to the events at Keilah provides further evidence that he has little regard for those who show him loyalty. His interest now is in retaining the status of kingship rather than in exercising the responsibility involved in being king. His joy at hearing the news is not prompted by the rescue of one of the towns for which he as king is responsible, but that David's sojourn there provides an opportunity to capture him. The action he takes is not to harass Israel's enemies further, but to seek to besiege one of his own towns – to harm loyal Keilah rather than to help. The addictive nature of power and its tendency to cause those so addicted to lose all sense of proportion is illustrated here. Any behaviour is considered acceptable if it means the retention of power and status. Given the continuing interest in the subject, it is hard not to assume that the author is conscious of the warnings conveyed in his writings. We, too, must be very careful lest our desire to hold on to office of any kind actually prevents us from carrying out the responsibilities of that office. In this instance, Saul has even deluded himself into thinking that his opportunity to get rid of David is God-given. However, David's informants prove as efficient as Saul's own. That it was Jonathan himself who acted as 'friend at court' for David, enabling him to have *heard definitely* of Saul's intended action, is only speculation, but that he had supporters in Saul's entourage is undoubted.

David's use of the ephod on this occasion seems hard to fathom. It is possible that the issue is timing. He knows that Saul is coming, but if the people of Keilah are going to hand him over, then he has a shorter time in which to get out. It is difficult to imagine that he would have stayed in the town, bringing danger on them, even if the inhabitants would not have surrendered him to Saul. In spite of their potential betrayal, they had sheltered David for a while and, in contrast to Saul, he had no intention of harming his own people. He and his gradually increasing band, now consisting of six hundred men, went back to the hills, this time in the southern area around Ziph. Even in such difficult terrain, a group that size would have been hard to hide. David's management and survival skills, as well as his own intelligence network bringing news of Saul's progress, would have been put to good use in his attempts to avoid Saul's continuing pursuit, providing further good experience for his own future role in leading Israel's campaigns. However, the text provides no doubt that the real reason that Saul was not able to find David, let alone capture him, was that *God did not give David into his hands* (14). The complex relationship between God's action and human responsibility is well illustrated here.

7. Enemies, real and perceived (23:15 – 24:22)

a. Good friends help us hold fast to our own principles (23:15–18)

We are provided with a great deal of information about Saul's persistent attempts to find and destroy David. Seven of 1 Samuel's thirty-one chapters are concerned with Saul's enmity towards David. The lessons to be learned from this damaged relationship and the events surrounding it are clearly seen as significant. Readers past and present are meant to take serious note of the destructiveness of jealousy, the dangers of a hunger for power, the necessity for obedience and the tragedy that can stem from allowing a personal agenda to make us forget God's priorities. One or two incidents are recorded in detail. On one occasion (23:15–18), as Saul got close, it seems as if the constant pressure was beginning to get David down. David was determined not to oppose Saul directly. However, as the number of men with him grew and his experience in handling the terrain increased, the temptation to turn and fight was perhaps becoming hard to resist. Jonathan, again indicating that he may have been involved in David's supply of information, knew exactly where to find him. Hearing of David's disheartenment, he risked leaving his father's encampment and, meeting up with David, *helped him to find strength in God* (16). Whether David needed strength to keep running from Saul or to hold on to his resolve not to fight is hard to determine. The more literal 'strengthened his hand in God' found in the AV and some other English versions conveys the sense of enabling David to hold fast to the task God had set before him, rather than just conveying a general sense of encouragement.

Jonathan, like David, firmly believed that God was in control, and his main desire was that God's purposes for Israel would be achieved. He was convinced that God's plan was for David to succeed Saul and therefore he trusted that God would bring this about, so there was no way Saul was going to be able to kill David. There was no need for David to fear or take precipitate action. David knew this too, but it must have been a tremendous encouragement to hear it again from Jonathan's lips. Even the strongest faith sometimes wavers and the value of an encouraging word from an understanding friend at those times cannot be underestimated. Jonathan knew that he could take only second place in David's kingdom and he was not at all troubled by that thought. Jonathan's statement that Saul, too, knew that David would succeed him is confirmed in 24:20, but Saul was very definitely troubled by the thought. It appears that Saul's desperate effort to remove David from the scene was a deliberate if hopeless attempt to thwart God's plans or at least to persuade God to change his mind. If there were no David, then surely God would look to Jonathan. Such an approach could come only from a man who has lost sight of God's sovereignty and lost control of himself.

The portraits of David, Saul and Jonathan are brilliantly drawn. This was the last meeting between David and Jonathan. Jonathan remained courageous and caring, sensitive, sensible and supportive right to the end; a true friend indeed.

b. The Saul who might have been (23:19–28)

On another occasion (19–28) Saul was offered help by local residents, perhaps fearful of their own safety or maybe simply wanting to serve their king (20). Behind the stories of Saul's obsessive and fruitless search for David lie intriguing glimpses of a possible alternative scenario where Saul gladly accepts David as his successor and works out his term supported loyally by the whole country. On this occasion Saul and David's intelligence agents appear to have been equally matched and the two forces came as close as the opposite sides of the same hill. This time David was saved, as the nation of Israel was saved on other occasions,[20] by a report of fighting in another area. Saul's response to this report provides a further glimpse of his potential and shows that he did, at least at times, retain some awareness of his responsibilities as king. One is reminded of Sméagol in Tolkien's *The Lord of the Rings*, where glimpses of lost potential keep appearing in spite of the apparently complete corruption caused by years of obsession with a powerful possession.

c. When the 'game' goes on for a long time it is easy to forget the rules (23:29 – 24:7a)

David's next haven was in the caves of En Gedi down by the Dead Sea,[21] where water and food were available as well as good hiding places. The

---

[20] E.g. 2 Kgs 19:9 where the Assyrian king Sennacherib left off his campaign against Israel to go and fight the Egyptians.

[21] The site of the *Crags of the Wild Goats* cannot be identified precisely but that area was known for wild ibex and this was presumably a known grazing point.

writer's vivid, evocative style again comes into play as we see Saul getting closer to David than at any time since the beginning of his search and yet totally unaware of it (24:3). Hiding at the back of the cave that Saul enters, David's men are sure that this is a God-given chance for David to deal with Saul, and David, apparently at least halfway convinced, creeps forward and cuts off *a corner of Saul's robe*. There is no record of the prophecy spoken of by the men and it may be that they have, perhaps unconsciously, expanded on the fact of which they were almost certainly aware, that David was ordained to be the next king. The tendency to elaborate on or reinterpret God's promises is a common one and it is to David's credit that his yielding to the pressure of his men was short-lived. He *was conscience-stricken*, not because he had damaged Saul's clothes, but because of what it symbolized. He had deliberately exercised power over Saul while Saul was still king. His taking a portion of the royal robes was a symbolic taking away of something of Saul's royalty. David knew he would wear royal robes, and Jonathan's gift of robes (18:4) had already symbolized that. But those robes would really be his only if they came as a gift from God and not as a result of his own grasping of them. David still saw himself as in Saul's service; Saul was his *master* and *the Lord's anointed*. It was his own failure to remember this, and perhaps even an awareness of a desire to harm Saul, that brought David up with a jolt.

Avoiding Saul without doing him damage had perhaps become something of a game for David, and he was shocked to realize that for a brief moment he had forgotten the rules. Not surprisingly, his anger with himself was transferred to his men and his rebuke of the whole troop was quite strong. For all of us there is a warning here that the battles we think we have won with ourselves can suddenly change direction, resulting in an attack coming from another front. The fact that David actually noticed what was happening is a measure of how much he reflected on what was going on in his life and helps to explain why he is regarded so highly in the Old Testament. His theology was, at least at his best times, not restricted to his poetry but was worked out in his life day by day.

d. Opportunity to harm may also be an opportunity to heal (24:7b–22)

Saul, unaware of all the emotional trauma and analysis of motives that was going on in the cave, calmly *went his way* back to his own camp. In that terrain sound would have travelled quite a long way and it seems certain that David allowed Saul to reach a safe distance before he called out to him. David is consistently portrayed as impulsive and emotional as well as a gifted leader and diplomat. It is not clear what prompted the impulse to make contact with Saul at this point. It could have been a desire to justify himself or maybe a sudden realization that although this could be seen as a God-given opportunity, it was not in fact an opportunity to harm or defeat Saul but to effect reconciliation. Any interpretation of God's involvement in our circumstances must be based on an awareness of the character of God and on his clearly revealed purposes. The opportunity to take a particular course of action – in this instance to kill Saul – does not mean that that particular action must be supported by God, who may in fact have provided an opportunity for something completely different. There are parallels here with Joseph's comment that although his brothers' action in selling him into Egypt as a slave was intended to harm him, in fact in God's providence it became an opportunity for good (Gen. 50:20).

David's speech to Saul is certainly an example of brilliant diplomatic skill. He begins with a very dramatic, even melodramatic, bowing down to the ground; both men were fond of extravagant gestures, but it may be that David wanted to make sure that Saul, even at a distance, could see exactly what he was doing. He knows that reconciliation depends on Saul realizing that David poses no threat to his position and he indicates his allegiance to Saul by action as well as word. For David, Saul was still *my Lord the king* (8). He panders to Saul's vanity by suggesting that it must have been jealous slanderers who persuaded Saul, because surely Saul was too sensible to think that David really was a threat. He completely reinterprets his own action in cutting off the piece of robe, portraying it as a deliberate means of conveying to Saul that he would never harm him even if he had the opportunity. Whether this was just a diplomatic tactic or whether David had managed to convince himself that he really hadn't had any of the motivation his conscience told him he had is not made explicit. The tendency to want to think the best of ourselves is universal and David was certainly not immune from it. He calls Saul *my father*, emphasizing the relationship between them, his own love and loyalty towards Saul and his appreciation of what Saul has done for him in the past. He was certainly not *guilty of wrongdoing or rebellion* against Saul. In fact, it was Saul who had wronged David in *hunting* him *down* in this way. David would be glad to allow *the LORD* to *judge between them* and it would be God and certainly not David who carried out the results of any judgment against Saul. David has turned the whole thing upside down by replacing what might have been expected to be a statement of repentance for his own sins into a statement of forgiveness for Saul's sins against him. He uses proverbs to point out how ridiculous it was for someone as important as *the king of Israel* to see as a threat a *flea* on the carcass of a *dead dog*, which was how unimportant David was in comparison. His final words were again to refer the dispute to *the LORD* as judge and to pray for his own vindication.

David's carefully crafted appeal did get through to Saul, who was particularly impressed by the fact that David could have harmed him but did not. In other words, he accepted that David had proved he was not *his enemy*. He, too, recognizes the relationship between them, calling David *my son*. He acknowledges that in any judgment between them it will be David who will be vindicated as he is *more righteous* than Saul. He finally acknowledges the reality of his own rejection by God and for the first time openly accepts not only that it will be David who will replace him as king, but that David will achieve the stability and security that Saul has longed to see in Israel and as yet has been unable to achieve. Like Jonathan he asks only that when David takes over he will be gracious to Saul's family. Once again the window is opened onto the possibilities of the 'might have been' scenario if only Saul's reaction here had been maintained. There is a hint in the account of a mourning for the unrealized potential in Saul's life and reign even after he has placed himself under God's judgment. Saul could still have known God's blessing, not as the founder of a dynasty but as a mentor for David, but he threw away the opportunity.

Those who fail must accept the reality and the consequences of their failure, but that does not mean there is no place of service for them. There is a great encouragement in these glimpses of possibility for Saul even if he himself was never able to follow them through.

Questions to ponder

1. What do we make of the coming and going of the 'Spirit of the LORD'?
2. Is it possible for leaders to avoid the temptation to form an aristocracy?
3. Was Jonathan's friendship with David a betrayal of Saul?

4. Could Saul's obsession have been overcome with different handling? Did he really suffer from mental illness and if so did that excuse his behaviour?
5. Should David have stayed or was he right to go?
6. Are there tools available for determining when and if a particular opportunity is God-given?
7. Which of David's strengths and weaknesses can be seen in this section?
8. David deceived Ahimelek. Can deceit be seen as a legitimate tool to be used in the service of God?
9. In what circumstances, if any, can it be seen as legitimate to set aside the law in order to achieve a higher purpose?

1 Samuel 25 – 31

5. David: the exiled nationalist

1. David and Abigail (25:1–44)

Saul's reconciliation with David was short-lived and we return in chapter 26 to his continuing mission to 'search and destroy'. However, once Saul had openly acknowledged David's claim, any doubt about the final outcome had been removed and the account can focus more on David and his wider activities. The power struggle between David and Saul was now virtually over and it was fitting at this point to record the death of Samuel, who had been so involved in the rise to power of both.

Samuel had exercised his own power well and had given great service to God and to Israel. It was fitting that a national gathering should take place to mourn his passing. It is interesting to speculate whether this took place during the temporary reconciliation of Saul and David and whether they were both present to mourn the death of their mutual mentor. Now neither his wise counsel nor his sad rebuke was available to either of them. Samuel was buried near his family home in Ramah.

The Egyptian custom of creating a shrine around the tomb of powerful leaders was never seen as appropriate in Israel. Even kings were only men among men, and death was a natural part of life, not a powerful force with sacral significance. The fact that only one verse is taken to describe both Samuel's death and any attached ceremonial is probably making the same point. However significant a leader might appear to be, no individual person is indispensable and God's purposes move on, worked out now via the next generation. It is not a sign of good leadership if the impression is given that when a particular person dies, retires or moves away, the work that person was leading will fall apart. There is little support in Scripture for the cult of personality which seems so popular in modern times. Samuel was undoubtedly a great loss, but not an insuperable one.

a. Examples to follow and to avoid (25:1–3)

We gain more insights into the pattern of David's life in exile during the times when he was not directly concerned with dodging Saul. The story of his dealings with Abigail and Nabal might be seen as interrupting the concern of the narrative with national leadership, but the continuing interest in the use and abuse of power is illustrated here in a different way. It has been suggested that within this chapter Nabal, whose name means 'foolish' or 'stupid one', is used to represent Saul in his attempts to destroy David. By means of this story Saul's actions and activities could be condemned as completely foolish without making any explicit comment about Saul himself. Following on from chapter 24, David's describing himself as Nabal's 'son' (8), and the fact that he could have killed Nabal but did not, may be seen as encouraging the reader to make this connection.[1] Having said that, the story makes sense in its own context and there is no real reason to doubt that the story also has validity in its own right by providing the reader with further examples to follow and to avoid.

Nabal, probably a nickname given to reflect his character rather than his actual name, was, we are told, *very wealthy.* The district around Maon was not fertile but there were areas of grazing land that make the title 'desert' slightly misleading. Nabal's wealth was built on his large herds of sheep and goats. That his extensive property was sited near Carmel, where Saul had set up a 'monument in his own honour' (15:12), may or may not be significant, but Nabal is certainly depicted as having a strong sense of his own importance. In many ways the couple are presented in almost cartoon fashion as absolute opposites. In a way that brings to mind the 'wife of noble character' of Proverbs 31, Abigail is introduced as the ideal woman, both *intelligent and beautiful,* liked and respected by their employees and a politically aware supporter of David. Nabal, on the other hand, was a loud-mouthed brute, *surly and mean in his dealings* and despised by his employees. He may have inherited the stickability of his ancestor Caleb (Num. 13:30; Josh. 14:6–15), but in him it came out as stubbornness and he had none of Caleb's likeable good sense. He was

---

[1] R. P. Gordon, 'David's Rise and Saul's Demise: Narrative Analogy in 1 Samuel 24 – 26', *TynBul* 31 (1980), pp. 37–67; cf. J. C. Exum, *Tragedy and Biblical Narrative* (Cambridge: Cambridge University Press, 1992), p. 106.

apparently a supporter of Saul, although his contempt for David may have just been an example of his general contempt for the human race. Nabal was not a nice man! It is not surprising that as the dispute between David and Saul became more widely known, people began to take sides. The plotting against Saul that he so feared was in fact made more likely by his own actions. Nobody takes sides against people who are working together. There is no doubt now that the sympathies of the writer lie with David and there is a strong implication within this story that anybody who was gifted and attractive, like Abigail, would be bound to give allegiance to David. However, such a thought remains unstated.

b. Everyone has the right to expect hospitality (25:4–13)

For David, finding food for six hundred men in a less than fertile area must have been a constant strain and this episode provides us with an idea of how it was done. It would seem that David's men acted as unofficial security guards in the area where they were based at the time, protecting the local people from attacks by outsiders and looting by local criminals. They did not act as brigands and took nothing that was not freely given, but they did expect to be rewarded when harvest time came round. If this is to be seen as a protection racket, it is a fairly gentle one. That their help was not entirely disinterested is seen by their reaction when Nabal refused to pay up. However, this approach was probably viewed by all as better than simply plundering local farms. For modern readers in the West where hospitality, often even among Christians, is seen as an optional extra rather than a universal obligation, David's request for support might be seen as something of a cheek. But in ancient Israel, as indeed in many less 'sophisticated' parts of the world today, both giver and receiver would take it for granted that visitors to a region would be offered at least some kind of sustenance. Many visitors abroad have experienced the generous hospitality of those in other continents who may have very little but will always willingly share that little with visitors, particularly Christian brothers and sisters from other places. Perhaps these people can understand the sense of isolation and rejection felt by visitors to the West who attend a church on many occasions without even being invited for a meal. Hospitality is taken very seriously within Scripture, and Nabal's refusal to provide supplies for David, like the inhospitable approach of the residents of Sodom to the visiting angels (Gen. 19), is seen as an unacceptable aberration. The New Testament injunction to practise hospitality (Rom. 12:13; cf. 1 Tim. 5:10; 1 Pet. 4:9) implies rather more than a gracious smile and a cup of coffee supplied after the morning service (good as those things might be!).

On this occasion, they had heard that Nabal was sheep-shearing. On a large estate, the feast celebrating the end of shearing would have been magnificent. Even with Nabal's reputation for meanness, there would be plenty to go round, enough for David's large band to be included without causing a problem. Perhaps that was why Nabal's farm was chosen. David sends a small, unthreatening group to remind Nabal of the way his men have protected the shepherds and to ask politely for some recognition of this, gently reminding Nabal of his neighbourly responsibilities. Nabal, in rather less than polite terms, tells them to 'get lost'.

Nabal's behaviour could, from one perspective, be viewed as the brave refusal of a loyal follower of Saul to give in to the bullying tactics of a rebel gang. He disowns any connection with David and responds to the *your son David* (8) with *Who is this son of Jesse?* (10) – he is certainly not a son of mine. One might see this as a reasonable response from a Saulide supporter who does not want to be tainted by association. However, the whole presentation makes it clear that the narrator, who so often describes events and leaves the reader to draw his or her own conclusions, in this instance wants the reader to be sure that that perspective is invalid. Certainly, Nabal had no evidence that David's men had behaved disloyally or in a rebellious way, and normal hospitality should have meant them getting some positive response, regardless of any help they had given to the shepherds. No, as far as the writer is concerned, Nabal's insults are to be seen as the unnecessary rudeness of an ignorant boor. David's men, perhaps illustrating the discipline that David had taught them, did not react but took the message back to David. Perhaps the requested contribution was never meant to be voluntary or perhaps Nabal's aggression meant that David's group could now be in danger. One thing, however, is clear: his insulting response was not to be allowed to stand. Four hundred trained men, the rest staying behind on guard, would have no trouble in dealing with a group of farmhands, however large.

c. Good and bad employers are known by their employees (25:14–22)

Meanwhile, back down in the valley, Nabal's servants went to find Abigail. They clearly felt that Nabal's response was both foolish and uncalled for, and they confirmed that David's band had protected them and presumably prevented Nabal from suffering considerable loss. The workers know, and they know that she knows, that it is no use talking to Nabal. However, they have no doubts that she will be able to deal with the situation.

Abigail, like a number of Old Testament women,[2] is seen as having a lot more sense than her husband. It says much for Abigail that, in spite of her husband's boorishness, she has such a good relationship with the men. Their confidence in her is repaid. David's curse in verse 22 is parallel to Saul's foolish vows (1 Sam. 14) and is perhaps intended to provide a further contrast with Abigail's calm good sense. Obviously her arrival with such lavish supplies would have made a big difference and one wonders whether Nabal was too drunk or just too dull to notice what she was doing – although it may simply indicate that the farm was so exceptionally well supplied that a loss even this large would not be significant. David's anger may have been assuaged by the smell of the food, but Abigail's very skilful and accomplished speech completely won him over. It contains as much diplomatic wisdom and awareness of the listener and his possible response as David's own speech to Saul in the previous chapter.

d. The power of diplomacy over violence (25:23–35)

She, as David had to Saul, acknowledges his position as *my lord* and her own as *your servant*. She accepts full blame for what has happened while at the same time dissociating herself completely from Nabal's actions and his position. It is David, not Nabal, whom she calls *my lord* (27). She, perhaps rather disloyally, dismisses Nabal as an irrelevant fool and makes it clear that if she had been present, it would never have happened. She plays on David's natural sense of justice, and his awareness of God's sovereignty. She knows enough about him[3] to realize that he will withdraw if he can be brought to see the lack of killing so far as God's intervention and to view his possible action against Nabal as merely revenge (punishment being unnecessary now the gift has been brought).

In her plea for forgiveness she launches into a remarkable political speech that clearly shows her understanding of exactly what is going on in the conflict between Saul and David. She makes clear her own

---

[2] Rebekah's easy manipulation of Isaac (Gen. 27) is one example of this. Manoah's wife (Judg. 13) and the Shunammite woman (2 Kgs 4) provide more positive examples.

[3] It is possible that David's refusal to act against Saul was a matter of public comment and, in Abigail's case at least, public approval.

conviction that David is God's man and will not only be given the throne but will be very successful in dealing with his enemies and will himself be kept safe by God. The clarity and passion in this speech go well beyond what would have been required as a defence of Abigail's employees. If this story has been retold as a politically acceptable way of critiquing Saul and vindicating David, then it could be considered possible that Abigail's speech has been rewritten to support that motive. However, it could equally well reflect the firmly held convictions of an intelligent and politically aware woman whose mind and gifts are stifled in her present situation. Abigail believes that it is David, not Saul, who is the future for Israel and that to take petty revenge against Nabal and his household would demean him and his cause. Perhaps Paul's instruction to the Christian believers, 'Do not take revenge, my dear friends, but leave room for God's wrath' (Rom. 12:19), resulted from meditation on Abigail's story.[4]

Her final request that he should remember her when God has brought him to power parallels Saul's request in chapter 24. In Saul's case it was a plea that his family not be destroyed. Abigail's meaning is harder to fathom. She did not need material help from David, so perhaps she was asking to be allowed to have some part in his regime; a strange request for a woman at that time but not unthinkable for someone of Abigail's calibre.

One of David's most endearing gifts was his ability to listen to critiques of his own behaviour.[5] He may have yielded too easily to unwise impulses, but he was rarely unwilling to recognize, regret and take responsibility for those impulses and the consequences of any action that might have followed. He is very aware that in this instance, as in many others, he might have gone on to act in haste and repent at leisure. He sees Abigail's arrival as a Godsend, acknowledging her theological astuteness and her understanding of his own character. He would otherwise have destroyed Nabal's farm and it would have been the wrong thing to do. The implications of her call to avoid unnecessary violence in the treatment of opponents are far-reaching, and David's treatment of Shimei (2 Sam. 19:22), for example, perhaps stems from his acceptance of Abigail's advice. Abigail stands as a challenge and an encouragement to intelligent women and men to use their gifts and to share the insights that God gives them.

---

[4] As well as, of course, on Deut. 32:35. Taking heed of both Paul and Abigail is certainly appropriate in today's world.

[5] Cf. David's response to Nathan's rebuke in 2 Sam. 12, although this came after he had yielded to his baser instincts rather than before.

Abigail did not allow her own difficult home situation to prevent her from developing her gifts.

There was no question in David's mind that Abigail had brought him God's word. The ability to hear God speaking and to listen to advice, even when it comes from unexpected sources, is a further sign of good leadership potential. In this instance, David readily agreed to Abigail's request, although his opportunity to *remember* her came rather sooner than expected.

e. Greed and temper bring their own reward (25:36–44)

Nabal was a prime candidate for a stroke, given his known temper and intemperate drinking, particularly if the kind of behaviour seen on this occasion was habitual. He suffered some kind of major seizure as soon as he heard the news of Abigail's action. As David had already agreed not to attack, it could not have been fear of that that upset him. Perhaps his rage that David had been given supplies after all proved too much for him. Nabal did not recover and ten days later he died.

David understood this as God taking the vengeance that was his prerogative and thus confirming Abigail's wisdom and validating David's own actions. The marriage that then took place may have stemmed from a mutual attraction or merely a mutual convenience. However, it gave David an opportunity to fulfil any obligation to protect Abigail from Nabal's family or from Saul and also gave him constant access to her astute advice (marriage was probably the only suitable way of bringing her into his council). It provided Abigail with the chance to exercise her gifts and express her political convictions. She gladly accepted David's offer in spite of knowing that she would not be David's sole wife and that life in a rebel encampment was likely to involve menial tasks (41). They had one son, known as Kileab (2 Sam. 3:3) or Daniel (1 Chr. 3:1), but nothing more is heard of him and he may not have lived beyond childhood.

Michal's remarriage is noted here. We cannot be sure of the time that has elapsed since David disappeared through Michal's window (1 Sam. 19:12), but it may have been several years. We know that Paltiel really did love Michal (2 Sam. 3:13–16), but we are not told of her attitude to him. It is possible that David's apparent neglect of Michal had turned her love for him sour and this second marriage was at her request. Saul had no legal right to give her to another husband without David's consent, but the action is understandable.

133

Ahinoam was the mother of David's firstborn son Amnon, but we learn nothing more about her. Perhaps this note about David's personal life at the end of chapter 25 is preparing us for the problems that would come at a later stage for David's dysfunctional family.

2. Saul: off the hook again (26:1–25)

The marked similarities between the account in this passage of David's sparing of Saul and the one in chapter 24, and the lack of any reference to the previous occasion, have led some to suggest that these are alternative accounts of the same event.[6] The parallel wording of 26:1 and 23:19 is certainly striking and could indicate conflation between two accounts. However, even here the area referred to by the Ziphites is quite wide and there is a strong probability that David would have covered the same ground on several occasions. There are also significant differences between this account and the previous one and the writer clearly felt that the inclusion of the second account was important. Given the continuing nature of Saul's persistent search for David, it is by no means inconceivable that there were several occasions when the stalked became the stalker. Also, given Saul's volatile nature and previous revoking of a sworn oath (19:6), it is not at all surprising that his acceptance of David's loyalty and right to the throne now appears forgotten.

a. Learning from experience (26:1–12)

Both forces have learned from experience. This time Saul takes his three thousand[7] men quickly to the appointed site. David's intelligence has remained good and he, having moved to a different site, is awaiting Saul's arrival. This encounter is by no means accidental. It is possible even that the Ziphites' information to Saul was this time a deliberate leak. David's incursion into the main Israelite camp and removing Saul's spear was clearly a pre-planned strategy. Perhaps the success of his previous speech in restoring Saul's sense of perspective led him to hope that a repetition of the same tactic would lead to a further breathing space before Saul's

---

[6] E.g. Klein, pp. 236–237; Caird, pp. 855–1176.

[7] It is possible, here and elsewhere, that 'thousand' is a name given to a battalion or a cohort of varying numbers and that Saul was accompanied by three such cohorts rather than literally by three thousand men. However, three thousand seems a not unreasonable number for Saul to take to retain an advantage over David's six hundred who were fighting in their own territory.

pursuit began again. Given the rough nature of the terrain and the detailed knowledge of it that David's enforced stays had provided, there would have been no problem in getting within sight of Saul's encampment. However, proceeding further was a very different matter. This particular mission did not warrant large numbers and David took with him just one volunteer, his nephew[8] Abishai, Joab's brother. He may not have been the wisest choice for a task that required stealth and self-control, but there was no doubting his bravery or his commitment. If it did come to a fight, he would be an excellent partner to have.

Saul and his army were asleep. That the whole lot, presumably including the guards who might have been expected to notice the arrival of the two outsiders, were so deeply asleep is seen as a result of the Lord's direct intervention. This explains how David was able to get so close and reinforces the fact that God was behind David, supporting his actions rather than protecting Saul. It may also be included as a defence for Abner, who is consistently presented as a good soldier and a faithful general. His support for Saul is always seen as praiseworthy, not blameworthy. It is not always wise or appropriate to criticize faithful followers of a foolish leader. Abishai may or may not have been told of David's plan in this instance and he may or may not have been with David in the cave on the previous occasion, but his reaction mirrors that of the soldiers there. Having come so close to the sleeping Saul without problem, surely this is a God-given opportunity to kill him. The confident Abishai knows he can do it with one thrust. This time David is not even tempted. Perhaps his previous experience coupled with his encounter with Nabal and Abigail has reinforced his conviction that it should be God himself and not any action on the part of David or his men that brings an end to Saul's reign. Saul's death might come from a supernatural act of destruction, in the middle of a battle or just in the natural course of life's journey, but it will not be at David's instigation.

It is interesting that David understands God to be at work in all these different ways. Diseases, ageing and foreign armies can be as much a part of the way that God works in his world as any apparently miraculous intervention. The lack of such intervention is certainly not to be seen as the lack of interest or involvement on God's part, nor as a sign that

---

[8] 1 Chr. 2:16. Given the fact that David was one of the youngest members of his family, it is likely that his older nephews were the same age or even older than he was. Joab is certainly presented as a contemporary of David.

individual members of God's community should take precipitate action which is beyond their responsibility. David has come solely to collect Saul's spear, the symbol of his kingship that Saul apparently never let out of his sight. This time, David, being clear about his own motivation and knowing that he intends to hand the spear back, has no trouble with his conscience (cf. 24:5). Whether the water jug was a particularly noteworthy one that could be recognized from a distance or whether it was just taken because David was thirsty isn't made clear.

b. Saying – or hearing – the same thing twice is not usually a waste of time (26:13–17)

The two men made their escape, *crossed over to the . . . top of the hill some distance away* and then shouted across and woke up the camp. David calls out, addressing not Saul but Abner, expressing surprise that a man with a reputation like Abner's has been so slack as to risk Saul's life by allowing intruders into the camp. If it had been someone without the loyalty to Saul felt by David, then the results could have been very different. It is Abner, not David, who might be thought of as deserving to face the death penalty for not caring about Saul's safety. The evidence of the spear and the water jug is irrefutable. Clearly David's approach is a ruse. Abner now drops out of the picture and Saul, for whom the interchange had presumably been intended all along, recognizes David's voice. Perhaps the early morning light or the distortion caused by distance had made it difficult for Abner to recognize David, but Saul knew the voice better or realized that nobody else would be likely to behave in this way. Saul's immediate reference to David as *my son*[9] must have reassured David that his ploy was likely to be successful. This reference, coming before rather than after David's speech in his own defence, makes more sense if the encounter described in chapter 24 did actually take place and Saul's memory of it has been reawakened by David's voice again calling from across the hillside.

c. Action brings reaction, and crime deserves a matching punishment (26:18–20)

Saul's support may already be won, but David nevertheless reiterates his arguments. He has done nothing wrong, therefore someone must have incited Saul to think that he had. If Saul's opposition to David really was

---

[9] Note again the contrast with Nabal in 25:8, 10.

God-provoked, then the best way forward was to bring a sacrifice. However, if human beings were responsible, then they deserved to *be cursed before the LORD* (19). The implication is still there that surely Saul could not have turned against David without some provocation, but there is also the sense now that if the antipathy had come from Saul himself, then he also was among those deserving to be cursed. David was beginning to think, as is made plain in 27:1, that if things were to continue in the same way, then he really would have to leave the country. Thus, those who turned Saul against him were in effect driving him away from the covenant community and from easy access to the shrines where the God of Israel was worshipped. David's subsequent behaviour shows that he did not accept the common understanding of Ancient Near Easterners that the power of the deity of a particular country was restricted to the territory of that country, so that to leave the country inevitably meant serving another god. But for those who did hold this view, driving him away from his native land, from his *share in the LORD's inheritance*, was in effect to say to him *Go, serve other gods.* This was a very serious thing and Saul needed to be aware of the implications of his behaviour. Following the principle often illustrated in the Old Testament of the punishment fitting the crime, any who did that certainly deserved the punishment they were applying to David. They themselves deserved to be removed from fellowship with God and his covenant people – that is, to be cursed. David again closes his speech by referring to himself as a harmless flea, beneath the interest of *the king of Israel* and not a fit subject for a hunting expedition.

d. Trust can be destroyed (26:21–25)

Saul's full response is even more positive towards David and more humbly recognizant of his own sin than on the previous occasion. His reference to himself as having *acted like a fool* is perhaps deliberately drawing attention to parallels with Nabal's behaviour in the previous chapter. He again calls David his son, promises not to harm him and invites him back into the court. David ignores these overtures, knowing only too well that Saul's good intentions are unlikely to last long. This time he does not even acknowledge a relationship with Saul, calling him not 'my father', but simply *the king*. He arranges for Saul's spear to be returned. He could have taken the kingship from Saul as he had taken this symbol of kingship, but by returning it in this way he made it clear to Saul and to all his entourage that he actually supported Saul's right to rule, at least for now.

David again makes clear his confidence that God is in control. As far as he was concerned it was God who had provided him with an opportunity not, as Abishai had thought, to kill Saul but to show that he had no intention of doing so. He had valued Saul's life and he asked, not that Saul in turn would value his life – by this stage he was apparently far too sceptical for that – but that the Lord himself would do so. After this point there is no further record of Saul's pursuit of David. It is just possible that this time Saul's repentance and change of heart towards David were real. But for David it was too late. There comes a point in a relationship where trust has been so damaged that it can never be repaired, and perhaps that point had been reached for David. At a later stage, Israel was to learn that although a merciful God would provide them with chance after chance after chance (Jer. 7:12–29), nevertheless in the end they would be allowed to carry the responsibility for their own behaviour.[10]

The final words in this final encounter between Saul and David (the two men were never to meet again) are given to Saul, perhaps at last exercising his role as king. His words provide another intriguing glimpse of how different things might have been. Given David's omission of the term 'father', Saul rather sadly perhaps calls David his son for the third time and gives him his 'fatherly' blessing. If Saul really had been able to accept David as his son, then, in spite of his own failure, and particularly given Jonathan's glad recognition of brotherhood with David, he could have still, in one sense at least, been seen as the father of a dynasty. Saul was indeed the source of his own destruction.

3. The Philistine sojourn (27:1 – 28:2)

That David had no faith at all in Saul's apparent change of heart is made clear by his rather drastic decision, given the circumstances of his previous visit to Gath, once more to seek refuge among the Philistines. He is convinced that Saul will try again to kill him. Although his experience of God's support and sovereignty might have assured him that Saul's attempts would be unsuccessful, there was always the possibility that on a future occasion David, or, more probably, one of his men, would not be able to resist the temptation to destroy Saul. If such an event were to occur, that would be as destructive to David and his future reign as

---

[10] 2 Kgs 17. In the New Testament, passages like Rom. 1 and Heb. 5 reflect the same idea.

anything Saul could do. Not only would David himself be wracked by guilt, he would lose any support he might have gained from those who had remained loyal to Saul and he would have set a precedent for rebellion against any king, including himself. He predicts that if he does leave the country, Saul will not follow him, and he is proved right.

It is not possible to determine whether Saul's search for David ended because he no longer saw David as a threat and, if so, whether that was because David had left the country or because Saul's repentance recorded in 26:21 had been genuine. What is clear is that David did leave the country and Saul did stop searching (27:4). It is interesting and may be significant that David's departure is presented as a result of his own reflection rather than as responding to any direction from God. The thought remains that had he stayed and had Saul's change of heart proved genuine this time, then David could have supported Saul openly and the battle at Mount Gilboa might have had a different result.[11] However, it is not a thought that is developed and the ensuing account treats David's continued service of God in Gath in a positive way.

a. Taking advantage of local cultural perceptions – right and wrong (27:1–7)

David's large company, the six hundred soldiers now, like David, accompanied by their wives and families, moved en masse to Achish's territory around Gath. It says much for David's ability to elicit trust and loyalty that they were all willing to go with him on what must have seemed to most as a move from the frying pan into the fire.

David's knowledge of Gath and his previous experience of being tolerated by Achish were probably the motivation for the particular choice of a place of exile. Also Gath was on the outer edges of Philistine territory and was more likely to give David opportunities to develop his real interests. Achish's welcome on this occasion and his willingness to allow David's group to live in his territory may sound incredible since he must have been aware of David's reputation as a scourge of the Philistine armies. However, although Achish may have been guileless and good-hearted, and David certainly took advantage of his good nature, he may not have been quite so gullible as it first appears. It was not uncommon

---

[11] It is possible that the heartfelt nature of David's lament about the deaths of Saul and Jonathan at Gilboa, recorded in 2 Sam. 1:19–27, is partially influenced by a sense of guilt at his own absence.

for groups of discontents from one country to hire themselves out as mercenary soldiers to a neighbouring regime. David had not caused any trouble on his previous visit and a recovered madman might even have been thought to bring good fortune. David's status as an enemy of Saul was now probably well known by the Philistines.[12] Even less-guileless counsellors may have encouraged Achish to welcome David, with his undoubted skills, as a potential member of his own armed forces.

David presents his request for a *place ... in one of the country towns* where he and his group can live as being entirely for Achish's benefit. David has obviously learned from the success of the tactic he used in persuading Saul that cutting off a piece of his robe had actually been a sign of his goodwill. It appears that the real purpose (to allow David and his men to carry out raids against Israel's enemies without restraint) had been in David's mind from the beginning. His ability to see the whole picture and to take account of the longer-term effects of particular decisions and to develop strategies in the light of all factors is a further clear sign of David's leadership ability. There may have been a risk in going back into Philistia, but it was certainly not a risk taken without careful planning and every attention being paid to minimizing the danger. The writer of Samuel has ensured that by the time David actually gets to be king no reader is left in any doubt that he has all the qualities required to make a great ruler.

Achish agreed to allow David and his group to stay in Ziklag and they lived there without any restrictions for sixteen months. The editorial comment that Ziklag has *belonged to the kings of Judah ever since* indicates that David won over the local people. When he moved on, it appears that they moved on with him. The loyalty of the group of Gittite mercenaries who were so helpful to David at a later stage (2 Sam. 15:17–22) was probably also developed during this time. David, as a warrior, may have been an enemy to be feared, but he had no racist objections to forming friendships with those from nations with whom Israel may have been at war.

b. Trust and deceit – fighting for the other side? (27:8 – 28:2)

The account of the Ziklag-based raids on surrounding territories reads like a story from a *Boy's Own*-style comic book. One can imagine the young

---

[12] Achish would certainly have been aware by this time that Saul and David were at loggerheads but may not have been aware that David would never actually act against Saul. He did not have Abigail's insight into David's character or his theology (ch. 25)!

soldiers laughing when the story was told as they drank together around the evening campfire. David used a Philistine base in order to wreak havoc on Israel's enemies. They did not, of course, target Philistine territory; that would not only have been a foolish and unnecessary risk but also an unacceptable breach of hospitality. However, the groups mentioned were most likely Philistine allies.[13] Each sortie probably tackled only a small group, and the policy of total destruction made sure that there were no witnesses to report on David's activities. David therefore was able to persuade Achish that he had been collecting tribute from desert communities belonging to Israel and her allies. Achish, only too glad to receive his share of David's booty, was more than happy to accept this and to allow David's activities to continue unhindered.

The Amalekites had been under ḥērem (see 1 Sam. 15) and David's killing of all he encountered brings that fact to mind. It is clear that they had not all been destroyed and that David had no qualms about taking plunder from these remaining groups. Such action would have been forbidden if the ḥērem was still in place. We cannot be sure of exactly how it was understood, but it is possible that once the initial attack to carry out the ḥērem was completed then the dedication lost its force. Achish was pleased to have David's forces as an extra guard in the border regions. He, as David had realized, was a trusting kind of man. He certainly *trusted David* (12), and had no doubts about his continuing loyalty.

It was inevitable that eventually a large-scale campaign against Israel would take place involving all the gathered Philistine forces. When this happens, Achish, convinced of David's support, takes it for granted that he will want to take part in the battle. His rather tentative *You must understand . . .* (28:1) is probably an apology not that David must fight, but that he will have to be part of Achish's army rather than commanding his own troop. David's reply of *you will see for yourself* is ambiguous, almost certainly deliberately so. Achish would surely see for himself what David could do, whether against Saul or against the Philistine forces. No deceit could be sustained in those circumstances. Achish completely misses the ambiguity and promises David promotion to lifetime service in the royal bodyguard, conveying a real honour as these were seen as the crack troops of the army.

---

[13] The Girzites are unknown elsewhere, but the Geshurites lived in the area south of Philistia. This is not the same Geshur as the one where Absalom spent time in exile across the Jordan (2 Sam. 13:38).

At this crucial moment, the story is interrupted. The reader is left in suspense, not knowing if David will find yet another way of avoiding the apparently inevitable discovery of his continuing loyalty to Israel. This is almost certainly a deliberate tactic of the gifted writer, but it also makes sense, before the record of what turned out to be Saul's final battle, to bring us up to date with Saul's position and to let us find out what has happened to Saul's always fragile state of mind during David's absence in Gath.

4. Saul's occult escapade (28:3–25)

The story of Saul and the medium makes sense only if certain facts are quite clear, and therefore we begin with an editorial comment setting out those facts. First, Samuel is dead. The reader is to be in no doubt about that; the repetition of the wording from 1 Samuel 25:1 is deliberate, although it is not clear whether this stress is to explain why Saul might have wanted to consult him via a medium or to emphasize the fact that, had Samuel been alive, he would never have tolerated such happenings. Second, all occult activity was viewed as detestable, as a completely unacceptable practice for any member of God's covenant community (Lev. 19:31; Deut. 18:9–13). Third, not only was Saul well aware of this, but he himself had taken action to ensure that no medium or spiritist would be allowed to practise within Israelite territory. It is interesting that even here, where Saul's allegiance to the covenant is seen to be weaker than ever before, we are reminded that in the past he did exercise his role as guardian of the covenant. The author does not shirk from recording the facts, but there remains a pervading sense of deep sadness at Saul's lost potential. There is no room within the community of God's people for rejoicing at the downfall of another. An ability well worth cultivating, even when noting failure, is the ability to recognize the 'might have been' potential of the one who has failed.

a. The task remains, but, with no vision left, that thought brings only terror (28:4–5)

The Philistines had *set up camp at Shunem* while Saul was based some 5 miles away at *Gilboa*, near Jezreel. The Philistine army originally mustered at Aphek (1 Sam. 29:1), which was where David left them, before marching north to face the Israelites at Jezreel. This means that chapter 29 precedes chapter 28 chronologically but it served the writer's purposes to record Saul's position first. Saul, too, had issued a national call-up. This was no minor battle to be carried out between the standing armies but a major showdown between the two nations.

It is not surprising that Saul was, to say the least, somewhat tense. The author does not mince words. Saul was not just scared, *terror filled his heart*. Saul, the strong warrior with a great reputation who had once been told that God would be with him in all he did on God's behalf (1 Sam. 11:7), could not even bring himself to believe that God would support his people in such a crucial battle for survival. Perhaps it was his obsession with David's supposed treachery that had enabled Saul to keep going. If this was so and if it was really true that he had finally acknowledged that David was not trying to depose him, then his *raison d'être* had been removed and he would have been forced to face up to the reality of his own inadequacy. Or perhaps the growing paranoia was leaving him incapable of any rational thought or action.

b. The dangers of constantly looking for guidance (28:6)

Saul must have known that the fight against the Philistines was inevitable and his own experience might have indicated that seeking further instructions or further reassurance from God at this stage was unnecessary. Once more the writer hints that, on occasions, searching for guidance from God can lend an aura of spirituality to what is actually an avoidance of taking the action that God has already clearly called for. This was obviously something that the readers really needed to understand. In this instance Saul no longer sensed the presence of God's Spirit and cried out for reassurance. He tried every means available to him to gain that reassurance, but there was no answer in dreams or through the use of the Urim or through prophets; the only thing he heard was a resounding silence.

Why it was impossible for Saul to receive the reassurance he longed for is not totally clear. God did sometimes speak through dreams, although in Israel there were no professional dream interpreters. Not all dreams were seen as sent by God (Jer. 23:25, 28), but if one of God's people did have a God-given dream, then it was assumed the meaning would be revealed by God himself and no interpreter would be needed.[14] But for Saul there were no such dreams.

---

[14] Joseph and Daniel both acted as dream interpreters but this was not in the context of Israel but to outsiders from cultures where all dreams were expected to have meaning. Both made it clear that they were not in fact dream interpreters but that God had chosen on these occasions to reveal certain things to these outsiders and he gave the interpretation through his servants.

The relationship between the Urim, which was available to Saul, and the ephod, which was not available because Abiathar had taken it to David (23:6), is not now clear. But in any case, not even the Urim worked for Saul. That Saul would have been in a fit state to hear or to accept anything that a prophet might have said is debatable, but no prophet spoke. Saul, in his desperation, felt he had no other choice than to consult a medium. The lack of logic in trying to discover what God was going to do by a means that was totally forbidden by God was lost to this terrified shadow of Saul's former self.

c. Last resorts involving deliberate wrongdoing are unlikely to help (28:7–14)

In spite of Saul's prohibition, occult practitioners still existed in Israel, reflecting the influence of Canaanite religions that remained a problem for Israel throughout the centuries (2 Kgs 21:6; 23:24; Isa. 8:19; Jer. 27:9). In this case either Saul takes it for granted that all mediums will be women, or he has heard a rumour that there is such a woman in the area. Saul *disguised himself* and searched out this woman *at night* – a clear indication that he was fully aware that his action was unacceptable. The woman's caution is understandable. She risks her life if she agrees to Saul's request to go against the Lord's commands in this way. It is ironic that Saul convinces her of his sincerity by swearing an oath in the Lord's name.

He asks her to bring up Samuel for him to talk to. Whether Saul in his terrified confusion was denying the reality of Samuel's death, or whether he really believed in the woman's powers and felt that somehow the dead Samuel might be more willing to reassure him than the living Samuel had been, is unclear. In fact, this whole account is, probably intentionally, shrouded in mystery. Was the woman a fraud or did she genuinely have some kind of clairvoyant skill? Was it really the dead Samuel coming back to life, or was it the appearance of an evil spirit or some kind of a trick? Was the woman's recognition of Saul based on her own insight or did his disguise drop for a second?[15] Did Saul really hear from Samuel or just deceive himself into hearing all the things that he knew and feared?

Two things, however, are clear. First, whatever happened seems to have been unexpected and disturbing not only to Saul but also to the

---

[15] Some versions of the Septuagint have Saul replacing Samuel in verse 12, suggesting to some that her horror resulted from realizing that her unknown visitor was Saul himself (cf. Caird, p. 1028).

woman. Second, Saul genuinely believed that he was actually talking to Samuel.

d. Consulting the dead doesn't help (28:15–20)

Saul expresses his own distress and explains that he has *disturbed* Samuel because *God has departed from* him and he has nowhere else to turn. The picture of Samuel being disturbed is consistent with the early understanding of the dead not as living but as in a sort of semi-existence in Sheol, a shadowy non-world or at best half-world. Samuel points out that as, in Saul's words, *God has departed*, then consulting Samuel as God's representative is a bit of a nonsense. He reiterates what Saul was told during Samuel's life about his sin, its consequences and his replacement by David. The only new information given confirms Saul's own fears that he and his sons will die and the whole *army of Israel* will be handed over to the Philistines. In fact, if this really was Samuel, his information was somewhat limited. It is true that Israel was defeated and Saul was killed, as were three of his sons. However, at least one son, Ish-Bosheth, remained to continue Saul's work temporarily and the defeat was by no means as comprehensive as Saul had feared.

Nevertheless, Saul, his terror compounded by hunger, for in his deranged state he had not eaten for twenty-four hours, found it all too much and he collapsed. Saul's excursion into forbidden occult territory brought him no joy, no reassurance and indeed no benefit at all but only further despair. There is a warning here which it seems the author intends to stand.

e. A good meal might help (28:21–25)

The account finishes in a very down-to-earth way. It is as if we are being reminded that what counts is real life. The woman sees the state that Saul is in and rightly discerns that what he actually needs now is something to eat. She can't do anything about his problems or his desolation but she can cook him a meal. Saul initially refuses, but after his men join her in seeking to persuade him, he does eat and they go on their way.

The parallel between this meal of meat and unleavened bread eaten at night before a journey and the Passover meal adds poignancy to the story. That meal was eaten in hope, this one in despair. It should be noted that as far as the political situation was concerned, nothing had really changed from the earlier period in Saul's life when Israel was facing threats from the Philistine armies. The change was in Saul himself. What he once faced with confidence he could now hardly face at all. It is important to realize that it is not always the circumstances we face that determine the way we react to them. It is to Saul's credit that in his final moments, in spite of his terror and its accompanying disablement, and in spite of the conviction that he was going to die, he did lead his troops into the battle.

5. David and Achish (29:1–11)

The site of the major encounter between Israel and the Philistines seems somewhat unusual. It was not held in the border area between the two lands, as might have been expected, but in the northern section of Israel's territory. Israel was apparently already camped at Jezreel, in the northern region, when the *Philistines gathered all their forces at Aphek*, some 30 miles (50 km) further south. It is possible that Saul had travelled north to subdue some of the other non-Israelite tribes in that area. Jezreel was well outside the Philistines' normal territory, but if Saul was successful in his attempt to consolidate his position in the north, this would certainly have been a threat to them. This could explain both why the Philistines travelled up as far as Shunem to take on the Israelites and also why Saul was so disturbed by what may have been the completely unexpected arrival of the amassed Philistine forces.

David, as part of a mercenary unit attached to Achish's army, marched alongside the Gittite troops. Achish had no doubts at all about David's loyalty but the other Philistine commanders unsurprisingly were suspicious. They obviously doubted David's loyalty to Achish, with some justification. However, even if his loyalty was genuine, to allow Hebrew forces to be part of the army that was fighting other Hebrews was an unacceptable risk. In this instance they were very well aware of David's reputation and skills, but the advantages of those skills were far outweighed by the havoc that David could wreak if he decided to turn against them. There was no way that they were going to allow David and his men to remain with their army.

a. Enemies are people too! (29:1–5)

The Philistines are often portrayed as boorish and foolish, but these chapters show why they were a force to be reckoned with and such a successful culture. There is an attractiveness both in Achish's naive guilelessness and in the commanders' realistic common sense and wisdom. The image of God was not entirely lacking in the enemies of God's people![16] The Old Testament does not portray the Israelites as wiser, more gifted or even as nicer than the people of the surrounding nations. Their specialness lay only in their relationship with God. When they turned away from God's covenant and ceased to reflect God to the surrounding nations, then they were indistinguishable from them.[17] It should not be a surprise to God's people today when they discover that non-believers can be both intelligent and pleasant. But this discovery should not lead them to assume that such people cannot at the same time be seen as in opposition to God, his Word and his people.

b. Dealing with disappointment (29:6–11)

Achish was obviously disappointed that he was to lose the support of David and his troops which he valued very highly. However, he was also realistic; it was clear that David's men were in danger of being harmed by other Philistines, so he encouraged them to leave the area speedily. His use of the name of Israel's God, Yahweh ('LORD' in English versions), in his oath (6) and his reference to David as an angel of God (9) are evidence of his respect for David and perhaps also a respect for David's faith. Maybe modern believers have things to learn from Achish. Strong convictions about the truth of one's own beliefs and the desire to bring others to faith in the true God can sometimes lead to a dismissive or even despising attitude towards those who do not yet share that faith. Respect for such people is often wrongly assumed to imply agreement with their views or a recognition of the possibility of alternative truths and thus a denial of God. Is it not much more likely that showing respect for people as people, whatever their views, will cause them to respond positively?

Whether David's attitude here should be emulated is a little more debatable. The question of how far one goes in order to defend one's own position has been a problem for generations of believers. David certainly had no qualms about deceiving Achish, in spite of the positive way that he himself had been treated. David proves to be a wonderful actor; his air of injured innocence in response to the decision of the rulers was obviously

---

[16] Abimelek (Gen. 20; 21; 26) and Cyrus (Ezra 1; Isa. 44 – 45) are two examples of non-Israelites who are portrayed very positively.

[17] Cf. Amos 9:7 where God is seen as working with Cushites, Philistines and Arameans just as much as with Israel.

very convincing. The ambiguity of his question *Why can't I go and fight against the enemies of my lord the king?* was lost on Achish. It is not really clear whether David was delighted to escape from being part of the Philistine army or genuinely upset that this opportunity to act on behalf of his king, that is, Saul, was lost. However, whether gladly or sadly, David and his party had no choice but to leave and their early return to Ziklag is shown in chapter 30 to have been timely.

6. Revenge for a haven destroyed (30:1–31)

David's band was presumably very tired. They had had a long march up to Aphek, followed by the stress resulting from the suspicion of the main Philistine armies. Then they had had the long march back home, possibly with the disappointment of having lost the chance to fight for Saul and thus maybe even restore their credibility in his eyes. They arrived home to find disaster and devastation. Their town had been razed, their families taken captive, and, not surprisingly, it was all too much for them. The description of them weeping aloud until they had no strength left to weep (4) gives a realistic picture of exhausted and emotionally distraught people. Presumably, although the writer makes a point of letting the readers know this information at the beginning of the account, the men themselves did not know at this stage that their wives and children had been captured but not killed. The Amalekites had followed a less violent policy than David's own 'leave no survivors' approach and possibly the reader is being encouraged to ponder on that fact. Similarly, the thought is there in the background that had Saul fulfilled his mission in chapter 15 to destroy the Amalekites completely, then this particular disaster would not have arisen.

a. Dealing with disaster: finding strength in God (30:3–6)

David's own family had been taken along with the rest, but this did not prevent the men from blaming him for the loss of their loved ones. Stoning David (6) would clearly not have benefited anybody, but logic tends to disappear in that kind of traumatic situation and the need to blame someone else is very real. It is not always easy, even for believers, to keep a right perspective or to resist the temptation to apportion blame. The men's desperation in their bereavement is understandable, but there seems to be more emphasis on David's distress prompted by his men turning against him than on his reaction to the loss of his family. However, in verse 4 we are told that David was among those who wept bitterly and it would be wrong to let our prior knowledge of his inadequacies as a husband and father cause us to read too much into what is said here.

Whatever the main focus of his distress, *David found strength in the LORD his God* (6). There are many psalms that reflect the way in which David must have felt at this point: attacked by enemies, accused by friends and totally at the end of his personal resources.[18] David's trust in God, expressed in these psalms, stemmed from personal experience of the strength given by God in such desperate situations. The Lord's strength is still available to us and we too can take encouragement both from David's experience here and from the psalms where he reflects on such experiences.

b. The energizing effect of hope (30:7–10)

David's use of the ephod at this point was an astute tactic; it diverted the men from concentrating on their loss or on David's guilt and they found renewed hope in the assurance that the attackers could be successfully found and defeated.

The use of the word *rescue* in verse 8 is significant. Their mission was not just to be one of revenge and judgment; there were prisoners to rescue. The six hundred exhausted men set off again with renewed vigour. In the barren and inhospitable territory, however, a third of them just could not summon up the energy needed to cross the Besor, apparently flowing through a ravine, which would involve a hard climb down and an even harder climb back out. These men stayed behind, presumably with the supplies that were too cumbersome to take across the ravine (cf. 24). The group would have taken sufficient supplies with them to support an extended campaign in the north and there was clearly enough left to supply a stranger with good nourishment (11–12).

c. The disastrous effects of complacency (30:11–17)

The remaining four hundred pressed on and came across a young Egyptian in an even worse state than they were. Whether his rescue was a genuine act of kindness or simply a way of gaining intelligence is not stated. It was probably clear that the man was not an Amalekite, but he may have had

---

[18] Pss 41 and 55 are good examples of this.

some recognizable Amalekite clothing – perhaps even marking him out as a slave. They thought he might have some information as to the direction the raiding party had taken, but it was only after he had recovered that they learned that he himself had been attached to the same group of raiders and knew exactly the route they had taken.[19]

The Amalekites appear to have been an exceptionally large and well-equipped party as all were destroyed *except four hundred young men who rode off on camels* (17). David's own four hundred may have been tired but they were well disciplined. Although it took a whole day's fighting, this large group of drunken revellers who had taken no precautions and were scattered over the countryside (16) were no match for David and his men.

David perhaps learned a lesson from the Amalekites. He was a careful strategist with a concern for the continuing safety of his men (2 Sam. 11:18–21), but Israel itself certainly was not immune to the dangers of complacency. Paul uses Israel's own past as a way of warning Christians to avoid overconfidence, concluding his argument with 'if you think you are standing firm, be careful that you don't fall!' (1 Cor. 10:12).

d. The importance of sharing any God-given 'spoils' (30:18–31)

David's rescue mission was remarkably successful. He recovered all the property and people taken from his own town and a whole lot more. The Amalekites had obviously taken the opportunity left by the absence of the main Philistine and Judean armies to wreak havoc in the southern regions. The account ends with a further indication of David's leadership and diplomatic skills.

The success of the mission brought its own problems. Who was going to share in the plunder? One can understand the desire of those who had actually been involved in the fighting to keep the rewards for themselves. After all, we have been told clearly that those who stayed behind did so because of their own weakness. They may have looked after the supplies, but that was a side effect rather than the cause of their absence. The conclusion of the writer that those who did not want to share were *evil men and troublemakers* seems a little harsh; selfish and greedy perhaps, but evil? However, David understood two things very clearly. First, that it was the Lord and not their own strength that had brought them victory. The

---

[19] His knowledge of the route may indicate that his master had expected him to follow after the band if he recovered, but the youth showed no signs of feeling any loyalty towards the Amalekites.

four hundred may have been involved in the fighting, but they had no more right to the plunder than those who had been left behind. It all belonged to the God who had *protected* them and *delivered . . . the raiding party that came against* them (23). Second, Israel stood or fell as a community. David's group may have been officially exiled, but they were Israelites and David wanted them to recognize the reality of community life. The plunder should be shared equally by all because all belonged to the community whether they had been in the fighting or with the supplies. The reference to the men as *my brothers* is almost certainly intended to bring to mind these community values. Equally, the reference to the now recovered two hundred as having stayed with the supplies is probably a deliberate attempt to restore the self-respect of those who had not been able to cope by indicating that even in their weakness they had fulfilled a purpose.

It is possible that Paul, in formulating his teaching in 1 Corinthians 12 about the many parts of the body which each have their own purpose, had been meditating on passages like this one. The desire of the men to keep the plunder for themselves was both a denial of community and a denial of God's part in their victory and as such is properly classified as evil. We do well to note that apparently minor sins like selfishness and greed have wide-ranging implications that could very easily lead to the downfall of God's people.[20] David's skill in persuading and reconciling his own men, recognizing that as a leader he had a responsibility to the whole group, was matched by his skill in relating to the Judean towns.[21]

The writer provides no insight into David's precise motivation but simply records the fact that he distributed portions of the apparently vast plunder to a large range of towns in the region. He may have been seeking to buy their future loyalty. He may have been reminding them of his presence and his role as a loyal Judean. He may have been acting out of compassion, providing necessary aid to a region devastated by similar raiding parties. He may have been providing payment for the help and support such towns had given him in the past when he and his men roamed over that area (31). Or perhaps he was providing a further object lesson for his men, showing that the concept of community involved not only their colleagues who had remained behind but the whole nation – or

---

[20] Jas 2:1–12 speaks in a similar way of the destructive role of the apparently minor sin of showing favouritism.

[21] Only a few of the towns mentioned here can now be identified with any certainty; for example, Aroer is now Khirbet Ar'areh.

at least the whole tribe. David probably acted from a combination of motives, but there is no doubt that he did win over the hearts of many in Judah. One is reminded of Jesus' parable of the manager using the resources he has to win friends and influence people (Luke 16:1–15). Sharing with others almost always brings great benefit – that giving is a greater blessing than receiving is not just a pious hope (Acts 20:35)!

7. Defeat and death in the north (31:1–13)

It is impossible to ascertain whether David's presence with the northern armies would have made any difference, although chapter 30's description of the successful attack against the much larger group of Amalekites suggests that his troops could have had a significant impact. Sadly, what is certain is that Saul's fears, which were confirmed at Endor, were shown to have been valid. The Israelite army were completely routed. The description of their defeat is telling: *the Philistines fought . . . the Israelites fled* (1). It is clear that some Israelites, the crack troops in Saul's bodyguard perhaps and Jonathan's personal forces, fought and fought well, but there was no real hope for them. The writer gives a very brief description of the defeat, concerned at this stage only with the fate of the royal family.

a. Life-and-death decisions are never easy (31:2–7)

Three of Saul's sons[22] were killed outright and Saul himself was critically wounded by an arrow. Too weak to resist any longer, unable or unwilling to escape, and afraid of being tortured further by the Philistines, Saul asked his armour-bearer to kill him. The brave and loyal soldier, afraid of neither the battle nor, apparently, death, was terrified. Perhaps the armour-bearer was aware of the significance of Saul as the Lord's anointed king and therefore could not bring himself to put him out of his misery. Perhaps he saw such a killing as murder and was unwilling to break the law, or he could not bear the disloyalty involved in killing one whom he was sworn to protect. Or perhaps his terror resulted from the thought that with the death of Saul all hope was gone. The writer does not make it clear,

---

[22] 1 Sam. 14:49 names Saul's sons as Jonathan, Ishvi (possibly another name for Ish-Bosheth, otherwise known as Esh-Baal: 1 Chr. 8:33) and Malki-Shua. 1 Chr. omits Ishvi, but adds Esh-Baal and also includes Abinadab. It is not clear why Ishvi/Esh-Baal/Ish-Bosheth was not present at this battle or escaped death. 2 Sam. 2:10 states that he was forty years old when he took over from Saul, so clearly he was not too young to be included.

but life-and-death situations do sometimes bring agonizing ethical dilemmas. The man's refusal to comply with Saul's request led to Saul taking his own life, an equally appalling action for anyone who was at all concerned about God's law. It is possible that the armour-bearer's suicide was a result of his despair at Saul's death. However, it may have been a final act of loyalty, the brave soldier wanting to make sure that Saul was not alone even in his denial of the life that God had given him. In verse 6 the writer specifically acknowledges his death along with that of Saul and his three sons – not necessarily affirming his action but just possibly recognizing and affirming the life and the loyalty of this particular unknown soldier. Any who have experienced the agony of watching the painful and inevitable end of a loved one and been faced with the terrible choice as to whether to assist the sufferer in hastening that end can feel great sympathy with the armour-bearer here. The text gives no support to those who would argue for the appropriateness of assisted suicide, but it does show a real awareness of the issues and the pain involved.

It is apparent that much of the army had fled, so *all his men* (6) who died with Saul refers to his own personal troops. The people of the surrounding towns and villages, now unprotected by Israelite troops, deserted their homes and left the towns to be occupied by the advancing Philistine armies. Often, and this has been seen many times in modern warfare, the enemy is able to advance more because of the mass panic and resultant flight of those being attacked than through any genuine victory. Perhaps there is a lesson here for those who face spiritual opponents. Often fear of supposed power can have far more devastating effects than the exercise of any actual power. Overestimating the power of the forces of evil can sometimes be at least as dangerous as underestimating them.

b. Desecration of the dead – even of the bodies of enemies – is always an offence (31:8–9)

The Philistines naturally wanted to take full advantage of their victory. They searched the battlefield for any weapons or plunder that might be found. In particular they took the recognizable head and armour of Saul to use in a public relations exercise, convincing their own people of the extent of their victory and further demoralizing the Israelites. The hanging up of the royal corpses on the wall at Beth Shan was another way of revelling in victory and shaming Saul. Beth Shan was a Canaanite town assigned by Joshua to Manasseh (Josh. 17:11) which had been occupied by the Philistines, possibly at this time, but there is evidence to suggest that Beth Shan (modern Tell el-Ḥosn) had not been in Israelite hands for any significant period of time.

In Amos, the desecrating of enemy corpses was seen as a reason for God's strong judgment coming on Moab (Amos 2:1). There seems to be a strong inbuilt sense throughout the world that the dead should be respected. The Bible reaffirms the properness of this respect – not in any sense affirming the superstitious practices associated with death in some cultures, but indicating the significance of the created life that was once lived. To desecrate dead bodies is somehow to deny the significance of their lives, which is, in turn, to deny God's creative activity. It is interesting that in Amos the problem was the burning to ashes (or 'lime'; cf. ESV) of the body of *Edom's* king: it was not just the desecration of an Israelite body that was offensive to God.

c. Even in the midst of defeat, God is still God (31:10–13)

The Philistines placed Saul's armour in the temple of the Ashtoreths (10). The Chronicler adds that they put his head in the temple of Dagon (1 Chr. 10:10). This act parallels the putting of the ark in the temple of Dagon (1 Sam. 5:2–7) and was probably related to their desire to show that Philistine gods were stronger than the Israelite God. However, the writer is almost certainly drawing attention to the earlier parallel when the end result made the initial Philistine rejoicing look very foolish. R. P. Gordon[23] suggests that in speaking of the Philistines *proclaiming the news in the temple of their idols* (9) the writer is using irony to suggest that these idols (a deliberately pejorative word) needed to be kept informed of what was going on in just the same way that the people did.

Israel might be defeated, Saul might have failed in his task of freeing Israel from the Philistines, but God was still God. This stands as a reminder to those of God's people today who live in situations where the church appears to have been defeated – either by physical persecution or by secularist indifference. God is still God!

Jabesh Gilead was the town rescued by Saul in what might be described as his finest hour (1 Sam. 11). To them he would always be a hero and the concept of his headless corpse left hanging on a wall was too awful to contemplate. The valiant men of the town, presumably not part of Saul's

---

[23] Gordon (1986), p. 203.

main army, braved the Philistine forces, took down Saul's body and gave it a decent burial. We cannot be completely sure of exactly what was involved in this process, although we are told they burned the bodies, then buried the bones. Amos 6:10 also speaks in an affirmative way of the burning of bodies, in contrast with the crime of burning the bones to lime mentioned above (Amos 2:1). Cremation does not seem to have been common in Israel, but it clearly had some function. It is possible that both here and in Amos 6 the danger of plague arising from bodies left unburied had come into play. Certainly in this instance the bones were left to be buried. The important thing was that Saul and his sons were given the respect that was due to Israelite royalty and the shame of the desecration of their bodies was wiped out. Jabesh Gilead may have repaid their debt, but the need to do so only brought them sorrow and mourning. They fasted for seven days.

1 and 2 Samuel make up one book, but this story forms an appropriate ending to the first half. Saul was dead and Israel was defeated. The Israelites' hope that the accession of a king would solve all their problems had proved to be baseless. However, the mention of Jabesh Gilead reminds us of some of the things that Saul did actually achieve. There had been successes like that which led to the love and loyalty of the people of Jabesh. There remained hope for Israel when the likes of Jabesh Gilead could still act with bravery and compassion. Also, of course, David was waiting in the wings. This apparent time of desolation, defeat and despair is by no means the end of the story.

Questions to ponder

1. What do we make of David's relationship with Abigail?
2. Was Saul's repentance genuine?
3. Was David right or wrong to leave the land?
4. Was it fair for David to deceive the good-hearted Achish in the way he did?
5. Why do you think the story of Saul's experience at Endor was recorded?
6. What actually happened there?
7. David took God's support for granted in his vengeance raid. Was this right?

8. Is the principle of 'equal shares in the spoil' relevant today? Are there circumstances within church life where it might apply?
9. Was there an alternative solution to the armour-bearer's dilemma?
10. Does the description of burial practices here have any relevance today?

2 Samuel 1 – 5

6. David: in control

1. Saul's death, the alternative account (1:1–27)

The start of the second book of Samuel mirrors the start of the first book in some ways. This time the despair is not that of a childless woman but of a bereaved nation. The first news that David received from the battlefield in the north came via a young man who described himself as 'the son of a foreigner, an Amalekite' (13), who 'happened to be on Mount Gilboa' (6) at the time when Saul was injured. This might mean that the young man had been captured by Saul's army or was part of the army, or that he was the son of a registered alien or of an Israelite woman and an Amalekite man. Whatever the case, it quickly becomes clear to the reader that his account of what happened is quite different from that recorded in 1 Samuel 31. The two accounts are presented side by side without any comment on their difference[1] (remember that 1 and 2 Samuel form a single unit). Readers are left to assess the evidence and draw their own conclusions. If the account in 1 Samuel 31 is correct, there must have been other witnesses on Mount Gilboa able to bring back the report. There is no doubt that the young Amalekite was also present. His possession of Saul's crown and armband proves that and it may be significant that there is no mention in 1 Samuel 31 of the royal regalia being taken by the Philistines along with Saul's armour.

---

[1] Ackroyd (1977), p. 20, and Mauchline, p. 127, both assume that there were two separate traditions concerning Saul's death and imply that the writer, unable to select between the two, includes both. However, given the writer's skill and insight elsewhere this does seem a somewhat unimaginative perspective. On the other hand, B. T. Arnold, 'The Amalekite Report of Saul's death', *JETS* 32 (1989), argues that the Amalekite was seeking to deceive David and that this ties in with an interest in the concept of deception in the narratives as a whole (as, for example, when David deceives Uriah in 2 Sam. 11 and Joab seeks to deceive David in 2 Sam. 14).

a. It is appropriate to mourn, even for the death of one who viewed you as an enemy (1:1–12)

David had no alternative account available to him at this point and he was eager to discover what the man had to say about the situation in the north. The news was that the army had fled and that Saul and Jonathan were among the many soldiers who had died. Thus far the report mirrors what readers have already been told. Perhaps David has some reason to doubt the Amalekite's word, or maybe he just wants to ascertain whether the deaths of Saul and Jonathan[2] are fact or rumour, but he does ask for clarification. The man's story is that it was he, rather than Saul's armour-bearer, who was the one asked to hasten what was perceived as the inevitable end of Saul's life. The armour-bearer's terror described in 1 Samuel 31 does not seem to have been a problem for him. He killed Saul, picked up the regalia and immediately left the region seeking David so that he could deliver the crown to him.

The first reaction of David and his entourage was grief. In spite of their exile, they were first and foremost Israelites and they mourned the national defeat, the widespread loss of life and particularly the deaths of Saul and Jonathan. It is often true that an exile has greater insight into and a greater affection for his or her country than the one who has never really left home. David's group was no exception to this. Saul may have perceived David as an enemy but, as David had tried to prove for the last few years, he had never viewed Saul as his enemy. His mourning was genuine. The New Testament provides insights into matters of death and life that David didn't have, but it still remains appropriate to mourn the loss of life and potential that comes with death, even the death of one who has treated us badly. It remains inappropriate to rejoice in an opponent's death, even when it brings new opportunities.

Once David had had time to get used to the army's defeat and the deaths of his one-time mentor and his great friend, he was able to ask further questions about the precise nature of what had happened and the origins of the informant.[3]

---

[2] There is no evidence at this stage to confirm Jonathan's death. This may be incidental or may be an indication that Jonathan was assumed to have stayed close to his father. That Jonathan's death is mentioned here but not that of his two brothers may relate to the fact that David's psalm of mourning also mentions only Saul and Jonathan.

[3] The wording of the question in verse 13 is not the same as that in verse 3. Here David asks not about the point of origin of his journey but about his personal background, perhaps an indication that David was seeking to make sure that justice really was served and the man would not be put to death unfairly.

b. Deceit does not pay (1:13–16)

Whether the Amalekite had killed Saul, or had simply witnessed the encounter between Saul and his armour-bearer and then Saul's suicide and had seized the opportunity to take the crown and armband from Saul's body before the Philistines came to plunder the dead, is left for the jury of readers to decide. The man describes how he was standing in the same place as Saul, 'with the chariots and their riders in hot pursuit' (6). It does seem odd then that he, linked with the Israelite army, even if only as a slave, should have escaped death. What is clear is that the Amalekite, with devastatingly faulty judgment, assumed that David would be pleased to hear of Saul's death and would reward the one who was first to pay homage to him as the new king. The young man's honouring of David (2) may have been nothing more than that paid to any tribal leader, but its extent – 'he fell to the ground' – probably implies that he was acclaiming David as king. There is no doubt that he knew who David was and had deliberately undertaken the long journey to seek him out in the shortest possible time.

David's reaction was unexpected – to the young Amalekite at least, if not to the reader who has repeatedly seen David's loyalty to Saul. Far from rewarding the young man, David questioned him further and then had him executed. At first sight this seems harsh. If the man was a foreigner, he could not have been expected to understand the complex implications of Israel's religion and politics. However, in this case he would not have been directly involved in this war, so his killing of Saul was a straightforward murder and, therefore, he deserved death. On the other hand, if the young man were indeed the son of a resident foreigner (cf. Exod 12:48; 22:21; 23:9) and had lived in Israel for many years if not from birth, as his understanding of the relative positions of Saul and David perhaps implies, then the situation would be different. But from David's perspective he still deserved to die. If he had been part of Saul's army, it is likely that he had heard something of David's view of the sanctity of Saul as the Lord's anointed. If the account of David's questioning is foreshortened and the phrase *I killed the Lord's anointed* (16) is an exact quote from the young man, then David's conclusion, *Your blood be on your own head* (16), makes complete sense.

It is ironic that if the young man had not killed Saul and only claimed to have done so in order to gain greater reward, then by telling the truth he might not only have saved his own life but actually have received a reward for bringing news to David. But now, his blood would indeed be on his own head, resulting as it did from his own lie. It is possible that the writer here is intending to suggest that the attempt to use deceit to buy reward or obtain influence is more likely to prove the deceiver's undoing than to bring any gain. It would certainly be possible to infer that lesson from the events described here.

c. Effective leadership of God's people never results from the illegal seizing of power (1:15–16)

In the accounts so far, David has been portrayed as wanting to ensure that if and when he did come to power it was not as a result of his own rebellion against Saul or through political manipulation of any kind. If David was to have any hope of winning over those who had continued to support Saul, it was vital that he was not seen to have had any complicity in Saul's death. The Amalekite's killing of Saul, seizing the royal insignia and bringing it immediately to David's camp could have been viewed by suspicious opponents as a prearranged plan. The immediate execution of Saul's killer would help to allay such suspicions. The Amalekite's confession that he had killed Saul, whether true or false, made his own death inevitable.

It is worth noting that the possibility of euthanasia – where the killing of Saul might be seen as a positive act, bringing him benefit by saving him from further pain or shame – seems to have had no place in the thought patterns of either Saul's armour-bearer or David. Killing was apparently seen as killing, whatever the motivation behind it.

d. Factions unite in community mourning (1:17–18)

There may have been an element of political motivation in David's action. His insistence that his own tribe of Judah be taught the hymn[4] that he wrote to lament Saul's death may also have been a politically astute move. Judah was not to be seen as anti-Saul or as being pleased that he had been removed from the scene, thus opening the door for the Judean David to take power into his own hands. They, along with all the other tribes, mourned the loss of their king. However, there can be no doubting the genuine nature of the grief reflected in the lament itself. Writing poetry

---

[4] The Book of Jashar where the hymn was recorded was some kind of official record. It is mentioned elsewhere only in Josh. 10:12–13 and may have been a collection of national poetry.

was always David's way of expressing his emotions, and the deaths of both Saul and Jonathan affected him deeply. He had, at least in the beginning, been treated as a son by Saul and viewed him as a father. With Saul's death he had finally lost the possibility of that relationship ever being restored. In this kind of situation there is mourning both for the loss of what had been and for the loss of what might have been. Jonathan had in a very real sense acted as a brother (26) to David. Over the years David had had many loyal followers but he apparently never again found a friend like this who valued his gifts, understood his weaknesses and loved him anyway. Yes, David's grief was real, and if the idea is there in the background that if David was a brother to Jonathan then he was also an appropriate inheritor of Saul's crown, it is there as a side effect of the lament rather than as its purpose.

The structure of David's poem of lament

- v. 19: Opening statement – the value of what is lost: *How the mighty have fallen!*
- v. 20: Reactions to the loss: Philistine women will rejoice
- vv. 21–22: Result of the loss: the land is defiled
- v. 23: The value of those lost: personal memories of Saul and Jonathan
- v. 24: Reactions to the loss: Israelite women weep
- vv. 25–26: Result of the loss: David's personal grief for Jonathan
- v. 27: Closing statement: *How the mighty have fallen!*

e. The national loss is great (1:19–25)

The lament of verses 19–27 speaks both of the value of the lives of Saul and Jonathan and of the impact of their deaths. Their deaths, and the deaths of so many of the soldiers who had fought with them, was a devastating loss to Israel. The nation's 'glory' had indeed been left behind on the mountain slopes (19, esv). Surely the land itself would be in mourning. How could the normal patterns of life, with dew and rain and crops (21), continue in that place where such a terrible disaster had occurred?

Saul had been concerned to avoid being abused or mocked before his death (1 Sam. 31:4); David was equally concerned that such mockery be avoided after his death.[5] Far from being suitable subjects for mockery,

---

[5] It was obviously impossible to prevent the Philistines from gloating about their victory; that does not take away from the reality of David's desire that they should not be given the opportunity to do so.

Saul and Jonathan were great warriors who had acquitted themselves well, making good use of their weapons before eventually being overwhelmed (21–22).[6] They had inspired love and loyalty and both, in Saul's case perhaps intermittently but nevertheless genuinely, exhibited graciousness. Saul's reign had brought some sense of economic and political stability to Israel, making possible the purchase of luxury clothing that would have been unthinkable in earlier times (24).

It was not just the men of the land who mourned their lost leader. The women of Philistia might be rejoicing at Saul's death, but for the women of Israel it was a tragedy leading solely to weeping. There was only a slight glimmer of comfort in the fact that at least Saul and Jonathan had been together in death as they had been in life.

f. Personal loss is great (1:26–27)

David's very personal grief for Jonathan creeps into the poem of national mourning (26). For David, accustomed from his youth to being the centre of attraction, the adulation of women was perhaps something that he took for granted. But that the son of the king should be his friend, even when the king himself turned against David, was something very special to David. A. Cook suggests that whereas Jonathan's sister Michal loved David the warrior but found David the dancing harpist more difficult to cope with, and Saul loved David the harpist but could not really accept David's success as a warrior, Jonathan loved and accepted the whole person.[7] Thus, if Cook is correct, the contrast here is seen, not with women in general, but with Michal in particular.

g. It helps to express grief

It is not surprising that in a lament of this kind there should be no element of hope expressed. There are several such laments in the Psalter where the very real feelings of anguish experienced by the psalmist are expressed without reservation. What is unusual about this lament, when compared

---

[6] Saul's shield may now no longer be polished and effective, but his sword was active right up to the time of his death. The literal translation of the last phrase of verse 21 is that Saul's shield is no longer anointed. However, nowhere else in the Old Testament is the word for 'anointed' applied to an object rather than a person and it is likely that the meaning here is simply that the shield was no longer fit for use. Of course, there may be an underlying implication that Saul himself was also no longer fit for use and that David, who during Saul's lifetime kept insisting on the continuing validity of Saul's anointing, was now accepting that the time had come for another 'anointed one' to take over. But the obscurity of the implication probably means that that was not David's intention here.

[7] A. Cook, '"Fiction" and History in Samuel and Kings', *JSOT* 36 (1986), pp. 27–48.

with other poems ascribed to David, is that it contains no reference to God. It is simply a reflection on human relationships. It is possible that David was still at the early stage of his grief where he was incapable of recognizing God's presence in anything that had happened. However, there is no indication here that he blamed God at all for the defeat or the deaths. Perhaps it is simply that this psalm was never intended to be used within the context of worship. Whether or not one has the poetic gifts of someone like David, the public expression of feelings about the death of a loved one and the recalling of that person's gifts and achievements can be a very helpful way of coming to terms with his or her death. One reason for the inclusion of this lament may be to indicate the appropriateness of such open expressions of grief and anguish in both a national and a personal context.

2. Power struggles: David and Ish-Bosheth, Joab and Abner (2:1 – 3:5)

a. Right timing is as important to God as right action (2:1–4a)

We don't know how long David waited before heading back into Israelite territory, but the phrase *in the course of time* seems to be the writer's way of showing that the proper period of mourning for Saul had passed before he did so. Even at that point David was sensitive to the fact that the Judeans at least were likely to see his return to the land as a claim to kingship and he did not want to be seen as inappropriately seizing power. He therefore *enquired of the LORD*, presumably using the ephod that was still in his possession (1 Sam. 23:6; 30:7), before making the journey. David seems to have been aware of the lessons provided within Israel's history that even when God has made his eventual purposes known, it is important to acknowledge that the timing is also in God's hands. Seeking to force God's hand, or seeking to sidestep his instructions in order to fulfil his known purposes, is more likely to bring disaster than to result in those purposes coming about more quickly. Abraham and the Israelites in the wilderness were among those who learned to their cost that this was so (Gen. 16; Num. 14).

Once David was given the go-ahead, he moved back to Hebron in central Judah and set up his base there. As expected, the local people anointed David as their king. They were perhaps encouraged in this by David's returning entourage who settled among them and were now a force to be reckoned with, but there is no indication that they were persuaded against their will. It is inconceivable that the story of David's anointing by Samuel had not by this time become common knowledge at least within Judah, and David had always been recognized as a gifted leader. The pattern of kings being recognized and appointed both by God and by the people was a regular feature of the system within Israel. Even today, leaders who seek to exercise power without acknowledging the need for these two factors to be in place (i.e. the recognition of God's call and the people's acceptance) are perhaps asking for trouble. The crowning of David as king of Judah, without any apparent reference to the other tribes, is an indication that the tribal unity forged by the appointment of Saul was very fragile.

b. The benefits of acknowledging faithful service (2:4b–7)

David's return to Judah gave him access to much more detailed information about the events both preceding and following the death of Saul. One of his first acts as king of Judah, having heard of their sterling work in caring for Saul's remains, was to send a message of thanksgiving and encouragement to the town of Jabesh Gilead, many miles away to the north and on the other side of the Jordan. This could be seen as a political act, seeking to gain respect and approval in other areas of the country, and in particular to win over a town that had been strongly loyal to Saul. However, as an isolated incident it comes across as a genuine response on David's part. He really was grateful that they had done this thing for Saul. It was probably something that he himself would have liked to be able to do. His message indicates that, as Saul was no longer able to repay his debt, then, if the occasion arose, David was willing to respond on Saul's behalf.

David was probably aware of the implication here that he was Saul's natural successor, but acknowledging with thankfulness and paying tribute to those who have rendered service plays an important part in the smooth running of any community. David's action is not to be seen as blameworthy simply because it may have also brought him advantage. Mixed motives are very common in all human behaviour, but fear of or guilt about the reasons behind our behaviour should not prevent us from taking action. Good deeds remain good deeds whether or not the motives behind them are mixed, and we would do well to follow David's example of sending messages of thanks and appreciation to those who have performed some particular act of service.

c. Is violence really necessary?

In Chronicles, we move straight from the account of Saul's death in 1 Chronicles 10 to the announcement that all Israel came together to proclaim David king (1 Chr. 11:1; 2 Sam. 5:1). The writer there is apparently interested only in the fact that David took over from Saul and not in the power struggles between David and Ish-Bosheth, or more specifically between Abner and Joab, which are found in 2 Samuel 3 and 4. The books of Samuel, perhaps in the context of their general interest in the nature of power, are much more concerned to describe the rivalry between the two gifted generals and to let the reader know that even for David the accession to power was not straightforward. Abner's role, first as Saul's faithful general and eventually in bringing the northern tribes into line with Judah and acknowledging David's kingship, is presented in Samuel in a very positive light but it is totally ignored in Chronicles.

When two books give us separate accounts of the same events like this, it helps us see the particular interests and purposes of the individual writers. Chronicles is less concerned than Samuel with the mistakes of the royal family, and it is possible that the fierce tribal fighting that took place before David ascended the throne of the whole country should be seen as a mistake. David had consulted the Lord before taking over as king of Judah, and had waited patiently for God to give him the throne that he had been promised so long before. Perhaps he should have waited a little longer rather than assuming that his rule over the whole territory would need to be achieved by war. We don't know what would have happened if David – and Joab, whose passionate and often violent loyalty to David was beginning to emerge – had waited just a little longer. However, Abner's action in taking the northern tribes into a coalition with the south seems to have been the result not of fear of force but of frustration and dissatisfaction with Ish-Bosheth as a ruler. It is possible that this would have happened anyway and many lives would have been saved. War – or confrontation in more everyday situations – may sometimes be necessary, but we should be very sure that we have reached that point of necessity before engaging in 'violent' action (or introducing 'violent' words), even in pursuit of an end result that we firmly believe to be part of God's plan. God is not usually in a hurry and he can be trusted to bring about his purposes without resorting to the kind of power-hungry manipulation that is pictured in the account in Samuel.

d. The rights and wrongs of loyalty (2:8–11; 3:1–5)

Three passages provide a brief summary of events leading up to the time when David began to reign over the whole of Israel in Jerusalem (2:8–11; 3:1–5; 5:1–5). In 2:8–9 we read of Abner as the one who *had taken Ish-Bosheth* and *made him king*. It appears that Abner was the power behind a rather weak throne. There is no mention of the tribes themselves anointing Ish-Bosheth as Judah had anointed David. However, the northern tribes in particular had been loyal to Saul and the army at least continued to be loyal to Abner and to the king he appointed. David may have had a good reputation throughout the land, but they were not yet ready to give up on Saul's line for a Judean. Judah was a large and influential tribe and it is possible that the others were afraid of being overwhelmed. Power struggles are not limited to fights between individuals, and throughout history there have been instances of minority groups within nations fighting to maintain their own identity. Readers are left to come to their own conclusion as to whether this is a good or a bad thing.

There is some difficulty involved with the numbers in the text of 2:10–11, which provides standard introductory statements to the reigns of the two kings, Ish-Bosheth in Israel and David in Judah. David spent more than seven years in Hebron and 5:5 indicates that it was not until the end of this time that he was crowned over the whole nation. However, Ish-Bosheth reigned for only two years, so where do the extra five years fit in? It may be that Abner waited for some time before making Ish-Bosheth king, perhaps because, as Saul's cousin (1 Sam. 14:50), he had some thought of claiming the throne for himself, or maybe there was a considerable gap after Ish-Bosheth's death before David took over.[8]

Chapter 3:1–5 reminds us that the account we have is only a summary and that David's ascendancy over *the house of Saul* took place over a long period of time. We are also given details of David's first six sons born to him while he was living in Hebron. Three of these, Kileab, Shephatiah and Ithream, are unknown elsewhere apart from the parallel verse in 1 Chronicles 3:1–3 where Kileab is known as Daniel. It may be that they died in infancy. Only one son is named for each wife. This may indicate

---

[8] That Ish-Bosheth was forty years old (10) at around the same time as David was thirty years old (5:4) could also be seen as a difficulty. The account of David and Jonathan's friendship gives the impression that they were around the same age and Jonathan was Saul's eldest son. It may be that that impression is wrong – friendships between those of different ages are not uncommon – or it may be, as Anderson suggests (Anderson, p. 35), that the forty was a symbolic or round number added because the original figure was missing.

that only the eldest son of each wife is recorded, or it may be a sign that David's relationships with women were passionate but in general short-lived. There is no doubt that David did have some difficulty in maintaining good long-term relationships with members of his family.[9] We are told nothing further of the four new wives that he took in Hebron, although 1 Kings 1 – 2 indicates that Adonijah's mother, Haggith, was known in the court.

e. How far should one go in pursuit of a good end?

The intervening verses of chapters 2, 3 and 4 include a range of specific incidents of death and deceit, intrigue and unkindness, murder and general mayhem, interspersed with elements of bravery and enterprise. Most of these are told in a vivid style with colourful detail that suggests that the writer, if not actually present, had been privy to eyewitness accounts. David remains in the background throughout most of these chapters. There is no doubt that certain unsavoury incidents formed part of his rise to power and the books of Samuel do not want to hide that fact. It is possible that David himself may have wanted to wait for God's timing, but there are strong indications that Joab did not share the same desire and it seems that David was rarely able to resist pressure from Joab.

These incidents are all recorded without comment. Readers are again, in effect, invited to assess for themselves what actions are or are not acceptable in the pursuit of a positive end result. However, there does appear to be a concern that the reader should realize that in general David himself was neither privy to nor supportive of these intrigues.[10] Although there may be underlying questions about the corruptive potential of all power, we are not to suppose that David himself, as he took up the throne of Israel, was anything other than God's chosen king. Having said that, perhaps the clear and continuing presentation of David's weaknesses which form such a feature of the books of Samuel is intended to help us realize that, although David could be seen as a great king, God's chosen ruler for this time and the one against whom other, later kings would be measured, nevertheless he was very far from being the Messiah.

---

[9] Cf. D. Clines, 'The Story of Michal, Wife of David', in Clines and Eskenazi.

[10] Cf. P. K. McCarter, 'The Apology of David', *JBL* 99 (1980), pp. 489–504; and D. F. Payne, 'Apologetic Motifs in the Books of Samuel', *VE* 23 (1993), pp. 57–66.

f. Diplomacy without flexibility does not resolve disputes (2:12–17)

Abner (Saul's general) and Joab (David's general) appear to have been equally matched in military prowess, strategic skills and determination. Their encounters bring to mind many similar encounters in ancient and modern history where two sides pay lip service to diplomatic or negotiated solutions, but have no real intention of making any kind of compromise. Here, as in most other such situations, the result is widespread and possibly unnecessary violence and death. In the first incident (2:12–16), which may have taken place before Ish-Bosheth was actually crowned king, Abner and Joab – accompanied by a militarily based diplomatic delegation – sat down around the equivalent of a conference table. Gibeon, which was in Benjaminite territory but well away from Ish-Bosheth's base across the Jordan at Mahanaim and quite close to Judah, was a good spot to hold this kind of 'summit' meeting. At Abner's suggestion a contest is arranged between twelve chosen champions on either side. Abner comes across as slightly more genuine than Joab in his desire to find an honourable solution to Israel's leadership problem, and it seems likely that the suggested contest was not just a rather gruesome game, but a way of determining the identity of the new king while avoiding widespread killing of Israelites by Israelites or even the loss of face by one side. However, the twenty-four young men were equally matched and instead of saving lives, their sacrifice led only to further and extended bloodshed.

Significantly, in this section no-one seems to give any thought to making enquiries as to what God's intention for Israel might be. Nor are there any signs of the careful wooing of the opposition that we saw from David in, for example, his approach to the people of Jabesh Gilead. It was as easy then as it is today to persuade ourselves that we are fighting for a righteous cause which justifies any and all actions when perhaps a very strong element of our motivation is simply personal ambition. As we read through the chapters of Samuel, there is no doubt about the writer's conviction that David was God's chosen replacement for Saul, but that does not mean that his every action is approved of and there is certainly an ambivalence in the description of the power struggle between Joab and Abner.

g. Ambition and overconfidence are unlikely to succeed against skill and experience (2:18 – 3:1)

This is the first time that Joab's younger brother Asahel comes into the picture. Possibly this was his first major battle. In 2 Samuel 23 he is mentioned as one of David's thirty 'chief warriors', but that could have been an honour awarded perhaps posthumously in view of his undoubted bravery and apparently remarkable speed. He was clearly as committed and as determined as his brothers, but he had not yet developed Joab's insights or an awareness of his own limitations. The refusal to take seriously the experience and skill of an opponent has been the downfall of many young enthusiasts within as well as outside God's people. Asahel wanted the glory of overcoming the great Abner and refused to be diverted into seeking more appropriate opposition. When it became clear to Abner that he could not outrun Asahel, he did his best to divert the young man, not so much from fear of reprisals but, so it would seem, more out of respect for Joab or recognition of Asahel's potential for Israel's future. He was unsuccessful, and so, inevitably and somewhat ingloriously, Asahel was killed.

In spite of Asahel's death, in general it was Joab's forces which had a clear advantage. However, after the deaths of 360 of Abner's men and only twenty of Joab's, the battle was suspended and the two armies returned to their respective bases. Perhaps Joab was genuinely convinced by Abner's diplomatic arguments that further killing was actually going to damage rather than enhance David's chances of successfully controlling the whole country. Perhaps he recognized that with Abner's troops rallying on a hilltop they had regained the initiative and Judah's initial advantage might be lost. The civil war is described as lasting *a long time* (3:1), but there are no further stories of battles and it may be that for much of the period the battle was one for the hearts and minds of the people, fought in the field of public relations. Over the next months, presumably within the northern tribes, support for Ish-Bosheth decreased and support for David increased.

3. Abner and Ish-Bosheth, the end of the line (3:6 – 4:12)

a. Trust works (or fails to work) both ways! (3:6–10)

There is no evidence that Abner himself had any pretensions to the throne. When he eventually lost patience with the weak and querulous Ish-Bosheth, he organized the transfer of power to David rather than seeking to take control himself. The *strengthening* of *his own position* (6) which occurred seems to have been more related to the growing popularity of an obviously gifted charismatic leader and to Ish-Bosheth's failure to exercise leadership than to any deliberate action on Abner's part. However, Abner must have been well aware that Ish-Bosheth's hold on power was totally dependent on his support, given because of a residual loyalty to Saul rather than any particular belief in Ish-Bosheth's ability or right to lead the country. It is never easy to decide how, when or whether to withdraw support from one who is incapable or unworthy of holding the position that he or she has been given. Loyalty is a valued and valuable commodity. However, misplaced loyalty can cause damage both to those continuing in positions for which they are unsuited and to those they are supposedly leading or caring for. Ish-Bosheth's leadership did not seem to be providing much benefit to either himself or his people.

It is interesting that when Abner eventually made his decision, it was not on any political, theological or even strategic grounds. It may be that Abner had been aware for some time of God's promise to David (18), or it may be something that he learned about only when he began to negotiate with David, but it is clear that this was not the primary reason for Abner's change of heart. His growing frustration boiled over when Ish-Bosheth, whom he could have betrayed at any time but had not, accused him of disloyalty. Whether or not Abner had slept with Rizpah – and there is a slight ambiguity in Abner's reply – the implication of Ish-Bosheth's accusation, that Abner had taken an action which showed that he intended to take over the throne, was completely unfounded.[11]

Abner's response was to take the action that he had probably recognized as inevitable from the beginning. He made the decision to acknowledge David as king over the whole land and to encourage the rest of Israel to do the same. Ish-Bosheth was not a gifted leader, had never really had the support of the people and without Abner's backing would not have been acknowledged as king in the first place. His insult provided the reason or the excuse that Abner needed. Once his own loyalty had been questioned, any residual responsibility he felt towards Saul's family came to an end. Trust is important in any relationship, but it always works both ways. It can be as easily destroyed by unjustified suspicion as it can by betrayal.

---

[11] The taking over of the women who had been wives or concubines of a former king was commonly seen as a sign that the throne too was or should be 'under new management' (cf. 2 Sam. 16:22; 1 Kgs 2:17). Ish-Bosheth's suspicion was not just a product of paranoid fear. However, Abner's power and ability were clearly such that he could have deposed Ish-Bosheth at any time but had deliberately made no attempt to do so. Perhaps his victory over the temptation to take over had been hard won, so the accusation of disloyalty was particularly galling.

b. A smooth change in government involves winning the hearts of the people (3:11–19)

There is no doubt that the decision was Abner's to make. Ish-Bosheth had no way of holding the nation together without Abner's support and he made no attempt to stop the process of reunification taking place. Nevertheless, the way in which the negotiations are described makes it clear that Ish-Bosheth was involved. Abner did not simply leave him to sink or swim. People who act as power brokers in the way that Abner did have a continuing responsibility to those they have placed in untenable positions. It appears that Abner envisaged Ish-Bosheth remaining as a tribal leader in the unified nation. This time, rather than simply acting for himself, Abner consulted widely among the tribes (17). If Israel was to become the strong nation that he genuinely desired it to be, it was important that the new king was 'owned' and recognized by the people as a whole, not just appointed as, in effect, a military puppet. David was to be affirmed as God's choice and the people's choice – the people this time being Israel as a whole and not just Judah. This was to be a willing and glad acceptance, a freely offered allegiance, not an unwilling or grudging acknowledgment from a conquered people. Special attention was paid to Saul's own tribe of Benjamin, as they were the most likely to oppose David's accession to the throne. Perhaps if David had at the beginning taken the action that Abner took now, then his kingship over the whole nation might have commenced earlier and with much less bloodshed.

c. Individuals are expendable? (3:12–16)

David made only one proviso. He wanted his first wife, Michal, to be returned to him.[12] We are given no explanation for this request. Presumably David felt that Michal's return to the court would be a sign of Ish-Bosheth's good faith. If, as the current head of his family, Ish-Bosheth agreed to Michal's return, he could not then argue that David's accession had been without his knowledge or against his will. Also, the continuing presence of Saul's daughter in the court could help to foster a sense of continuity with the previous regime. Although Michal had at one time loved David (1 Sam. 18:20), there is no mention of him ever seeking to visit her, or indeed any indication that he had spared her a second thought in

---

[12] David had never actually divorced Michal, which is perhaps why the normal prohibition of remarriage (Deut. 24:4) does not come into play.

the intervening years, and we are not told what she felt about him now. She had married again; whether this was by her own choice or not is not known, but neither she nor her new husband Paltiel, who certainly loved her, were given any choice in the current situation. Paltiel's distress is described with great feeling. It is clear that as far as both David and Abner were concerned, political expediency was more important than the personal feelings of either Michal or Paltiel. David's high-handed treatment of Michal here may go some way to explaining her reactions at a later stage (2 Sam. 6). We, as readers, are again left to make the judgment as to whether or not callous disregard for the feelings of individuals is acceptable in the service of a 'higher' cause.

d. Terrorism is not justified even in a good cause (3:20–27)

The negotiations having been successfully concluded between Abner and David, and with all sides agreeing to the terms with happiness and mutual respect, Abner and his team set off to return home. His task now was to make arrangements for the national ceremony that would confirm David's position within the land and proclaim to outsiders that Israel was once more a united nation and a force to be reckoned with. The scene is set for a positive and peaceful handover.

At this point, Joab returned to Hebron (22). His extended absence leading a raiding party is a salutary reminder that the Philistine threat had by no means been removed. Joab was horrified by the action that David had taken and immediately determined to sabotage the arrangements. Probably Joab felt he was acting on behalf of the nation and with David's best interests at heart. It is possible that his long rivalry with Abner, exacerbated by the death of Asahel, meant that he was unable to see Abner as anything other than a dangerous enemy. He himself could not envisage David becoming king of the whole nation of Israel by any means other than military conquest, and he was totally convinced that Abner's whole approach to David had been an elaborate hoax. It seems clear that in the light of this he saw his own subsequent actions as completely justified. It seems equally clear that neither David nor the writer of 2 Samuel shared his perspective!

Any peaceful and positive end to a situation of fierce antipathy is going to involve some compromise and some letting bygones be bygones. Joab was unwilling to accept this and, although in spite of Joab's action David did still become king of all Israel, the foundation was laid for a continuing rivalry and mistrust between the tribes that would cause major problems for both David and Israel later on.

The thought lies in the air that Joab, although he was in his own way totally loyal to David and had no desire to claim kingship for himself, nevertheless was unable to accept that such significant decisions had been made not only without his participation but with his enemy Abner playing such a significant role in brokering the deal. There is always a danger of 'kingmakers' being more power-hungry than the kings themselves. Those who do not seek to be figureheads can easily justify their own fierce ambitions and their own uncompromising violence on the grounds that they act only in the interests of others. In this context, it is hard not to come to the conclusion that Joab is portrayed within this account more as a terrorist than a peacemaker.

Abner's death is described briefly (27). Throughout the world and history we find a common convention that the personal safety of those who seek to negotiate terms is guaranteed. Abner came back to participate in further negotiations with Joab without fear and without precaution. He was killed, not on the battlefield and after a warning, as Joab's brother Asahel had been, but covertly and cold-bloodedly. There was no doubt in the mind of the writer, and he wishes there to be no doubt in the mind of the reader: this killing was a vengeful murder.

e. A good leader must deal justly with friends as well as with enemies (3:28–39)

The rest of chapter 3 deals with David's response to the news of Abner's death. Joab may have ignored any possible consequences of his actions, but David knew only too well that Abner's death lessened the possibility of a smooth takeover from Ish-Bosheth. He makes clear his displeasure at the action Joab has taken and dissociates himself from it as much as he possibly can. He mourns for Abner personally, as he would for a relative, and insists on the kind of public ceremonial that would be appropriate for a member of the royal family. His actions certainly convinced the people – presumably those from the north as well as his own Judeans – of his sincerity. They believed that he had had no part in Abner's death, nor even any desire for it. Joab's foolish action had not removed the possibility of David's kingship over all the tribes of Israel.

The discussion of David's treatment of Joab is worthy of note. He is quite clear that Abner's death was murder and that Joab is guilty. He makes a public statement of this, calling down a curse on Joab and his family (28–29) and asking God that any consequences resulting from the guilt of Abner's death should fall on them rather than on the innocent David or on the people (39). He insists, with some irony, that Joab himself should take a major and visible part in the mourning for Abner. However, he takes no direct action against Joab. The penalty for murder was quite clear and David had no qualms about executing those responsible for the death of Saul (2 Sam. 1) and for the death of Ish-Bosheth (2 Sam. 4). Nowhere in the law is the pronouncement of a curse allowed as a replacement for proper punishment. The people may have been satisfied by the action that David took, but the writer is still raising questions about who is in control and what power means. The king's primary responsibility was to uphold the law (Deut. 17:18–20) and the law applies to all alike. There was to be no special treatment for kings and certainly not for the friends and relatives of kings. David's 'leave it to the Lord' approach may sound spiritual, but Scripture does not allow for God-given responsibility to be set aside in the name of pseudo-spirituality.[13]

David's statement to his men that Zeruiah's sons were *too strong*[14] for him (39) is ambiguous. Is the mention of Zeruiah, David's sister (1 Chr. 2:16), meant to imply that the family ties were too strong to break? Was David in awe of a dominating older sister and afraid therefore to act against her sons? Was David suggesting that Joab and Abishai were physically stronger than him? Was Joab in reality as much in control of the southern region as Abner was of the north and was David, therefore, as much a puppet king as Ish-Bosheth? Was it that David felt so dependent on Joab's skills as a general that he was unwilling to lose him for any reason? The surrounding texts do not give the impression of David as anything other than in full control of his kingdom. However, for some reason he did not fulfil his kingship responsibilities in relation to Joab and he was fully aware that he had not done so. David's final prayer that the Lord should repay the evildoer has primary reference to Joab – David will not deal with Joab's crime but God will. It may be that for the writer, and even possibly for David himself, there is also the implication that God should deal with David for failing to fulfil his responsibilities.

---

[13] In Mark 7:9–13, Jesus makes it clear that it is unacceptable to set aside God's commands (in that case, the command to honour parents) in the name of service of God.

[14] 'Harsh' or 'rough' is probably a better translation here than 'strong', and the implication may be that Joab and his brothers take a harder stance on issues than would be David's preference.

David's failure to handle Joab is reflected later in his failure to deal effectively with his own sons. In both instances it was a failure that led to continuing problems for David and for the people. The ability to recognize and confront the failures and weaknesses of friends is an important element of any leader's skill base. David falls well short here, as elsewhere, of the messianic ideal presented in Isaiah 11:1–4.

f. 'Helpful' action that is in itself unjust is not helpful at all (4:1–12)

The record of the death of Ish-Bosheth and David's resultant action described in chapter 4 is almost a rerun of the record of the death of Saul. In some senses Ish-Bosheth's death did make it easier for David, and it is not perhaps surprising that the two military leaders Baanah and Rekab felt that David would be pleased with their action. They misjudged both David and the situation. The death of Ish-Bosheth compounded the problem that David had after the death of Abner. It was becoming increasingly hard for his kingship of the northern tribes to be seen as a welcomed handover rather than as a feared, unavoidable and probably unwelcome takeover. It was again vital that David dissociate himself completely from their action and so, like the Amalekite in chapter 1, they were immediately executed. David concludes that those who kill an innocent man in circumstances where he should have expected to be safe themselves deserve a shameful death. His conclusion serves to raise further questions about his lax treatment of Joab.

The mention in 4:4 of Jonathan's son Mephibosheth and his disability is an aside preparing us for further reference to Mephibosheth at a later stage. The NIV rightly places it in brackets.

We are at last ready to hear of David's coronation over the whole country. One can understand why the Chronicler did not include the material from 2 Samuel 1 – 4 in his account. It is hard to portray the reign of David as glorious when it had such an inglorious start. However, the writer of the books of Samuel obviously thought that it was important for the reader to understand that there is significance in the way power is attained as well as in the possession and exercise of power. It is clearly important that we have a realistic view of leaders and their teams. That leaders have made mistakes, even bad mistakes, does not prevent them from exercising good leadership at other times, as David clearly did. That leaders at times exercise good leadership does not prevent them at other times making serious mistakes, as David equally clearly did.

4. Nationwide power achieved and endorsed (5:1–25)

a. Leadership needs to be recognized properly (5:1–5)

The style of chapter 5 is rather different from the vivid descriptions of events in the camps and the courts that have filled the previous few chapters. It reads more like editorial comment than eyewitness account. Verses 1–5 provide an official summary of the start of David's reign and a standard brief record of his dates,[15] verses 6–14 tell of the institution of Jerusalem as capital and verses 17–25 describe the final, or at least fairly final, defeat of the Philistines. It seems likely that the information in this chapter was gained from national records. Much of the material is repeated virtually word for word in Chronicles.[16] In general, the writer of Samuel seems more interested in the implications of specific incidents and in character portrayal and relationships than in official records. Nevertheless, an overall understanding of political and national events is essential to an understanding of the specific stories, and every now and then these summary sections from national records are included. God's purposes are always worked out in the context of history and it is very difficult for anyone to understand the Old Testament without having some awareness of the historical context in which the individual accounts, stories and prophecies were situated.

The point emphasized in verses 1–4 is that David is a proper representative of the whole nation. He belongs to one tribe, Judah, but he is related to all. He has proved his credentials as a military leader and clearly he has received God's call and backing for the task of leading the nation. It is on this basis that he is acclaimed as king over the whole nation. No details are given of the *covenant* (3) or 'compact' made between the king and the tribal elders, but it appears to have been an agreement setting out the terms of the king's reign, recognizing the rights and responsibilities of all sides. David and his supporters, particularly Joab (chs. 2 and 3), may have taken violent action in the pursuit of kingship, but the ideal is always clear. The king's reign is validated by the agreement and with the cooperation of the whole people. Like all good leadership, it should not be something simply imposed from above. There is irony in the fact that Solomon's reign,

---

[15] Parallel to the introductions to later rulers in the books of Kings (e.g. 1 Kgs 14:21; 15:1–2; 16:8, 29; 2 Kgs 14:1–3; 18:1–4).

[16] 5:1–3 = 1 Chr. 11:1–3; 5:6–10 = 1 Chr. 11:4–9; and 5:11–25 = 1 Chr. 14:1–16.

which although extremely effective in human terms eventually led the people away from worship of the Lord (1 Kgs 11), began not with a covenant but via a palace revolution, and similarly Rehoboam lost control of the northern tribes because of a refusal to accept the necessity for making a covenant with them (1 Kgs 12).

b. Establishing a brand-new capital city helps to unite rival groups (5:6–9)

Given the later importance of Jerusalem, both politically and theologically, the description of its capture is remarkably brief. Chronicles refers to the appointment of Joab as official army commander after his having been the first into the city (1 Chr. 11:6), but omits the references here to *the blind and the lame* (6, 8). David seems to have been particularly annoyed by the Jebusites' taunt that the city was so well defended that even a weakened, disabled army could hold David off. There is possibly an implication here that David himself included a number of *the blind and the lame* within his initial raiding party to turn the taunt back onto the Jebusites. Certainly the city that they thought was so well defended was in fact taken without difficulty.

The description of the building works around the city is equally brief. Hiram did not become king of Tyre (11) until later in David's reign and it seems clear that the development of the city took some time to complete. However, the institution of Jerusalem, *the fortress of Zion – which is the city of David* (7), was apparently accepted as the capital of the nation very easily. There is no hint of opposition to the siting of the new national centre. Perhaps it helped that even though Jerusalem was in the south, it was in the territory originally assigned to Benjamin, and also, as it had never been conquered by Israel, it was in every sense a new capital city.

This was a genuine new start for the whole nation and not just a matter of the northern tribes being associated with a Judean court in Hebron that already existed. For any merger to be successful, whether of states, businesses, churches, Christian organizations or even of two people in marriage, it is important to find ways of showing that the new institution really is new; that there has been a merger and not a takeover.[17]

---

[17] The 'leaving and cleaving' exhortation in Gen. 2:24 makes this point in relation to marriage.

c. Any power over God's people is God's power and must be exercised in God's way (5:10–25)

The two statements found here in verses 10 and 12 are recorded in quite separate places in Chronicles (1 Chr. 11:9; 14:2). By bringing them together here, the writer places a strong emphasis on the fact that David's regime was instituted and enabled by God and that David himself recognized this. It was because *the LORD God Almighty was with him* (10) that *David became more and more powerful*. David's power was dependent on God's support and that support was given *for the sake of his people Israel* (12). The reader is to be absolutely clear at the beginning of David's reign that David was ruling the people of God as God's representative and with God's support. Saul began the same way and, as the story of David's reign begins to unfold, the question is raised in the mind of the reader as to whether David, like Saul, will begin to focus not on the reason why he has been given power but on the power itself and the need to retain that power. David begins as *a man after* God's *own heart* (1 Sam. 13:14). We have to read on to discover whether he will remain that way. The next verse (13), telling of David's taking more wives and concubines, may simply be providing information about David's sons (14–16),[18] but perhaps the writer placed it here deliberately to show that the answer to the question of David's continuing faithfulness is not a foregone conclusion. The king who reigns according to God's principles is not one who takes many wives (Deut. 17:17). It may be significant that after the initial reference before his anointing, the text never again refers to David as a man after God's heart.

Saul had been anointed to deliver God's people 'from the hand of the Philistines' (1 Sam. 9:16), but he had failed in his task. David had been given the same commission (2 Sam. 3:18). Again the question is raised as to whether David will succeed where Saul failed. The initial answer this time is much more positive. The Philistines, hearing of David's accession, took immediate action to ensure that their comprehensive defeat of Saul's forces was not reversed. This time, the failure was theirs. We are given brief details of two incidents following a similar pattern. The Philistines attacked; David *enquired of the LORD* (19, 23); David followed the Lord's instructions; the Philistines were defeated comprehensively. The timing

---

[18] Chronicles adds that the first four of these were the children of Bathsheba. It then includes two extra names and states that those named were the children of David's official wives; there were several more who were born to his concubines (1 Chr. 3:5–9).

of these two incidents is uncertain and they were clearly not the only battles. However, we are told later that 'in the course of time, David defeated the Philistines' (2 Sam. 8:1) in such a way that although they or their descendants may have caused occasional problems,[19] they were never again a major threat to the people of Israel.

It is interesting that although both victories are seen as a result of God's intervention, David again consults the Lord and then introduces a completely different strategy (23–24) rather than simply repeating his tactics from the first victory (20). Every situation is clearly different and God may have different plans for tackling situations which at first sight seem very similar. It is not enough simply to do what has been done before. Sometimes when we move to a new sphere of ministry, there is a temptation simply to repeat what we did last time, or perhaps to repeat what has been done in some other large and successful church or institution. It is good to learn from the past and from others, but it is also important to take note, as David did, of the fact that each situation is new and God takes seriously the needs of each individual circumstance.

Questions to ponder

1. What lay behind David's decision to execute the Amalekite? Was it fair?
2. Was Ish-Bosheth an offender or a victim?
3. Did David's political acumen or his spiritual discernment take priority in his actions relating to the Amalekite and to Ish-Bosheth?
4. How relevant are the character portrayals of, for example, Abner and Joab?
5. What light does this section shed on the problem of deciding the nature and timing of action taken to fulfil what might be seen as God's purposes?
6. What was it about Joab that made him 'too strong' for David?
7. Thus far, has David proved to be a 'man after [God's] own heart'?

---

[19] E.g. 2 Kgs 18:8, where Hezekiah is described as defeating the Philistines.

2 Samuel 6 – 10

7. David: in covenant

1. The ark comes to Jerusalem (6:1–23)

a. There is a difference between assuming and ascertaining God's will (6:1–2)

Chapter 5 describes from an organizational and military point of view how David began to act as king. He was commissioned to free the land from the Philistines and that commission began to be fulfilled. In chapter 6 he turns his attention to what could be called the religious side of his responsibilities and, for the first time since it was left for safekeeping at Kiriath Jearim (1 Sam. 7:2),[1] the ark of God comes back into the picture. It is noteworthy that when considering what action should be taken in response to the large-scale Philistine advance (5:17–19), David's first thought was to 'enquire of the LORD'. No such enquiry is mentioned relating to the decision to bring the ark into Jerusalem. Given the way events work out, this omission may be significant. In 1 Chronicles 13 the Chronicler gives more details of the circumstances in which the decision was made and makes it clear that there was widespread consultation, although most of that appears to have been with military commanders about *how* the action should proceed, rather than with religious leaders about *whether* it should proceed. The statement to the national assembly in 1 Chronicles 13:2, 'if it seems good to you and if it is the will of the LORD', is somewhat rhetorical, inviting acceptance rather than comment.[2] When

---

[1] There is also a somewhat obscure reference in 1 Sam. 14:18–19 to an abortive attempt by Saul to use the ark.

[2] Chronicles places the account of the defeat of the Philistines (1 Chr. 14) between the accounts of the two attempts to bring the ark into Jerusalem (1 Chr. 13 and 15). It is possible that here, too, the specific enquiry as to the nature of God's will is being contrasted with the general desire to follow that will.

religious or spiritual matters are involved, it is easy to assume that God's preferences or requirements are obvious and to take it for granted that what we have decided to do must be the 'right thing'. It appears that David made this kind of assumption. God had been with him in the setting up of Israel's new capital city. It must surely be right that the great symbol of God's presence with Israel, the ark of God, should be housed in Jerusalem. This would set the final seal on David's reign as God's chosen king for Israel. How could God not want such a thing?

It was decided that the ark would be brought up from Baalah of Judah (an alternative name for Kiriath Jearim) to Jerusalem. David was obviously very involved in the proceedings and the unstated implication is that he himself had taken the initiative and organized this celebratory procession. David took it for granted that the best and right place for the ark was in the newly instituted capital city. This assumption was not without basis. It would certainly make sense for the most significant religious object within Israel to be sited in what was at least beginning to be seen as the most significant site. The ark was special, *called by the Name, the name of the LORD Almighty, who is enthroned between the cherubim on the ark* (2). It was the symbol of God's own presence with Israel. It was also assumed, therefore, that the moving of the ark should take place with as much splendour and ceremonial as they could muster. Both these assumptions may have been right, but what was missing was any record of consultation or seeking out of God's opinion in the matter. In fact, it could be inferred that David was behaving in the same way as his predecessors and subconsciously or otherwise seeking to use the ark for his own political ends. If the ark was situated in David's capital, it would be far easier to convince the people that God was behind David's kingship and that decisions made by David should be viewed automatically as God-inspired.

b. God deserves the best; but who decides what that is? (6:3–7)

The writer's underlying interest in power, in who was actually in charge, again comes to the fore. David was God's man, but this did not mean that David could presume that he understood and could control God's purposes. God could not and can never be manipulated in that kind of way. Saul, and many others throughout Scripture, discovered that truth at a cost. So did David. The emerging events could be seen as providing evidence that the writer's omission of any reference to God's instructions really was deliberate and the reader is being called upon to evaluate actions as well as to note them. This remains a possibility, whether or not David's own motivation was primarily or even partially to glorify God in the best way that he could envisage.

Even if the 'thousand' of verse 1 is a general term for a troop rather than a literal thousand men, thirty troops involved a very large number of men for what was largely a ceremonial duty. However, Baalah of Judah was still very close to Philistine territory and David could have been indulging in a show of strength, making sure both that the Philistines were aware of his growing supremacy and that there was no chance of an invading group preventing the success of his enterprise. In this case, a real desire to honour God and provide the ark with the best possible journey could also justify the use of a large section of the army.

Certainly the ceremonial was magnificent. The ark remained for the moment in the custody of the same family who had been guarding it for several years (1 Sam. 7:1). Two of Abinadab's sons, Uzzah and Ahio, guided the brand-new cart that had been provided specially – the top of the range of available transport. The whole people, including David, were making the most of the fantastic music and the whole great occasion. They *were celebrating with all their might before the LORD* (5). Nobody, including David, had any doubts that this was a religious celebration, a wonderful way to worship and serve God. Therefore, the shock at what happened at Nakon was profound. Uzzah, with the clear intention of preventing a disastrous accident, touched the ark. Dramatically and immediately he died. How they knew that this was as a result of God's anger is not explained, but nobody, including David, had any doubts that it was.

c. Our God really is awesome! (6:7)

There is no discussion in the narrative of the reason for Uzzah's death. The Hebrew in verse 7 is somewhat obscure but the NIV's *irreverent act* gives the sense of it. It is possible that Uzzah's instinctive action may have given the impression that God needed to be protected by his people rather than the other way round. On the other hand, it may simply have been that touching the ark was seen as infringing God's holiness.

Our conviction that God is 'nice' and would never do anything that we might not like makes passages like this one very difficult for us. We perhaps need to grasp much more clearly what it means to say that God is holy. It is certainly important to realize that religious service and theo-logical understanding must work in tandem. Knowledge of God and of his revealed purposes must form the background to action supposedly taken on God's behalf and to all worship of God. God in his great mercy often did not strike down the Israelites and does not strike us down, but passages like this force us to take seriously how strongly God feels about our placing our preferences before his revealed will. Many of us have a tendency to judge the validity of a particular worship service by how much we have enjoyed it. This indicates that sometimes our understanding of the awesome nature of God does not go too far beyond the songs we sing.

It is likely that part of the problem here was that the wrong procedures had been followed. Samuel does not emphasize this point and problems only arose when Uzzah took action, not when the procession started, but there is a strong hint that setting aside tradition in favour of the most up-to-date method can sometimes have unforeseen side effects! The last time we heard of the ark, in 1 Samuel 6, it was carried back from the Philistines on 'a new cart' (1 Sam. 6:7). Here again a 'new cart' (3) is used and it seems very likely that our attention is being drawn to the use of Philistine methods rather than the procedures laid down in the law. On the second attempt to bring the ark to Jerusalem (recorded in 1 Chr. 15), the instructions in the law were strictly adhered to and the ark was carried on the shoulders of appointed Levites (Deut. 10:8). The text in 2 Samuel 6 is less explicit, but verse 13 also records that this time the ark was carried. God's instructions were not to be so lightly dismissed.

d. Are we right to be angry when God seems not to appreciate our best efforts? (6:8–11)

We see in this passage a remarkably astute observation of human nature, in particular of David's nature. We are told that David was first angry (8) and then afraid (9). It would probably be true that at first he was absolutely furious and then completely terrified, but the understatement makes the point. The reader is left to interpret the anger – was it because David had been totally convinced that everything he was doing was for God's benefit? He was trying to put God's ark in the best possible place. What right then did God have to step in and spoil their celebrations in this way? David, once he stopped acting impetuously and began to reflect on what was happening, did have tremendous insight – even into himself and his own motivations. Perhaps it was at this point that he began to be afraid. He knew in his heart that God could not be manipulated. He was perhaps honest enough to admit that his motives had been mixed, that he may have been enjoying his own precedence and the trappings of kingship more than seeking to serve God. He knew that his motives were always likely to be mixed and therefore, with a typical move from one extreme to the other, he gave up the whole enterprise. The ark was placed with a Gittite family, but we are not told whether these were resident foreigners or some who had been with David in Gath. Neither are we told if Obed-Edom and his family had any choice in the matter, but what is very clear is that having the ark in their house brought them great blessing.

David had learned one set of lessons. He was sure now that the ark was not to be touched inappropriately, but more importantly that God's holiness was not to be compromised even with good motives. He was even more convinced than before that God was not to be manipulated or taken for granted and that what really counted was God's power and not David's, God's kingship and not David's. However, there were still more lessons to learn. Maybe there had been a superstitious attitude that suggested that it was the ark itself as an object that was dangerous or a sense that the ark should really never have been moved from where it was. The blessing of Obed-Edom's household convinced David that neither of these factors applied. He had not really understood what was going on, but became convinced that now really was the appropriate time to bring the ark to Jerusalem.

e. Exuberance and/or dignity (6:12–23)

The second procession was, if possible, an even more glorious celebration than the first. It involved great sacrifices,[3] making sure that all involved realized that it was the Lord God who was in control of what went on and he only who was being worshipped. The ark was eventually set in its new place, further sacrifices were made, the whole crowd was presented with a special celebratory picnic and everyone went home. David's gift to the people also added to the sense of national unity and identity which the celebration itself was helping to reinforce. The main motivation may have been to increase the popularity of and support for David's government, but the kind of positive national awareness that such occasions bring are good for a country. In today's world, similar examples of positive national celebrations are seen when a country wins a huge sporting event

---

[3] It is sometimes suggested that what we have here is really part of an annual feast involving a ceremonial procession. However, there is no doubt that the ark was moved into Jerusalem at some stage and there is nothing in the text which precludes this from being seen as the account of that first occasion.

like soccer's World Cup, or when there is some kind of national jubilee festivity that increases a people's awareness and affirmation of their own national identity.

David's personal involvement in the celebrations was wholehearted. His dancing was exuberant and, having set aside the more bulky clothing and wearing only the short ephod,[4] his appearance was not dignified and could perhaps legitimately be described as indecent. Whether David's actions should be seen as an exuberant expression of worship that in itself glorified God or as over-exuberant self-glorification is not really the point. As the magnificent procession approached Jerusalem, what Michal saw when she glanced down from her window was David looking undignified. She did not see the celebrating nation or the demonstration and recognition of God's glory; she did not notice the ark or rejoice in the acknowledgment of God's presence. She saw only David behaving in a way that she viewed as indecent. It could be argued that David deserved some kind of rebuke, but it is very easy for bitterness to blind us to things of real significance and cause us to focus on what might be seen as irrelevant details.

In mentioning the window, the writer might be reminding us that Michal did have some cause to be bitter. There are brief references to the start and finish of Michal's marriage to Paltiel who loved her (1 Sam. 25:44; 2 Sam. 3:13–16), but this is the first real insight that we have had into Michal as a person since 1 Samuel 19:12. On that occasion she was also watching through a window as David, at that time her much-loved husband, disappeared into the darkness after she had helped him escape. He apparently made no attempt to see her again until she was taken away from Paltiel, for reasons which it is hard not to see as purely political, and returned to David, this time as one among many wives. She had seen her father and most of her brothers killed in battle and her remaining brother murdered. Yes, Michal had reason to be bitter. But in allowing her bitterness to blind her to God and his glory she became her own worst enemy. Anger and the inability to forgive have a habit of harming the one who feels offended more than the perceived offender.

For Michal, David's indecent exposure was an unacceptable setting aside of his royal dignity; for David, it was an unintended side effect of his

---

[4] The ephod was a short robe usually referred to in the context of priestly dress, so it is possible that David here is associating himself with the priesthood. This garment is quite distinct from the ephod used to enquire of God whether a particular action should or should not take place.

wholehearted worship of Yahweh. For Michal, royal dignity was perhaps all she had left; for David, it was completely irrelevant in the light of God's glory and power. We are left with the strong impression that Michal's bitterness, however much it arose from the despair of her own circumstances, is unacceptable. We are not told if Michal's barrenness was a punishment sent by God or a result of a deliberate decision on her part or on David's part to avoid sexual relations. What is clear is that Michal was to be cut off from any further involvement in royal dignity that might have come from being the mother of a royal son, and that the heir to David's throne was not to come from Saul's family. This somewhat sour note at the end of the account of the day of national rejoicing finally shuts the door on Saul's reign and opens the way for the account of God's covenant with David.

2. God's covenant with David (7:1–29)

The encounter between David and the prophet Nathan that is described in this chapter could be seen as one of the most significant meetings recorded within the royal history. The account sets out the beginnings of the temple and of the Davidic covenant, both of which had a profound effect on Israel's religious and national life for many centuries. It also contains deep theological insights into God's purposes within history and the way he relates to human beings.

The timing is somewhat vague. David was *settled in his palace* (1) and the surrounding enemies were no longer an immediate threat. Presumably the battles described in chapter 8 had already taken place. It does seem to be the case that when the Davidic covenant was instituted, David had been a successful king for some time. It is not David's kingship as such that is being affirmed here but the validation of the Davidic dynasty. David, unlike Eli or Samuel or Saul, was going to be succeeded by his son and his son's son.

The chapter does contain narrative but the style is much more restrained than that of the chapters up to chapter 6 and after chapter 9. It may be that because of the significance of its contents, this section was edited at a later stage in order to further emphasize its theological importance.[5] The chapter centres on a wordplay that, unusually, works in

---

[5] Parts of both chapters 7 and 8 are repeated word for word in 1 Chr. 17 and 18, so it is probable that both writers were making use of other national records in their own accounts. It is quite clear that the writers of Samuel made use of sources, but the editing of material to emphasize particular points does not mean that the material loses validity as a historical record.

English as well as it does in Hebrew. David is not to build a house (building) for God, but God will build a house (dynasty) for David.

a. What to do with a 'good idea'? (7:2)

The story is simple. David has another good idea about the ark. It is now housed safely in a special tent in Jerusalem, but surely it would be better placed in a beautifully constructed permanent building. Deuteronomy 12:10–11[6] provides a possible basis for this view. Perhaps made wary by the results of his previous 'good idea', David's first action is to consult the prophet. Nathan plays a major role at a number of stages in David's life and appears to be a national prophet, able to be consulted by and to challenge the monarch. Nevertheless, he enters the narrative without any formal introduction. We know nothing of his family or his background; we know only that he is a prophet apparently well known to and perhaps well used by David. He may have been permanently based at the court, but each of his appearances (2 Sam. 7; 12; 1 Kgs 1) seems to have been unexpected and it may be that he was based elsewhere and visited occasionally.

The lack of information about Nathan may be a deliberate way of indicating that it is the message rather than the bearer of the message that matters. There has always been a tendency among God's people to make celebrities of those who speak for God. It is probably a tendency that should be resisted! There is no further mention of the ephod being used as a method of ascertaining God's will. It seems that if a prophet was available to mediate God's word, that took precedence over the more mechanical procedure involved in using the ephod.

b. Good ideas are not always right for now (7:3–5)

The idea also seems good to Nathan and he has no hesitation in reassuring David, *go ahead and do it, for the LORD is with you*. The words bring a reminder of the initial commission to Saul where he also was told to do whatever came to hand, confident of God's presence with him (1 Sam. 10:7). It seems that for both king and prophet, and by implication for ordinary believers too, the normal procedure was to act and to speak on the basis of human thought and decisions made in the light of the knowledge of God and of his previously revealed will. The exception to this came when God gave a direct and specific revelation. There is no clear

---

[6] The strong links with Deuteronomy are very clear in this chapter (see the Introduction).

distinction between the word of the prophet and the word of God. An oracle was assumed to have God's authority and to be God's word whether it was revealed directly to the prophet or not. However, this incident makes it very clear that when a direct word did come it overrode Nathan's own professional prophetic judgment. In most cases the ideas that seem good are good – but that does not mean that they are always to be acted upon immediately. It was vital that God's prophets be ready to listen and take heed if exceptions were revealed to them.

There is no indication that Nathan, in reassuring David, was acting as a false prophet. It is interesting that he showed no hesitation in returning to David with the information that God had given a direct revelation and his initial conclusion had not in fact been adequate. Only foolish leaders stick to an entrenched view or refuse to change a position out of fear that their credentials might be doubted. Even a true prophet like Nathan some-times got it wrong and needed to be corrected.[7]

c. No building, not even the temple, should be seen as the 'be all and end all' of worship (7:6–13)

The first part of God's message to David given via Nathan informs him that he is not to build a temple and sets out some of the reasons for this. First, it could cause theological misunderstanding. God is not and never has been limited to a particular site. The tent in which the ark was placed provided a useful symbol that God was present with the people, but its portability also symbolized that God was with the people wherever they were. The temple could and eventually did provide equivalent ways of maintaining the same truths, but it could also lead people to a false trust in the building itself. It was important that before the temple was built the people understood exactly what it did and did not symbolize and signify. It was a place where they could meet with God, but not the only place that God could be found. They had clearly not yet reached the stage where they could understand fully what was involved. The use of any and all religious objects and symbols must be undertaken carefully with serious thinking about what kind of understanding or misunderstanding might stem from that use. A painting or a sculpture might be a helpful means of encour-aging the worship of God, but in some circumstances it could also lead

---

[7] Another example of a prophetic word that was superseded by a further message from God is found in 2 Kgs 20:1–5 and the parallel passage in Isa. 38:1–6. Isaiah brought a message that Hezekiah was about to die, but shortly afterwards was told to tell Hezekiah that he was to be granted another fifteen years of life.

those who revere it to begin to worship the object itself. We must always question whether this really is the right time or place for the institution of a particular ritual.

Second, God had not asked for a temple. David had made the mistake in the past of assuming that he knew what it was that God wanted. Human values do not always reflect God's values and the implication must be avoided that God possessed less glory because his ark was placed in a tent rather than a beautiful and expensive modern building. Perhaps David talked with his sons about the dangers involved in the temple project. Certainly, in the prayer of dedication (1 Kgs 8:22–53) Solomon makes it very clear that the temple was not to be seen as something that limited or restricted God or his glory. Solomon was also told that a further reason why David was not allowed to build the temple was his involvement in military campaigns (1 Kgs 5:3; 1 Chr. 22:8–9), but there is no sign of that reasoning here.

d. Not getting one job doesn't mean that there is no job to be done (7:14–17)

David was not to build the temple. It is always disappointing when a dreamed-of project, something that we assumed was visionary, is shown, at least as far as our own participation is concerned, to be just a dream and not God's purpose for us after all. It is not an uncommon reaction to such a disappointment to feel rejected or even let down by God and to refuse to hear or accept any alternative future scenarios. But David did not react like this; rather he heard Nathan through to the end. As he listened on, he learned that not being appointed to a particular job was in no sense a rejection. God had by no means finished with him or with his family. On the contrary, he was presented with a clear affirmation of his leadership and of its continuing results within both his own family and the whole nation of Israel. The David of chapter 7 seems much more humble and thoughtful and ready to heed God's word than the exuberant, hasty, 'bull-at-a-gate' populist figure of chapter 6. Perhaps he was beginning to benefit from his growing experience and from the lessons of his past.

e. A 'special' relationship with God is always there for a purpose

The term 'covenant' is not used here, but God's words were clearly understood in those terms by David (2 Sam. 23:5). Psalm 89, which is closely linked to this chapter, also uses explicit covenant terminology. Almighty

God was setting up a specific relationship with David and his descendants. This was not a replacement for the Abrahamic covenant with all of Abraham's descendants. Indeed the promises to Abraham of a secured land and worldwide influence come to the fore during David's reign, as Psalm 89 makes clear. Nor was it a replacement for the Sinaitic covenant instituted at the time of Moses. David and his descendants were in no way to be exempted from the requirements of that covenant. Rather, God had chosen them for the privilege of being his instruments in enabling Israel to live within that covenant. In the end, the Davidic covenant failed at the point where either David's family or the people of Israel assumed that God's relationship with the king was a replacement for his relationship with the people or that the responsibilities of the people could be taken over by the king. Any view of leadership that involves the leader relating to God on behalf of the led or taking over the responsibilities of the individual believer cannot be seen as adequately reflecting the biblical pattern.

Within God's message given via Nathan there is a fivefold focus. First, God had already chosen and blessed David, using him in the context of the continuing choosing and blessing of Israel. Second, the choice of David to lead Israel involved also the choice of his descendants. Third, David's vision of a magnificent temple to be built for God would be fulfilled, but by David's son rather than by David himself. Fourth, no individual descendants of David could take their position for granted; those who failed in their responsibilities would certainly be punished. The father-son element of the relationship with God that was involved in the Davidic covenant also included discipline. Fifth, in spite of the possibility of individual failure there was an eternal element to God's promise. David, through his descendants, would have a permanently significant place in God's kingdom. The messianic implications of this passage are obvious to Christians but they are picked up elsewhere in the Old Testament too, notably by Jeremiah in chapter 33:14–17. The understanding that there was to be a 'great David's greater son' who would come as Messiah stems originally from this chapter.

f. The importance of the 'wow' factor (7:18–29)

David was not to build the temple, but it is not surprising that he was overwhelmed by the brightness of the future that was laid out before him. His prayer of response also serves as a summary of what went before and it is possible it was edited at a later stage. Nevertheless, there is still a strong sense of the 'Wow!' that David felt at that time and there is no reason why any of it should not have been spoken by David. He begins, 'Wow, just look at what God has done for me and my family!' and continues, 'Wow, just think about who God is and what he has done for his people!' The 'wow' element of prayer is perhaps something that God's people need to recapture today. The awe that David expresses as he ponders on God's involvement in his life and reflects on the nature of this great God should surely be reflected in the hearts of all those who have been conscious of God's presence and action in their own lives.

The second half of David's prayer, where he pleads with God to *do as you promised* (25), is not a sign of doubt that the promise will be kept. It is rather a realistic and encouraging fumbling to find the right words to express what David felt. David had been promised that his name would be made great (9). He prays that in keeping this promise God's *name will be great for ever* (26). He knows that his descendants may fail and doesn't want to focus on that, but his prayer that *the house of your servant will be blessed for ever* (29) perhaps reflects his desire that any failure won't be too significant. In asking God to do what he has said, David's prayer is in effect a precursor of Jesus' instruction to his disciples to pray 'your will be done' (Matt. 6:10).

3. War and peace (8:1–18)

a. God-given victory (8:1–14)

In general, the writers of Samuel are concerned with specific incidents and the way in which they affect the lives of specific individuals. However, it is important that these incidents are seen in context. Therefore, occasionally we have sections like this that provide a summary of the background situations in which the specific incidents took place and the individual lives were lived.

In the course of time (1) – we are not told how long or in what order – David, with the help of his armed forces, defeated the Philistines and the Moabites, the king of Zobah and the Arameans, the Ammonites, the Edomites and the Amalekites. He also made alliances, for example with the king of Hamath. He gained tribute both as involuntary contributions from the nations he defeated and as voluntary gifts from those that became allies. The amount of detail provided about these conquests does vary a little but all the stories are told with brevity. The point of this account is to make sure that the readers notice that Israel was secure at last. Her boundaries were no longer threatened and she even had influence in surrounding lands. The fear and insecurity that had lasted from the initial conquest, throughout the time of the judges and even during the reign of Saul was now over. Now the Promised Land really was Israel's. They were beginning to see something of the area's wealth. The hopes that the Israelite elders had had when they asked for a king had been fulfilled. The monarchy, for a while at least, was working: *the LORD gave David victory wherever he went* (6, 14). This final reference is probably an editorial addition making sure that the reader is fully aware of God's involvement in the successful establishment of the nation. David might have been the instrument that God had used, but the victory was most definitely the Lord's.

b. Winning the peace (8:15–18)

For a nation to be successful it has to win the peace as well as the wars. The last verses of the chapter tell us, if possible even more briefly, of the structure and personnel involved in David's government. The key point is that David was concerned to do *what was just and right for all his people* (15). The implication here could be that David took personal charge of the justice department. In any case, we are being informed that his motivation was not greed or personal power but service; service of God and of the people. No leader can function without backup and here we have a list of some of the key people involved in the regime. There are a number of lists like this scattered through the accounts (2 Sam. 20:23–26; 1 Kgs 4:3–6), and it is interesting to note the gradual change of names as time goes on. For example, 1 Kings 4:3–4 tells us Jehoshaphat remained as recorder well into the reign of Solomon, but Benaiah had by this time taken over from Joab as head of the armed forces. The combination of continuity and change is important in the life of every institution or organization, including churches. Without regular changes the institution can become moribund, but where there is no continuity there is also no stability. The problem is usually deciding who should be changed and who should remain as a long-term fixture!

It is not surprising that the leaders of the army and the senior priests are mentioned in these lists, but it is perhaps more surprising to see the regular mention of the *recorder* as a significant national figure. However, the making of historical records was seen as vital. The Old Testament is very clear throughout, and Samuel is no exception to this, that the God of Israel is involved with history. It mattered that the people could look back and see what God had been doing with them, whether he had acted in blessing or in rebuke. They could not learn the lessons from history if there were no records. Believing communities in the present day have much to learn from this. Biblical teaching is presented in the context of biblical history. It is of course essential, therefore, that we have an understanding of the shape of that history in order to gain an adequate grasp of the teaching. The stories recorded are not incidental to the message; they are essential to the message. But modern Christians could also profit from a critical awareness of their own history in terms of the church both as a whole and also as individual communities. God may not work with us in the future in exactly the same way as he did in the past, but we can certainly learn from earlier events. However, we can do this only if we have some kind of knowledge of such events. Perhaps we should appoint recorders in our churches today!

The reference to David's sons as priests is a little confusing and the NIV marginal note may be correct in its interpretation of this as 'chief officials' (18). There is clearly a distinction between their role and that of Zadok and Ahimelek,[8] and we have no evidence that any of David's sons were involved in traditional priestly activities. David had been assured that he would be succeeded by one of his sons and it could be seen as a wise move to introduce them to political life at an early age and allow them to be part of the decision-making of royal life. However, David's failure to appoint one of them as his officially recognized heir caused major problems at a later stage and Absalom for one felt strongly that he was underused (2 Sam. 15:3–4). The training of future leaders is a vital part of community life, but there are many issues involved in this that do need to be investigated. It is rather speculative to suggest that David's use of his sons in this way was another good idea that went somewhat wrong, but it is a possibility![9]

---

[8] Elsewhere Zadok is linked regularly with Abiathar, who is himself described (1 Sam. 22:20) as the son of Ahimelek. Of course, names do recur throughout the generations, but it is a strong possibility that in this instance the two names have been transposed.

[9] Ps. 110:4 ('You are a priest for ever, in the order of Melchizedek') could imply that the king was seen as having a priestly role distinct from that of the Aaronic priests, but there is no real indication that this should apply to the royal princes before they were appointed king.

4. Friends and enemies (9:1 – 10:19)

In chapter 9 we see a return to a more lively style of writing centring on individual incidents and characters. The stories almost all relate to life in and around the royal court. There is a strong similarity in the way these stories are written and it is probable that chapters 9 through to 20 were part of a single document.[10] It has been suggested that the main interest in these accounts is in the succession. The reader is being presented with the question of which of David's sons will be the next king. However, not all the stories have this focus and it may be simply a continuation of the overall interest in power struggles and the nature of power.

a. Keeping promises (9:1)

The first of these stories reintroduces the question of David's relationship with Saul's family. There is a certain amount of ambiguity in the account and the story is told with no added editorial comment. It can be read as a lovely story illustrating David's inherent compassion and the fulfilment of his promise to Jonathan to care for his family, although it does seem to have taken rather a long time for David to remember his promise. It can be read as a further demonstration of David's political acumen, seeking to win over the perhaps waning support from erstwhile Saulides from the northern tribes. It could be read as a further insight into David's character, acting impulsively and generously when something comes to mind but not always having the commitment to follow through when the moment has passed. Probably there is an element of many things and neither political motivation nor previous neglect necessarily lessens the picture of generosity seen here.

Given the amount of time that has passed since Jonathan's death and the nature of their relationship, it does seem strange that David appears to have no knowledge of Jonathan's remaining family.[11] However, it was not uncommon in the Ancient Near East for all those associated with a previous regime to be killed when a new and unrelated king was installed. It is possible that Mephibosheth's carers had deliberately kept secret his continuing existence and his whereabouts.[12] In fact, Saul's associates had

---

[10] This document also included 1 Kgs 1 – 2.

[11] The timing of this incident and in particular its relationship to the execution of Saul's descendants described in chapter 21 is not entirely clear.

[12] Lo Debar was situated in a disputed area on the east side of the Jordan, well away from the reach of court gossips.

in general been left in peace and his family lands were still being farmed by a steward, Ziba, who in the process had apparently become wealthy in his own right. Given the later encounters with Mephibosheth and Ziba (16:1–4; 19:24–30) there may be a hint here that Ziba deliberately revealed Mephibosheth's whereabouts in the hope that he would be removed from the picture once and for all and with that his right to what Ziba may now have seen as his own farm. Ziba's failure to mention his name and the deliberate reference to his disability may indicate that Mephibosheth was regarded by Ziba with contempt. The editor again makes no direct comment, although the direct reference to Ziba's large household (10) may support the view that Ziba's motives are being deliberately questioned. There is a brief mention in verse 4 of a man called Makir. References to people are rarely incidental; for example, Makir appears again later in the narratives in a more significant role.[13]

b. Learning from predecessors (9:2–13)

The story itself is simple: David seeks out Jonathan's family. Ziba helps him find Mephibosheth. David restores the family lands to Jonathan's son and welcomes him into his own family. However, it seems that the writer is deliberately emphasizing a number of points. First, that Mephibosheth is no threat to David, both because he is disabled and also because, like his father, he is quite willing to recognize David as king and *to pay him honour* (6). His description of himself as *a dead dog* (8) is reminiscent of David's earlier references to himself (1 Sam. 24:14; 26:20) when he was trying to assure Saul that he was not a threat to him. Second, Mephibosheth is treated as a son by David, as David had once been treated by Saul. It is hard not to see these links back to Saul as deliberate. David, in welcoming Mephibosheth, is imitating Saul's good points and, in not treating Mephibosheth as a threat but gladly giving him back his ancestral lands, is avoiding imitating Saul's bad points. The reader is being drawn towards the conclusion that, perhaps unlike Saul, David really was a worthy king. The modern reader may also conclude that it is a good thing to reflect on the behaviour and attitudes of predecessors, seeking to imitate the good, to avoid the bad and to recognize the difference between the two.

Mephibosheth could have been seen as an enemy, but was treated as a friend. Contrastingly, chapter 10 tells the story of how David was treated

---

[13] In 2 Sam. 17:27–29 we read of the support that Makir gave to David during his flight from Absalom.

as an enemy when he could have been seen as a friend. The editors seem to have deliberately placed these chapters together before chapter 11, where Uriah, who had proved himself to be very much a friend, was betrayed by David and treated as an enemy. Identifying the difference between friends and enemies, recognizing the need to turn enemies into friends and finding ways of doing that are key skills for any national leader who wants to govern a stable regime. David had these skills, but he didn't always use them. The picture of David as a gifted and attractive character but with a number of serious flaws is beginning to build up. It seems as if readers are being asked not so much to decide whether David should ultimately be classified as good or bad, but rather to accept the realistic picture of David, good and bad, as a man whom God could use and did use.

c. Can old grievances be set aside? (10:1–5)

The precise relationship between Israel and Ammon at this point is a little obscure. The last we heard of Nahash was when his forces were soundly defeated by Saul at Jabesh Gilead (1 Sam. 11). The nature of the *kindness* that he showed to David and when he showed it remain a mystery. It may be that Nahash gave support to David at one time because he saw him as a fellow enemy of Saul. Whatever it was, David had decided that it was time to bury the hatchet with Ammon and again, as in chapter 9, repay a kindness shown by a father by befriending the son. He used the opportunity of a change of ruler to extend the hand of friendship to Nahash's son Hanun. The implication that there are times when old grievances should be set aside and new friendships forged with old enemies cannot be avoided. But like many modern combatants in acrimonious conflicts and like Joab (2 Sam. 3:22–28), Hanun's advisors were unable to put the past behind them. They could not believe that David did not have ulterior motives, and in the context of the Ancient Near East there is some justification for their suspicion. However, their inability brought a great cost on themselves and their nation.

Hanun's action in shaving off half their beards and cutting off half their garments might be seen as a rather coarse joke by the modern Westerner. But it is important not to underestimate the extent of the humiliation and the nature of the offence to the delegation. In many cultures the beard is a sign of adulthood and masculinity; to be forced to shave was completely degrading. The public disgrace caused by this and the destruction of the garments – remembering that it is unlikely on a reasonably short trip like this that the soldiers would have taken a change of clothing – was not to be borne. Regardless of whether this was his own immature response to his advisors' suspicions or whether it was at their instigation, Hanun's deeds could only be seen as deliberate and unprovoked aggression. a clear declaration of hostile intentions.

It is a hard thing to accept when a generous and perhaps costly gesture is thrown back in one's face. If David's motives were pure, and the text strongly suggests that this was so, then his reaction to the rejection and humiliation is understandable.

d. Aggressive action has a habit of escalating (10:6–19)

The reaction of the Ammonite forces indicates that Hanun's action had not been part of a deliberate plan to declare war. However, on hearing what he had done, the generals realized the significance and immediately took pre-emptive action. Large mercenary forces from surrounding areas were hired to supplement their own army and gathered together to resist the expected invasion. In fact, David seems to have responded more to this military threat than he did to the original offence. This chapter provides a clear demonstration of the way in which attempts to avoid defeat can in fact sometimes cause conflicts to escalate and defeat to become much more likely.

The account of the ensuing fighting and the defeat of both Ammon and the Aramean mercenaries provides impressive evidence of Joab's skills. The Aramean leader Hadadezer apparently saw the defeat of the hired troops as a threat to the credibility of the whole Aramean war machine and brought more sections of the army into play, but these too were routed. With David as king and Joab as general, Israel was virtually un-beatable. The opposing forces eventually recognized this. The Arameans decided that whatever the Ammonites were paying, it wasn't enough, and the groups that had been vassals of Hadadezer changed their allegiance and put themselves under David's regime. It is possible here that the editor, as well as describing Israel's supremacy at this time, is also pointing out the transitory nature of that kind of military power. Support that can be bought is just as likely to be sold on elsewhere.

Perhaps David's recognition of the effectiveness of his partnership with Joab in military operations was the major reason behind his failure to deal with Joab's excesses seen already in chapter 3 and again in chapter 11. Joab was undoubtedly a loyal Israelite and a great general. His statement in

2 Samuel 10:12 is slightly ambiguous. Is Joab assuming that *what is good in God's sight* will be their victory or not? It may have been simply good psychology, providing further encouragement to the men to fight bravely with the assurance that the Lord was behind them.[14] Rulers throughout history have used religious language to rally the troops even when they themselves had few or no religious convictions. It is possible that Joab really did share David's belief that it was service of God that counted, but the phraseology used raises as many questions about Joab's faith as it answers. Within this chapter there is more focus on Joab as the director of the campaign than on David. It is possible that this is deliberately done to provide an introduction to the next series of stories about events in Jerusalem.

Questions to ponder

1. Is there anything today that expresses the kind of symbolism seen in the ark and the temple? If so, what are the equivalent accompanying benefits and dangers?
2. Why might the covenant in chapter 7 have been seen as a replacement for Sinai?
3. What questions arise from David's relationships with Michal, Mephibosheth and Hanun? Was it David's political acumen or his spiritual discernment that took priority in his actions relating to them?
4. To what extent is David being presented as a role model in these chapters? If he is, is it as a model for all believers or just for leaders?
5. Are there lessons to be learned from the Ammonites?
6. Can victory for God's people always be assumed to be 'what is good in his sight'?

---

[14] Joab's encouragement to fight for the people and for God provides a reminder of Gideon's call to his small army in Judg. 7:15–18. Perhaps Joab had been studying military history?

2 Samuel 11 – 13

8. David: out of control?

1. Adultery and murder (11:1–27)

a. When is a king not a king? (11:1–2)

There is no doubt that the writer is making a specific point in 11:1. In the fighting season *kings go off to war . . . But David remained in Jerusalem*. It seems that David was a man of huge but fairly short-lived enthusiasms; an excellent initiator of projects, but not quite so good in maintenance mode. He was a gifted soldier, but preferred it when there was an edge to the fight, when he was competing against the odds. Once Israel gained supremacy and the battles seemed to have a foregone conclusion, David appears to have lost his appetite for the fight. Joab was an excellent general and therefore at first sight it seems to have been a sensible decision to delegate all military responsibility to him so that David himself could concentrate on home affairs. However, it must be remembered that the main function of a king at this period was as a military ruler. Saul had been appointed primarily in order to remove the Philistine threat. David had inherited that role. The threat may have lessened and changed, but it still remained. In staying at home David was ceasing to behave as a king. Had power gone to his head? The unfolding story does not provide a reassuring answer. When leaders begin to view their leadership in terms of status rather than in terms of task, it is more than likely that they will begin to fail at the task and therefore to cease, in any meaningful sense, to be leaders.

It soon becomes apparent that in remaining at home David was not overwhelmed by heavy government duties! In the early evening, that is, neither at night nor in the heat of midday, he had been sleeping and was now wandering around the rooftops of the palace surveying his kingdom.

He caught sight of a beautiful woman; presumably at that distance she was identified as beautiful by her figure rather than by her face. There is nothing in the text here to justify the picture of Bathsheba as behaving deliberately in an alluring manner and setting out to seduce the unworldly and innocent David. She was in her own courtyard where she might reasonably expect to be private and was undergoing ritual bathing to cleanse herself after her menstrual period (4). Part of the reason for informing us of that fact is to make it clear that she could not have been pregnant before David slept with her.

b. Disloyalty and loyalty: who was the faithful servant of the Lord? (11:3–13)

David wanted the woman. He found out who she was, sent for her, slept with her and sent her away. This is a description not of a great love story but of a seedy one-night stand. Bathsheba may or may not have been a willing participant in this. There is no way of telling whether she was flattered by David's attention or felt coerced and unable to refuse the king's command. The writer makes no judgment about Bathsheba's guilt, but there is no doubt at all about David's. Whether or not Bathsheba was willing makes no difference to the extent of David's guilt. David knew that Bathsheba was married. He also knew that her husband was a brave and committed soldier[1] who, as might be expected, was away from home with the army. He would not therefore be a barrier to David's lust, and the question of loyalty to his own loyal follower does not seem to have entered David's head. David behaved as if his own desires were the only thing that mattered. He wanted Bathsheba so he took her. His obligations to other people and to God and God's law were set aside. David's passionate nature, his wholehearted commitment to the task in hand which was used so well in the service of God, could also be used in the service of his own lust. As far as we can tell, once Bathsheba left, David put the incident out of his mind and would have forgotten all about her – if it had not been for one thing: she was going to have his baby.

It could be assumed that it was to David's credit that he took some kind of responsibility when he heard Bathsheba's news. But there is no sign of

---

[1] 2 Sam. 23:39 names Uriah as among the great warriors of David's army. As a senior army officer he would almost certainly have been known to David personally. If, as is likely, Bathsheba's father is the Eliam also mentioned in 2 Sam. 23:34 as a warrior, then she was the granddaughter of David's friend and advisor Ahithophel. David's betrayal in this incident was widespread.

repentance or acknowledgment of guilt in his actions. He simply sought to find a way of avoiding any consequences, either for Bathsheba, or more pertinently for himself. If Uriah could be brought home, then the world could be persuaded that the baby was his. It would have been a brilliant solution if it were not for the fact that Uriah took seriously his obligations to David, to his own men and to God and his law.[2] There is a dark comedy in the way that the story is told. Even being made drunk did not make Uriah set aside his principles. David could take away Uriah's wife and even take away his life, but he did not have the power to take away his integrity. The contrast with David could not be more marked. Uriah the Hittite[3] was a more faithful Israelite than David, Israel's king.

c. The tangled web of deceit and sin (11:14–15)

David's next action seems inconceivable. Any who have read David's story so far will be aware of his generous nature, of his care for the men under his command and of his commitment to Yahweh. And yet he had no qualms about ordering Joab to arrange for Uriah, whose only crime was being righteous, to be killed. He had become so focused on this particular problem that he lost all sense of perspective. This abuse of power seems as great if not greater than any of Saul's acts of disobedience. Questions inevitably arise. Was David going the same way as Saul? Could this king possibly still be seen as the man after God's own heart in the way that the young David was (1 Sam. 13:14)? Had his desire to retain power become more important than his desire to serve God?

d. Beware of unenvisaged consequences (11:16–27a)

Chapter 12 provides us with at least the beginnings of an answer to some of those questions, but before that we have the record and reporting of Uriah's death. It is worth reflecting on the immense skill of the writer of these narratives. There is brilliance bordering on genius not just in the lively and evocative writing style but also in the deep insight into character, circumstances, consequences and implications. All this is exemplified in this little section. Again the circumstances are recorded

---

[2] The 'no sex while on duty' rule was a basic principle of war that David himself had previously supported (1 Sam. 21:5; cf. Deut. 23:9–14).

[3] Uriah's name means 'Yahweh is light'. It is likely that he or his parents had been converted to Yahwism and absorbed into Israelite life. It is possible that the rigour of his religious commitment stemmed partly from a desire to show that his ethnic origins in no way lessened his loyalty.

simply and straightforwardly. Joab receives his letter, sends Uriah on what is effectively a suicide mission and dispatches a messenger to inform David of what he has done. David hears the news, sends an encouraging reply, eventually marries Bathsheba and, from his point of view, the chapter on this incident is successfully closed.

However, our understanding of the bigger picture is greatly enhanced by this incident. We learn that normally David was deeply concerned for his men and was completely opposed to suicide missions; that normally he was a restraining influence on Joab. The implication is that normally David was a good king. This incident should be seen, as it clearly was by Joab, as an aberration. Our picture of Joab is also confirmed. We see a dedicated fighter who was more concerned about victory than about people. He was a hard man who had no problem with taking action to his own or David's benefit even if it bent or broke the law; a man who was only too glad to be allowed off the leash for a while; a clever man who knew how to manipulate people – perhaps especially David – and circumstances to his own ends. We learn that there are consequences to every action. David may not have foreseen how events would go, and Joab's complex message indicates that he realized this was probably the case, but Uriah was inevitably not the only person to die because of David's request. Other women lost their husbands, other parents lost their sons. Normally these unnecessary deaths, which had no effect on the course of the campaign other than hastening its end, would have provoked strong anger from David. In this instance there was not even a mild rebuke, only calm compliance and encouragement. David appears to have sold out his principles. A further consequence, almost certainly perceived by Joab with his understanding of David's character, was that Joab now had a permanent hold over David. This was not so much that Joab could reveal David's sin, but that David would no longer be able to take the high ground. He was not by nature a hypocrite and having been complicit in Joab's excesses on this one occasion would find it hard to restrain or rebuke him on other occasions. David would not be the only one to suffer because he had lost any ability that he might have had to keep Joab under control.[4]

Bathsheba, we are told, mourned for Uriah. There is an explicit reference to this, in addition to the comment about the ritual period of mourning. She grieved for Uriah. He was a good soldier and a good man

---

[4] Joab's apparently unpunished murder of Amasa in 2 Sam. 20 is an example of this.

and his death did not go unnoted or unmourned. Only David and Joab knew that his death was something more than that of an unfortunate but inevitable casualty of war. Bathsheba mourned for her husband as a hero, not as a victim, and we are given no reason to doubt that her mourning was real. Her genuine grief probably points to her unwilling cooperation in verse 4, although it is possible that she, like David, had simply not foreseen the consequences of their action. Once Uriah was dead then David, probably seeing himself as a generous provider, married Bathsheba, acknowledged the child as his and apparently put the whole incident behind him.

e. Results that satisfy us do not necessarily satisfy God (11:27b)

Many of the narratives in the books of Samuel record events without editorial comment. Readers are usually left to analyse and judge behaviour for themselves. However, in this instance there was to be no room for any doubt. The chapter closes with a powerful understatement: *the thing David had done displeased the Lord*. Whether God's displeasure stemmed more from the avoidance of responsibility by remaining in Jerusalem, the adultery, the murder or the abuse of power is not elaborated on at this stage. What is absolutely certain is that David, in spite of being king and in spite of the eternal promises God had made to him, was not above the law. We are all, without exception and particularly not excluding leaders, responsible to God for our actions and must take responsibility too for the consequences of those actions. None of us, however blessed by God, however gifted, however high in status, however used by God in the past, can rest on our laurels and assume that for us anything goes.

2. Condemnation and punishment (12:1–31)

a. God treats us as individuals (12:1–4)

Often, when a message of condemnation comes it is quite explicit. For example, it was clear to Eli from the beginning what God was saying to him when the message came both via the prophet and via the young Samuel (1 Sam. 2 – 3). But when Nathan was sent to David to convey a similar message of condemnation he approached it rather differently. He told David a story. It was not uncommon to use a fictional story in order to present a case study of a real situation. Joab and the woman of Tekoa use the same technique in 2 Samuel 14. David would have quickly realized what was going on, even if he assumed it was a normal case being presented for judgment. As the director of the department of justice, he would have been faced with many such cases and it is not surprising that he did not automatically relate Nathan's presence to his own behaviour. It is clear throughout Scripture, particularly with prophetic messages, that God works with different people in different ways. Different methods are appropriate at different times depending on the recipient, the circumstances and the point of the message. There is a lesson for all of us here, particularly if we feel it is incumbent upon us to deliver a message that the recipient may not be too pleased to receive. It is possible that any lack of positive response might be the result of our failure to discover the best method of delivery rather than simply a stubborn refusal to hear. Perhaps we need to put as much prayer and thought into the way we deliver a message as we might do into whether it needs to be delivered at all – at least by us.

In this particular case it seems that the real issue was not what punishment David might receive. What was really important was that both he and the people – and all future readers of the text – fully realize not only that David's behaviour was completely unacceptable and that God would not tolerate it, but also just why it was so wrong. The fable is told simply in only three verses (2–4). A miserly rich man, faced with the need to provide hospitality for a traveller, rather than using one of his own animals took instead the well-loved pet lamb that was the only animal belonging to a poor neighbour. To provide hospitality for a passing traveller was seen as the responsibility of the town as a whole and therefore the rich man could have persuaded himself that there was no reason why it should be him rather than his poor neighbour who should give up a lamb. There may be an implication that the poor man was willing to fulfil his obligations even at such a great cost. However, the poor man may have been a vassal of the rich man and therefore had no choice in the matter. The information given is scanty and, as with all such parables, there is no need to try to make all the details fit. The main point is quite clear.

b. It is important to recognize the seriousness of our offences against God (12:5–10)

David immediately saw the meanness and cruelty of what was involved in the story and was appalled and angry that this might have happened in his kingdom. He had no doubts whatsoever that such behaviour was totally unacceptable in God's sight. Anyone who would behave in that way deserved the severest punishment. With typical exaggeration, he spoke of the death penalty, although the real punishment was a fine of four times the value of the lamb[5] (not much cost to the rich man, but life-transforming to the poor one). Nathan's terse *You are the man!* must have been a great shock to David, but the story had prepared him for hearing the actual message from God. His almost immediate recognition of what Nathan was talking about may mean that his conscience had already been speaking to him. Are we as ready to hear the unpleasant message and to apply it to ourselves?

David had committed both adultery and murder – it may have been difficult to prove that Uriah's death was murder, but David was left in no doubt that that was how God saw it. These offences were clearly condemned, but the use of the story helped to bring out the fact that the abuse of power involved and the contemptible meanness of what David had done were equally abhorrent to God. God had given David so much and yet he still thought he had the right to take what belonged to someone else. In breaking the law, not only did he despise the word of the Lord, he despised God himself by acting as if the gifts God had given him were insufficient. The one who had been granted the privilege of a special relationship with Yahweh had, in effect, spat in God's face. The enormity of David's sin at last dawns on him. He has sinned not only against Bathsheba and Uriah, which would have been bad enough, but *against the Lord* (13). He has acted as if God and his word are of no account. As a result of his behaviour he is told that *the sword shall never depart from your house* (10). The book of Kings, which records the history of the monarchy after David's death, could be seen as relating the continuing tension between this prediction and God's promise in 7:15 that 'my love will never be taken away from him'.[6]

c. Consequences can be very far-reaching (12:11–15)

The immediate consequences of David's behaviour, including the unnecessary deaths of several good soldiers and Joab's increasing power over

---

[5] Lev. 6:1–7 commands that the penalty for cheating someone is to pay back the amount cheated plus an extra 20% compensation, but David clearly thought that the punishment for this crime should be more severe. Zacchaeus perhaps saw himself in the same category as the rich man here when he also agreed to pay back four times the amount he had taken (Luke 19:8).

[6] Cf. F. H. Polak, 'David's Kingship: A Precarious Equilibrium', in H. Graf Reventlow et al. (eds.), *Politics and Theopolitics in the Bible and Post-Biblical Literature*, JSOTSup 171 (Sheffield: Sheffield Academic Press, 1994), pp. 119–147.

David, have already been noted. Here we begin to see a further range of ever-widening effects. David, in setting an example of adultery and violence, had ensured that a pattern of violence and adultery would be loosed, if not upon the world, certainly upon his own family and within Israel. The distinction in this section between punishment and consequences becomes somewhat blurred.

It seems as if David is not going to receive a direct punishment for his sin. He himself had proclaimed the judgment that such a person deserved to die, but in Nathan's words *The Lord has taken away your sin. You are not going to die* (13b). Mercy and justice go hand in hand in the Old Testament picture of God. Punishments do not always take place in the way that the law seems to call for. Perhaps the mercy shown by God to David in this instance is presented as a deliberate contrast with the lack of mercy shown by the rich man in the parable, or by David to Uriah.[7] Nevertheless, all the consequences of David's actions will be allowed to stand. His sons will follow their father's example and be caught up in violence and adultery. David's own wives will be taken – not in secret but *in broad daylight* (11). He who has tried so hard to avoid scandal will be openly shamed.

Modern readers may be disturbed at the thought that the rape of David's wives should be seen as a suitable punishment for David's sin. The distinction between punishment and consequences is very important at this point. Absalom learned from his father's example and acted in favour of his own interests, regardless of how that might damage other people. The taking of David's wives was not a direct punishment for David's sin, but it was an indirect consequence. Scripture is very clear that in most instances God will allow the consequences of our actions to stand, even when other people get hurt in the process. Resentment and rivalry between stepchildren and half-siblings in multiple-marriage situations like David's are not a punishment for those marriages but are a regular consequence. David's sons Amnon, Absalom and Adonijah all died violently in incidents that were, in one way or another, related to the exercise of power and control. All his sons, including Solomon, seem to have learned more from David's example of setting aside the law in his own interests than from his genuine repentance and service of God. We are created as responsible human beings and we must bear that responsibility. It is not a punishment

---

[7] Cf. G. Coats, '2 Samuel 12:1–7a', *Int* 40 (1986), pp. 170–173.

for drink-driving when a child is killed, but the child remains dead, the parents are devastated and the driver has to live with it for the rest of his or her life. As in so many other cases, David did not foresee or intend the continuing consequences of his action but he remained responsible for them. In some senses, for David, living with those consequences was a greater punishment than the deserved death penalty might have been.

Again, for many modern readers verse 14 causes serious problems: *because by doing this you have shown utter contempt for the LORD, the son born to you will die.* The difference between punishment and consequences is not easy to identify here, but it must again be maintained. The term translated *because* in the NIV does not elsewhere function in a causative way and the implication of cause and effect here should probably be avoided. The two facts that David has despised the Lord, or caused the enemies of the Lord to despise the Lord (NIV mg.), and that David's son will die are placed side by side, but the connection between them is left open. It appears that the death of David's newborn son was going to be used as an object lesson for the 'enemies of the LORD'. David's behaviour, as one who represented Yahweh, had given the impression to outsiders that Israel's God did not care about justice and would allow his regent to behave in whatever way he liked. The death of the boy would show them that this was not so. Within their understanding this would perhaps be seen as a justifiable punishment for David. In fact, it may be that the timing was just coincidence and it could even be suggested that for the baby, death was a better option than a life coping with the traumas relating to his birth. It is possible for us to find solutions like this that help us to cope with an uncomfortable text, but any such solution can only ever be speculative. The problem that remains for us may not have occurred to ancient readers and the text neither raises nor deals with these issues. It is perhaps not appropriate to introduce that kind of modern question into a context where it would not necessarily have arisen.

d. God will act as God wants, but this doesn't mean we are not free to ask (12:16–23)

David's behaviour after the child fell ill is described in dramatic and fascinating detail. It is clear that his actions were incomprehensible to those around him. In the first place, why would anyone be so concerned about one child? After all, babies died all the time and David already had many other sons. Those in David's household were probably only too aware of the situation and if they too saw the child's illness as a punishment from God they would assume that it should be accepted without this excessive grief, fasting and prayer. No wonder they were afraid to tell David when the boy died, and no wonder they were completely dumbfounded when David then stopped mourning and got back to normal life.

The writer here clearly wants everyone to understand something both of David's character and of his understanding of God and God's character. David knew that God was not an oppressive autocrat but that he was living and active, relating to people and responding to prayers and actions as they arose. While the baby lived it was possible that God would *be gracious* (22) and show mercy in the way that he had done before. Maybe some other way could be found for the consequences of David's sin to be worked out, some other way that the 'enemies of the LORD' could be brought to a proper understanding of God. Once the baby died, David accepted that no other way was possible. Therefore prayer and fasting were no longer appropriate and David was able to set aside his grief and move on.

David's prayer was not an attempt to blackmail God into doing what David wanted, but a way to express to God his own feelings and seek out God's will. David recognizes both God's freedom to act in whatever way he thinks best and that human prayer may play a part in the decisions God makes. There are occasions when it is right to keep on praying (Luke 18:1–8) and there are occasions when it is right to accept the inevitable and move on (2 Cor. 12:8–10). The important thing is to recognize the difference between the two. David, in this if in nothing else in this lamentable episode, stands as a model for later believers.

The statement *I will go to him, but he will not return to me* (23b) may indicate that David had a firm belief in the afterlife. Jesus does not use this incident in his answer to the Sadducees' rather cynical question about the wife who had had seven husbands, but he does make it clear that a careful reading of the Old Testament indicates the reality of life after death (Matt. 22:23–32; Mark 12:18–27; Luke 20:27–38). However, many scholars believe that it was not until later in Israel's history that there was any developed understanding of the afterlife. David's statement may be prophetic and indicate confidence in a future resurrection, but it is also possible that he himself understood the statement simply to mean 'I will die one day, but he will not again become alive.'

e. Repentance is vital but it does not remove the consequences of an action (12:24–25)

There is no doubt that David was genuinely repentant; Psalms 32 and 51 provide ample evidence of this. He regretted his action and wished it had never happened, not simply because he didn't like the consequences but because he had grasped what it meant that he had 'sinned against the LORD'. But the fact remained that it had happened and David also recognized that, although it was possible to be forgiven, there was no going back from the incident or from its consequences. He had to start again from this point, not from the time before he had sinned. David's understanding and experience can be a tremendous encouragement to those who are also facing the consequences of a deeply regretted action. However much we might wish to return to the situation as it was, that is rarely possible and we have to move on from the current situation – not the wished-for one.

It would only have compounded the offence if David had spurned Bathsheba and left her as a childless and probably unmarriageable widow. He therefore *comforted her*. Another son was born and they named him Solomon. The alternative name, *Jedidiah*, given to him by Nathan, means 'loved by God'.[8] It was almost certainly seen by David and by Nathan as a recognition both that David could now put the sin behind him and that this son would not suffer, at least not directly, as a result of David's sin.

There is no mention here of any oath pronouncing Solomon as David's heir (1 Kgs 1:13). We have no way of telling whether this is simply an omission, whether the oath was an invention used by Nathan and Bathsheba to ensure Solomon's succession, or whether Nathan as an old man had persuaded himself that the pronouncement of God's love for Solomon was in fact a promise of kingship. There is a danger for all who have been involved in bringing knowledge of God's blessing, or indeed judgment, to expand on or read more into the message than was ever intended.[9]

f. One failure need not negate a lifetime of service (12:26–31)

The last few verses of chapter 12 take us back to the siege of Rabbah that we first heard about in 11:1 when we were told that 'David remained in

---

[8] Jedidiah is literally 'loved by Yah', but this is almost certainly a shortened form of the name for God: thus the NIV margin's 'loved by the LORD' is correct.

[9] G. H. Jones's theory (Jones, pp. 40–46) that Nathan was a native of Jerusalem and therefore saw Solomon, who was born in Jerusalem, as the ideal successor to David is interesting but unproven.

Jerusalem'. The whole episode with Bathsheba and Uriah is thus bracketed by a reference to what might be seen as the real business of kingship: that is, fighting enemies. This bracketing should perhaps act as a warning against placing too much emphasis on one individual incident. What happened in between has much to teach us and cannot be ignored, but it should not be seen as the measure by which David's life and achievements are judged. Chronicles, where the account concentrates on the progress of the kingdom rather than the personal life of the king, makes no reference to Bathsheba, other than as the mother of David's sons (1 Chr. 3:5), or to Uriah, other than as one of David's mighty warriors (1 Chr. 11:41). There is a direct parallel with 2 Samuel 11:1 in 1 Chronicles 20:1, and with 2 Samuel 12:31 in 1 Chronicles 20:3, but the intervening events are not mentioned. The reference to Joab leading out the army and David leading them back shows an awareness that something happened in between, but the Chronicler did not see it as necessary to his purposes for the reader to know what that was. We do need a realistic awareness of the failures of God's servants (including ourselves), but we must beware of letting such failures get out of perspective.

Joab is presented as having many faults, but his military skills and his loyalty to David are undoubted. He could have used any success at Rabbah to boost his own power base, but instead he encouraged David to take up his responsibilities and ensured that the glory for the victory, and also the substantial booty, went to David. The writer's ability to present objective as well as insightful pen pictures of the characters described is consummate. He knows Joab inside out and clearly presents the good and the bad without, at least at this stage, making judgment. Scripture avoids the tendency to divide people into heroes and villains, recognizing instead that even those with severe faults should not be written off as if they had no contribution to make, and vice versa.

The Ammonites were now a spent force. Hanun's refusal to accept David's overtures of friendship (10:2) proved disastrous for his nation, reinforcing the lesson that actions have consequences. Saul in effect lost his job because he took plunder from the Amalekites. David apparently received no rebuke at all either for retaining the booty or for keeping the population alive and using them as forced labour. The difference is that Saul's attack on the Amalekites came under the *ḥērem* regulations, whereas David's attack on the Ammonites apparently did not. Actions which are completely inappropriate and consist of a clear breach of God's law in one situation may sometimes be acceptable in another. The reader is again challenged to recognize the difference between the two. Disobedience to God always deserves condemnation, but one must be clear that the particular command really does apply in that situation.

3. Crime, revenge and parental failure (13:1–39)

a. What does love mean anyway? (13:1–3)

The account of Amnon's rape of Tamar is frighteningly realistic. It is portrayed as high drama. The obsessive, passionate young man; his *shrewd*, apparently amoral accomplice; the doting, credulous and ineffectual father; the generous, incredulous, dishonoured and devastated sister; the silent, vengeful brother: all the characters are only too believable. Amnon, David's eldest son,[10] *fell in love*[11] *. . . became so obsessed . . . grabbed . . . raped . . . hated . . . with an intense hatred.* His friend and cousin Jonadab took it for granted that Amnon ought to get what he wanted and helped him do so. The deceit involved makes it quite clear that both young men knew that what they were plotting was wrong. This was no spur-of-the-moment offence; it was a deliberate and well-planned assault on a defenceless woman. There was no consideration at all in their minds as to what effect their plan might have on Tamar. That was completely irrelevant. Amnon was following in his father's footsteps. He wanted, so he took. The repercussions of David's own sin were going on and on. The thought that Amnon might ask David if he could marry Tamar seems not to have been in the mind of either boy. Amnon wanted to sleep with Tamar; he didn't want to have any kind of relationship with her.[12] We are told that he *fell in love with* Tamar, but it is clear that his understanding of love had nothing in common with the model of love revealed in God's love for his people and expected from them in relation to others. Amnon showed no signs at all of loving his sister *as himself* (cf. Lev. 19:18).

---

[10] He was born to Ahinoam of Jezreel, the first woman David married after leaving Michal behind (1 Sam. 25:43–44).

[11] The Hebrew here simply says 'loved' so that *fell in love* is something of an interpretative rendering.

[12] Although the law forbids it (Lev. 18:9), apparently marriages between half-siblings were still sometimes permitted, as they were in the time of Abraham and Sarah. It is probable that they were frowned upon and Amnon might have assumed that David would refuse permission. However, there is no indication that he ever thought of asking.

b. The dangers of indulgence (13:4–9)

Jonadab's plan was a clever one. He, like the writer, had a good knowledge of people and their reactions. He knew that his uncle David would be indulgent towards Amnon, particularly if he pretended to be ill. Clearly Tamar would not normally have come visiting Amnon and some kind of plot to cause her to do so was necessary. As in many Middle Eastern cultures today, it is likely that it would normally have been unthinkable for Tamar to be allowed to visit Amnon in his personal quarters. However, Jonadab rightly predicted that David could be persuaded to make an exception. As Jesus indicated in relation to the Sabbath (Mark 2:27), rules are made for the benefit not the detriment of people and it is sometimes right to bend those rules for the greater good of all concerned. David's experience of this when Ahimelek gave him the prohibited consecrated bread to eat is also affirmed by Jesus (1 Sam. 21:6; Matt. 12:4). Rules can be broken, but they are there for a purpose and self-indulgence is not an acceptable reason for making an exception. David's fault was not necessarily in breaking the rule, but it is clear that his easy generosity to his son caused great damage to his daughter. So often today, Christians fall into one trap or another. Either we legalistically refuse to bend any rule, even if doing so is clearly beneficial to all concerned, or we see all rules as an infringement of freedom and set them aside to suit the convenience of any and all. In both instances we ignore the consequences. But it is as important for us as it was for Amnon and for David to recognize and take responsibility for the consequences of our actions. If David had agreed that Tamar should go but only if he himself accompanied her, for example, then the situation would have ended very differently.

This is the first time we have seen David in relationship with his children and the picture comes into focus of a father who is unwilling to interfere with his sons' pleasures (1 Kgs 1:6). David perhaps has no reason to doubt Amnon, but it is clear that his understanding of his son, both of his motives and of his capabilities, is very limited. David takes at face value his request for Tamar to come and bake him some *special bread* (6), the equivalent of a nourishing soup or a vitamin-enriched meal that might be expected to comfort and build up the strength of an ailing patient. It never occurred to David that the request for Tamar to do it while the sick Amnon was looking on might have been seen as suspicious. It also apparently never occurred to him to take into account Tamar's feelings in the matter. She was not asked, she was told to go, although of course this may be because he never doubted that she would gladly respond to such a simple request.

c. Tamar's feelings: ignored by Amnon (and Jonadab and David) but noted by God (13:10–20)

The scene was set, the rape took place on schedule and, as might be expected with that kind of obsessive desire to possess, Amnon's 'love' turned to 'hate'. He wanted the virgin Tamar, not the soiled woman she had now become – even if it was he himself who was responsible for the soiling. Tamar had pleaded with him before the rape but *he was stronger than she* (14). There is no doubt at all that she was unwilling; that the offence was against her and not just against the law. The writer's focus on the use and abuse of power continues. With a groundless hope that there might be some element of humanity in Amnon, Tamar pleaded with him afterwards to lessen the offence by marrying her. He completely ignored her desperate begging and had her thrown out by his servants as irritating baggage, of no account at all. It is possible that Amnon was shocked by what he had done and that his turning against Tamar stemmed initially from self-loathing, but if so, that in no sense lessens the offence or its effect on Tamar. It is interesting that the writer here makes no attempt to excuse, limit or even explain Amnon's behaviour. It was inexcusable and is presented as such.

For readers, perhaps women in particular, the one element of light in the dark tunnel of this account is the writer's deep insight into Tamar's feelings here. Amnon, the surrounding society and even David might have thought her feelings irrelevant, but the writer, and by implication God himself, most certainly did not. We see Tamar as a person in her own right. We note her generous nature as she cooks for her supposedly sick brother. We feel her incredulity turn to dismay as she realizes what his intentions are. We sense her dismay turn to hopeless desperation as it becomes clear that Amnon has no intention of listening to reason. We watch her despair turn to inconsolable misery and self-loathing as she is thrown out and becomes indeed *a desolate woman*, permanently isolated in her brother Absalom's house. We notice the pride with which she wears her *ornate robe* as she approaches the house; it proclaims her as one of the most eligible women in the country. We weep with her as she rips her clothes and covers herself with ashes, her great shame apparent to all. There is no lessening of her misery but there is nevertheless some comfort in realizing that this woman was known, this woman did count. Here, as in so many other places in Scripture,[13] we see a patriarchal society critiqued by the text even in the act of describing it. We are all influenced by the culture, the worldview, of the society in which we live. It is vitally important for us to recognize that God's view of the world is sometimes very different and to learn to critique even as we observe our own cultures.

d. Justice is served neither by useless anger that takes no action nor by violent revenge (13:21–39)

King David . . . was furious. We are not given any information as to where his anger was directed. Was it towards Amnon for behaving in this way? Was it, as sadly sometimes happens, towards Tamar for inspiring Amnon's lust? Or was it towards himself for failing to prevent such a thing happening? The reference to his title emphasizes his royal responsibility rather than his parenthood. He was noticeably extremely angry – he ranted and raved – but in the end he did nothing about it. Neither as king nor as a parent did he take any action to punish Amnon or to alleviate Tamar's situation. By contrast we are told of Absalom's silent hatred. For a long time he also took no action, but hated and waited and planned revenge for his sister's disgrace.[14] The writer makes no explicit comment, but we are left with a strong sense that neither David's nor Absalom's response was adequate or appropriate.

The inevitable next scene plays itself out two years later. Absalom's hatred had not lessened in the meanwhile. He shared many of his father's gifts including the ability to inspire loyalty, but he did not share David's capacity for letting go of the past and living in the present. Perhaps David's lack of action added fuel to Absalom's revenge.

There are remarkable similarities between Absalom's plan for revenge and Amnon's original plan, perhaps deliberately so on Absalom's part, but certainly noted by the author. David again is involved, this time ensuring that Amnon is led into the trap. Verse 26 suggests that David is suspicious but is not able to resist Absalom's pressure. All the king's sons are invited to Absalom's harvest celebration and Amnon, all suspicion of Absalom

---

[13] For example, Hagar, the foreign woman slave who is only ever 'that servant' or equivalent. Neither Abraham nor Sarah ever refers to her by name, but God does (Gen. 16; 21). Similarly, the announcement of Samson's birth (Judg. 13) makes it very clear that although the testimony of women was often discounted by men, including Manoah, the angel of God did not share that approach.

[14] It is possible that Absalom was also motivated by personal ambition and the desire to remove his older brother (2 Sam. 3:2) from the scene, but that is not the focus of the account.

lost in the abundance of good wine, is killed. Jonadab too is involved again. He appears to have avoided the party, remaining behind with David, but his insight comes to the fore once more. The rumour reaches David that Absalom has killed all his brothers. Jonadab is sure that it will only be Amnon, and he is proved right. After that we hear nothing more of Jonadab but are left with the impression of a great talent wasted.

Although David had taken no action in defence of his daughter, Absalom is not willing to risk him taking action in defence of his son, and so he flees. David, with typical wholeheartedness, mourns for his son every day. The ambiguity about which son he mourns for is almost certainly deliberate. Perhaps even David himself was not sure. Three more years passed; David's pain at the loss of Amnon eased but his reaction to Absalom remains ambiguous. His spirit longed to go to Absalom, but it is not clear whether this was in a positive sense or to go out against him. The term is more often used in this negative sense but the more positive implication of the NIV is possible. Perhaps David himself didn't know. The drama of life in this dysfunctional family was clearly not yet over.

Questions to ponder

1. What questions arise from David's relationships with Bathsheba, Uriah and Joab?
2. What was the essence of David's sin?
3. Can Nathan's approach be seen as a model for Christian counselling?
4. Is it possible to distinguish between the punishment and the consequences of David's sin?
5. What do these chapters teach about the importance of taking responsibility for the consequences of our actions?
6. How should David have dealt with Amnon? Did David's inaction deserve punishment?
7. Was Absalom right to take action when David did not?
8. In these chapters can David be described as 'a man after [God's] own heart'?

2 Samuel 14 – 20

9. Absalom: a usurping son

1. Absalom in Geshur and Jerusalem (14:1–33)

There are six chapters in 2 Samuel covering events relating to Absalom's rebellion against David. In contrast, Chronicles makes no mention of Absalom at all, apart from three 'in passing' genealogical references. Perhaps the Chronicler felt these stories could deflect the attention of the reader from the main point of observing the growth of the kingdom. But in Samuel these events provide ideal material for the authors to explore further their interest in relationship with God lived out in the context of personality, potential and power.

a. Learning from stories – and from friends (14:1–22)

A whole chapter is dedicated to explaining how it was that Absalom and David were, at least on the surface, reconciled. Quite why Joab took such an interest in Absalom's return to full participation in life at court is never explained. Did he see Absalom's potential and want to make sure that he was prepared for future leadership? Did he fear that a discontented Absalom could make more trouble for David from outside the country than he was likely to do at home? With Amnon dead, Absalom was the heir apparent, so did Joab want to make sure that he maintained his influence with the next monarch? Or is the implication of verse 1 that as usual Joab's primary concern was for David? Joab was very different from David but he understood, perhaps more than anyone else, how David's mind worked. David might have had mixed emotions about Absalom, but the situation was tearing him apart. His attention was thus diverted from his job of running the country. Perhaps Joab felt that one way or another the situation had to be resolved before things went any further. He copied Nathan in approaching David with an analogous case study, but this illustration involved somewhat more guile and clearly displays Joab's ability in theatrical direction.

Joab knew of a Tekoan woman who had a reputation for wisdom but who had never met David. He needed somebody who was not only a good actress but who could grasp a situation quickly, be confident enough to deal with David and be able to speak on her own initiative as events panned out. Joab provided the script for the first part of her interview, but she would have to carry it on depending on David's response. We find another example in 2 Samuel 20:16 of a similar 'wise woman' who had influence in her own town and was probably regularly used as a kind of elder stateswoman. As in the case of Deborah (Judg. 4 – 5) and Huldah (2 Kgs 22:14–20) there seems to have been no problem about accepting advice or even teaching from a woman. The Tekoan woman was dressed as a widow in mourning and sent to David with a plea for mercy for her son who had supposedly killed his brother. David could see clearly that the death of the second son, however much it may have been deserved, would bring double devastation on the mother and agreed that the execution should not be carried out. Again the issue comes into play as to whether and when rules should be bent for the benefit of all concerned. The woman pushed David to reaffirm his decision twice more so that the point was really clear to him and to any bystanders before she introduced the parallel with Absalom.

As soon as the woman began to give David advice about his own situation, the penny dropped and he rightly guessed that Joab was involved (19). This probably means that Joab had been pushing him for a while to bring Absalom back. David had refused to listen to the direct approach but now he agreed to allow Absalom to return to Jerusalem, although not to any participation in palace life. Did David feel that he had been pushed into a corner by Joab's manipulation? Having pronounced mercy on the Tekoan woman's fictional son, did he fear being seen as hypocritical if he refused to have mercy on Absalom? The two situations were not in fact parallel; an unplanned death in a fight is not the same as a premeditated murder. The mention of Absalom's sons in verse 27 also shows that, unlike in the case of the supposed widow's son, the succession was already assured.[1] The

---

[1] 2 Sam. 18:18 tells us that Absalom had no sons, so it is possible that the three mentioned here in fact all died in early childhood. It is ironic that the parallel with the story becomes more accurate than was intended.

decision to show mercy in the one case would not have formed a legal precedent forcing David to take similar action in the other. However, Joab's plan was very carefully worked out. He formulated a scenario where showing mercy was a good thing to do and where he could be reasonably sure that David would pronounce in that way. Joab had presumably calculated that this scenario, even though different, was close enough to Absalom's situation to make David fear the charge of hypocrisy if he did not allow him home.

b. Manipulation changes circumstances, but does that make it right? (14:23–33)

That David made the decision reluctantly is indicated by his refusal to have anything to do with the returned Absalom for a further two years. It may be that David resented being manipulated. It may be that he felt Absalom's exile had masked his reluctance to take any action against his sons, but with Absalom's return his failure to exercise discipline, whether judicial or parental, was made clear to all. It may be that he still felt guilty that he had precipitated Absalom's crime by turning a blind eye to Amnon's. We are not given quite enough information to get inside David's head at this point and of all the Samuel narratives this is perhaps one of the hardest sections to understand why it was chosen for inclusion in the text. What are we supposed to gain from this account? How should we respond to it? David was deceived and manipulated again, as he was by Amnon and then by Absalom in the previous chapter. The interest continues in the way in which people exercise power over others and the reader is certainly being invited to reflect on the process of manipulation, its morality – or otherwise – and its consequences. The writer demonstrates David's ability to recognize that he is being or has been manipulated in contrast with his apparent inability to resist the process. Absalom's return was undoubtedly in accordance with Joab's will and purposes, but whether it was in accordance with God's purposes is much less certain. The woman's scripted statement presents Absalom's banishment as 'against the people of God' (13). Joab almost certainly encouraged her to speak in spiritual terms to put further pressure on David. Religious manipulation has never been uncommon and can be extremely effective. If a particular course of action is presented as God's will, then it is easy to assume that that must be so and it takes a strong person to resist such pressure. Who wants to be seen as going against God's will? This may be why that kind of manipulation is treated so seriously in Scripture.[2] In this instance, any real attempt to analyse the issue in terms of what God might require is notable by its absence.

The chapter closes, providing a further example of brilliant literary skill, with another account of manipulation. This time it is Absalom who manipulates Joab – by the somewhat less-than-subtle method of burning his barley field – into facilitating an interview with David. One can imagine the frustration that Absalom must have felt as he brooded idly in Jerusalem with no role in public life to provide him with the acclamation that he craved and not even getting the satisfaction of explaining how he felt to David. How different the future might have been if David had shown real forgiveness to Absalom and welcomed him back gladly. The dysfunctional nature of David's family to a large extent must be seen as David's responsibility. Given David's lack of any action against Amnon and the fact that Absalom had already served three years in exile, he must have seen his treatment as unjust. It is easy to see how deep resentment against David may have built up in his heart. Through Joab he challenges his father in effect to 'charge him or let him go'. David, when faced with the alternative of accepting Absalom or executing him, finally backs down and the two are apparently reconciled. From what we have already seen of David's character we can predict that from his point of view all is now forgiven and forgotten, the incident is over, the chapter is closed. From what we have seen of Absalom's character we can predict that from his point of view that is far from being the case. Thus the account of the rebellion in the next chapter does not come as a surprise. The prophesied consequences of David's adultery (2 Sam. 12:10) and the consequences of his failure to deal adequately with either Joab or his sons are beginning inexorably to work themselves out. Let the reader be warned!

Sandwiched in between the two pictures of manipulative activity is some further information about Absalom which also prepares us for the next chapters. He was a handsome charismatic figure who was physically outstanding, with a remarkable head of hair that seems to have been such a matter of pride to him that he even weighed it. We are also told that he had three sons and a daughter. The latter, who shared her father's physical beauty, was the namesake of her aunt and there is an element of pathos in

---

[2] The punishment that Moses was given, for striking the rock instead of simply speaking to it, seems very harsh until one realizes that he was misrepresenting God. His action made it appear that God was angry, when God himself had not suggested such a thing. To take God's name in vain is a serious matter.

this reminder of what it was that originally drove Absalom into the bitter, revengeful, power-hungry man that he became. *The king kissed Absalom* (33). It may be significant that there is no record of Absalom kissing the king.[3]

2. The plan of campaign (15:1–9)

a. An excellent public relations exercise; but was it godly? (15:1–2)

How long it was before, *in the course of time*, Absalom put his well-thought-out plan into action we can't be sure, but the plan was four years in the making before Absalom finally felt ready to bring it to a decisive conclusion (7). The plan emerges as a masterpiece of strategy, diplomacy and public relations. It provides strong confirmation of the fact that Absalom was gifted not only in his looks! It is easy to see why Joab felt that Absalom should be brought back and groomed for kingship. He had discernment, foresight, intelligence and social skills to back up his natural charisma and the obsessive patience that we have already witnessed.

The chariot with its escort of fifty accompanying runners could be seen as merely the manifestation of a massive ego, indicating that Absalom wanted everyone to be as aware of his high status as he was. However, the rest of his behaviour suggests that there was more to it than that. Certainly it brought Absalom into the public eye. In a modern context his picture would have regularly been on the front pages of every newspaper. Any chat show worth its salt would have had an interview with Prince Absalom. Even in that context, those who had not seen him would certainly have been aware of who he was, what he looked like and any of the latest gossip. It took great effort to maintain this high level of visibility. We are told that *he would get up early* (2) and presumably work long hours on the job. Modern politicians know how much work needs to be put in on the 'hand-shaking and baby-kissing circuit'. Absalom was not imitating Jonathan, the previous heir apparent to the throne in Israel, who usually had only one armour-bearer with him. He was, however, following a custom common among the royalty of surrounding nations. He was encouraging the people to think of him in royal terms. The reader is again left to ponder

---

[3] W. Brueggemann draws out the parallel between this verse and the parable of the lost son in Luke 15:20–24. Absalom greets David as a servant but David treats him as a son. The difference is that there is no sign that Absalom saw any need for repentance (Brueggemann, p. 298).

exactly what royalty should look like in a kingdom where God is to be recognized as the ultimate ruler. There is a strong underlying hint that it should not look like this. It is important in the modern world for Christians to take note of the advice of public relations experts, however, it is equally important to make sure that our methodology remains in line with our theology. Creating Christian 'celebrities' may not always be the best way forward.

b. Neglected tasks pave the way for uprisings (15:3–4)

Absalom's public relations exercise was not just a matter of raising his visibility and emphasizing his status. There were two other key elements to his campaign. First, he found an unexceptionable way of both boosting his own reputation and credibility and damaging David's without actually having to take any action. There was nothing illegal or immoral about what he was doing and even if David's wise advisors such as Ahithophel and Hushai suspected his motives, one can imagine David looking on proudly and being glad that his son was so popular. Like a politician speaking from the opposition benches who can criticize government policy and make large unsubstantiated promises of what would be done if only they were given the power to do it, Absalom sought to win over the nation. Perhaps at first he only wanted to force his father into giving up his role as head of the justice department and allowing Absalom to take over as a *representative of the king* (3). However, his approach of suggesting to all and sundry that their particular claims were *valid and proper* suggests that he had popularity rather than justice in mind from the beginning. It should be noted that this kind of campaign was likely to work only if there was some truth in his allegation that justice was actually hard to find.[4] Perhaps David had become a little bored with pronouncing on legal cases in the same way that chapter 11 indicates he had become bored with military campaigns. There is always a danger that those who have received public acclamation in the early stages of their careers[5] will rest on their laurels, forgetting that continuing support is dependent on continuing fulfilment of the assigned task. Absalom certainly had experience of inaction and what he saw as injustice on David's part.

---

[4] It may be that there was a marked suspicion that David was favouring those from his own tribe of Judah and that Absalom's question about the complainants' home towns was therefore especially relevant.

[5] As David did, for example in 1 Sam. 18:7.

c. Celebrity status is not all there is to leadership (15:5–6)

The second element in Absalom's campaign was to persuade the nation that he was a man of the people. His 'marketing' exercise made them very aware that he was a prince. His public relations exercise won their hearts, for those who came in awe to see this great celebrity and to *bow down before him* were treated as equals. One can imagine the excited reports when they got back to their own villages: 'He actually spoke to me!'; 'He was just like an ordinary person!'; 'He treated me as if I were royalty too!'; 'He'll make a great king one day.' Absalom may have come back into Israel under a cloud of suspicion, guilty of killing his brother and obviously disapproved of by David, but he had transformed himself into a hero in the public mind.

The way the account is written, and in particular the final assessment in verse 6 that *he stole the hearts of the people*, shows that even if it was only with hindsight, Absalom's motives were understood, judged and found wanting. He had many, many gifts marking him out as a suitable future king, but he lacked one crucial characteristic: integrity. David had realized that seeking to depose Saul would be more likely to harm rather than help his own future kingship; that showing loyalty would make it easier in the long term to gain loyalty from others. This lesson had passed Absalom by. Through Samuel we learned the lesson that human beings 'look at the outward appearance, but the LORD looks at the heart' (1 Sam. 16:7). No explicit statement is made, but one can't help feeling that readers are being led towards the conclusion that in this context charisma and cleverness might come in the same category as outward appearance. Many of Absalom's contemporaries might now have been convinced that Absalom was the right man to replace David; readers of Samuel will at this point be fairly sure that he was not. There is maybe a warning here for the modern reader to be wary of those potential leaders who seek to win our hearts by flattering our egos and telling us everything that we want to hear. There are many similar warnings given to Israelites within the prophetic books.[6]

d. Blame does not always lie exclusively in one place (15:7–9)

After four years of his subversive activity, Absalom apparently decided that the time was right to launch his campaign proper. He was sure that

---

[6] E.g. Isa. 30:10; Jer. 6:10–15; 14:13–15; 29:8–9; Ezek. 13:16; 22:28; Mic. 3:5–11.

the vast majority of the population were now on his side. It may be that strictly speaking Absalom is telling the truth in verses 7–8. Perhaps it was way back during his time in Geshur that his plan to overthrow David began to evolve and he did make a vow to go to Hebron. However, there is no doubt that his statement, like so many that we have seen in the last few chapters, was deceptive. He intended to deceive David into assuming that his trip was a religious pilgrimage and he was successful in doing so.[7] David seems to have no suspicions at all as he gives Absalom his blessing, although the writer is probably underlining the irony as, at the very point where Absalom is planning war, David tells him to *Go in peace* (9). Whether David is exhibiting praiseworthy innocence or blameworthy naivety here is left for the reader to decide. It might seem strange that Absalom has waited so many years before making the relatively short journey to fulfil this vow, and even stranger that Hebron should have been the place where he had pledged to go when the ark was now housed in Jerusalem. Maybe this is evidence that the ageing David had given up asking questions about what was happening in his kingdom.

There is no doubt that Absalom's rebellion is presented from the beginning as ill-conceived and wrong. But that does not mean that David's reign was above criticism and as the story unfolds we shall see that David himself was aware of that. It may be right to fight off opposition but it is probably always a good thing to ask whether the opposition has in fact arisen because of failure on our part. But the critique of both Absalom and David in this section is also accompanied by a critique of the people whose hearts were won over so easily. It is not only leaders who are held responsible for their actions.

3. The revolution begins (15:10–23)

a. Flattering invitations sometimes come with a hidden cost (15:10–12)

As well as his open public relations activities, Absalom had been setting up underground cells throughout the country. These supporters, awaiting his command to arms, were now put on red alert. Absalom also took with him to Hebron a substantial contingent of guests from the Jerusalem

---

[7] It is ironic that a religious pilgrimage was used as the excuse for finding an opportunity to anoint the young David (1 Sam. 16) and another is used to provide an opportunity to unseat him.

court. His supposed pilgrimage would no doubt have included the grand feast that could accompany a fellowship offering (Lev. 7) and provided cover for him to take so many guests without arousing David's suspicion. This group of two hundred also went with him without suspicion, in all likelihood only too glad to have been put on the guest list by the popular young prince. They were probably well chosen as the kinds of crowd-pleasers who, although unlikely to have joined Absalom's camp of their own accord, were also unlikely, when they found themselves at the heart of a rebellion, to assert their independence and leave. They would be hard-pressed to convince Joab, if not David, of their ignorance about Absalom's intentions.

Thus the pattern of manipulation once more raises its ugly head and a further warning about the danger of being over-influenced by flattering invitations hangs in the air.

The plan to take two hundred courtiers with him (11) was a brilliant one. It is always easier to gather crowds once the first group is already in place. Absalom's campaign got off to a great start and went on from strength to strength. He was indeed proclaimed *king in Hebron* (10). Many who, perhaps like some of the Jerusalem two hundred, were not at all sure about what was going on were either swept along with the crowd or were too afraid to speak out against what appeared to be the majority view. The importance of making decisions and taking action on the basis of thought-out principles and not just peer pressure is underlined here – if only at this point with a dotted line.

Ahithophel, *David's counsellor* (12), was a wise man who, whether or not he had been directly informed of Absalom's plans, had almost certainly grasped what was going on. Unlike the guests from Jerusalem, he responded to Absalom's direct summons and came with eyes wide open. It is possible that Ahithophel was Bathsheba's grandfather; both her father and Ahithophel's son were named Eliam and the name is not used outside those two contexts (2 Sam. 11:3; 23:34). If so, then it is also possible that from the time of David's affair with Bathsheba Ahithophel began to resent David and to question whether David really was qualified to be king. If Absalom's implication was correct and David was increasingly neglecting his job, it is perhaps not surprising that a man of Ahithophel's undoubted skills could be persuaded to support Absalom and maybe even to convince himself that this was God's man for the job. David was again reaping the consequences of his own actions.

b. Peer pressure can be resisted (15:13)

It was inevitable that as soon as Absalom's intentions became known, the message would get through to David (13). There had been many people who remained loyal to Saul even at his lowest ebb and David had been far more popular throughout the nation than Saul ever had. There were still very many supporters, certainly many more than Absalom had calculated for, who were not swayed by the tide of popular opinion and whose loyalty could not be bought. It is sometimes assumed that peer pressure or the influence of some new charismatic figure is impossible to resist. That assumption was as false in the time of Absalom as it is today: difficult or costly maybe, but impossible? No! Followers are responsible for their actions and responses and will have to bear the consequences just as much as leaders.

c. Powerlessness sometimes enables (15:14–18)

At this point, when faced with an imminent crisis, we see David once more coming into his own. When faced with a clear urgent task and fighting against the odds, just like in the old days, David is at his best. It is fascinating that in the books of Samuel much of the material that presents David in a positive light comes from the time during Saul's reign, before he came into power, or here when Absalom had, for the moment at least, apparently stolen his power. Again the writers' underlying reflection on the nature of power comes into play. There is the hint of a suggestion that even if the possession of power does not always corrupt in moral terms, it can disable in other ways. However, for the next three chapters, up until the point where Absalom is killed and the threat removed, David is once more the able, active, incisive and spiritually discerning leader that he was in his youth. There is an inherent sadness in the account that David's new lease of life apparently does not last beyond the time of the rebellion and, as we read on, we see that the indecisive, less-active David returns.

But in this instance, as soon as he receives the news, David springs into action (14). He can see immediately that for Absalom to succeed, he will need to put David and those close to him out of the picture. Also David knows that Jerusalem, although well protected, can be vulnerable to siege. If they are to defeat Absalom, it will not be from the city, and in any case to stay there would inevitably cause large numbers of casualties on both sides – and as king he still has responsibility for both sides. He therefore quickly gathers together his household and leaves. Little more than a passing reference is given to the ten concubines left behind and this could be a further indication of David's somewhat cavalier attitude to women and his less than ideal model of family life. Certainly these women suffered as a result of David's action.[8] As far as the military were concerned, there was no question of the majority of the standing army who were under Joab's command abandoning David. These forces, along with six hundred troops from Gath – who had apparently defected to David's side following on from his time spent among the Philistines – marched out with David eastwards towards the wilderness across the Jordan. To travel west would have taken them into Philistia, which although not the power it used to be was unlikely to provide secure shelter. The northern tribes were apparently where Absalom's main support base was found and in the south was Absalom himself. The eastern route over the Mount of Olives was the only option. Absalom's strategy had been well planned.

d. Loyalty given is loyalty gained (15:19–23)

David was happy for these Gittites and other foreign troops to fight for him on behalf of God and the people of God. But this was going to be a civil war, not a religious war. Why should the Gittites be caught in the crossfire? They did not owe David anything and would be much safer if they stayed behind and offered support to *King Absalom* (19).[9] Given the pressure of the situation it appears that this was an instinctive, spur-of-the-moment, generous response on David's part. But the Gittites were loyal to David and made it clear that they had no intention of deserting him. This positive consequence of David's past actions in showing kindness to such peoples is recorded alongside the negative consequences of other actions. The *whole countryside*, who *wept aloud* as David and his group passed by, seemed on the one hand to have loved and supported David and yet on the other hand to have assumed that Absalom had the upper hand and was likely to be successful. Their support was vocal, but not apparently practical. The threat to David was a real one; the possibility of Absalom being king was strong. The rebellion had indeed started.

---

[8] 2 Sam. 16:21–22; 20:3. There is no support in the law for a king to keep concubines, but it was a common practice in the Ancient Near East for a large harem to be set up to provide evidence of a king's status and power. David seems to have been influenced more by the surrounding culture than by the kingship rules of Deut. 17. It may be that it made little difference to these women if they were used by David to boost his ego or by Absalom to boost his.

[9] In fact, in spite of David's statement here, throughout the whole narrative David is still referred to as king. In the mind of the writer David has not been deposed and he retreats as king, not as ex-king.

4. Friends and enemies (15:24 – 16:14)

a. God is sovereign; his support is not influenced by the carrying of religious symbols (15:24 29)

Zadok and the religious hierarchy stood alongside David as much as did Joab and the military hierarchy. With such backing it seems that the popular dissatisfaction with David's regime must have been very high for Absalom to have stood any chance at all of rallying support. Perhaps people had forgotten what David's capabilities were. His spiritual insight and his political acumen might not have been much in evidence in recent years, although we do see both illustrated very clearly here. The priests and Levites, by offering sacrifices and bringing the ark with them, were demonstrating their conviction that David was God's anointed king and that God was on David's side. But David resisted this attempt to manipulate the people by spiritual means and to seek to manipulate God. He had been there before and was not about to make that mistake again. He knew his own faults, or at least some of them. He knew that there was a possibility that this rebellion was God's way of punishing his failures, that Absalom might be meant to replace him just as he was called to replace Saul. He didn't think that that was so, but it was a possibility and therefore he sent the ark back. If God was going to act on David's behalf, he would do so whether or not the ark was with him.

The ark was not to be seen superstitiously as a kind of invincible talisman. God is not to be treated as a personal bodyguard whose main role is to protect us from our own mistakes and who is forced to take action at the times when we think he should. He is still the sovereign ruler of the universe who is more than capable of working out his purposes. Also, God was not only the God of David but the God of Israel and would remain so whether or not David was still king. The ark was not David's personal property and so should remain in Jerusalem. If David had somehow lost sight of the fact that God was with him at all times and in all places regardless of his role in society or his possession of sacred objects, he had certainly regained the conviction now. With the loss of power David appears at his most powerful, certainly in terms of spiritual understanding. We can learn from him the danger of thinking that God's support for human enterprises is or can ever be controlled or demanded by his people.

b. God gives the victory – usually via intensive effort on our part (15:30–37)

However, David's unwillingness to use spiritual manipulation did not mean that in his attempt to defeat Absalom he was unwilling to use all means possible including subterfuge and deceit. David was convinced that God would determine the victor in this fight. However, until it was demonstrated that David's defeat really was God's will, David was going to do all within his power to achieve victory. Trusting God and taking appropriate action are never seen in Scripture as mutually exclusive possibilities (e.g. Neh. 4:9). We can sometimes be paralysed by the thought that because God is in control he is the only one who acts and we should just sit back and let him do it. Scripture gives very little support to that view.

David needed informers within Absalom's camp, which he was certain would be set up in Jerusalem once he had left. Who better to act in that capacity than the priests and their sons? He also needed a fifth columnist who could infiltrate Absalom's government and manipulate the situation to David's benefit. At this juncture his friend and advisor Hushai comes into the picture (32–37).[10]

c. The support of friends brings hope (15:30–37)

David's retreat from Jerusalem caused him great distress. It was far from the triumphant beginning of a campaign where victory was confidently expected. He was *weeping . . . his head was covered and he was barefoot* (30), all signs of ritual mourning. Part of the grief was undoubtedly the betrayal of Absalom, part of it was simply the sadness of leaving his beloved city, but part of it too was hearing that Ahithophel had gone over to Absalom's side. Perhaps bound up in the sadness was an awareness of Ahithophel's motivation, an awareness that this wise man of previously undoubted integrity had decided that David was no longer fit to be king. But also there was a conviction that Ahithophel's advice was always good. In many instances leaders are only as good as their advisors and having Ahithophel alongside brought real credibility to Absalom's campaign. David's prayer that God would *turn Ahithophel's counsel into foolishness* (31) comes in that context.

---

[10] There is no mention in Chronicles of these events, but the reference to Ahithophel as 'the king's counsellor' and Hushai as 'the king's confidant' (1 Chr. 27:33) maybe indicates that the writer was well aware of what had gone on. It is possible that 'king's confidant' was actually an official government appointment.

The arrival of Hushai as David reached the top of the Mount of Olives must have seemed to David an obvious answer to his prayer and a great encouragement. Hushai was bright enough not only to be able to convince Absalom that like Ahithophel he had also left David behind, but also to grasp how Ahithophel's and Absalom's minds worked and to make sure that any advice Ahithophel gave was set aside. With Hushai, Zadok, Abiathar, Ahimaaz and Jonathan in place, David must, perhaps for the first time since he heard the news, have been able to envisage the possibility of Absalom's defeat. Although so many in the nation had turned against him, the fact that he did still have faithful friends would in itself have provided him with the strength and reassurance to keep going. We must not underestimate the importance of the loyalty of friends in a situation where we feel betrayed.

d. The danger of support that comes with strings attached (16:1–4)

David's next encounter on the journey away from Jerusalem was with Ziba, the steward who was responsible for Mephibosheth's estate. He came bringing a large number of very welcome supplies. It is not clear at this stage whether Ziba was indeed wanting to support David, and his statement about Mephibosheth was an unpremeditated grasping of the opportunity to further his own cause, or whether the whole thing was a plan to defraud Mephibosheth.[11] If Absalom did succeed, then there was a strong likelihood that he would not support Ziba against Mephibosheth, and if he did decide to take positive action against Mephibosheth, he would also take it against Ziba, and Saul's estates would be removed from both of them. Ziba's decision to cast in his lot with David is therefore a logical one. If David wins, he has ensured royal affirmation, and if David loses, he will probably be no worse off than if he had stayed at home. There is no doubt that Ziba's apparent generosity – and the gift he brought was most certainly generous – was at Mephibosheth's expense, and there is no doubt that his conclusion that Mephibosheth was not there because he thought he would gain the throne is extremely unlikely if not incredible. By no stretch of the imagination could Mephibosheth have thought that Absalom's rebellion might result in himself becoming king, and in any case, Mephibosheth had shown no signs at all that that was something he

---

[11] Ziba, as a known Saulide likely to feel antipathy to David, may have been aware in advance of Absalom's plans. Certainly his collection of provisions would have taken some time to prepare and his appearance on David's route may have also been carefully planned.

would have wanted. David demonstrates the capacity that most of us have to believe the worst of others immediately.

David's question *Why have you brought these?* possibly does reflect some suspicion on his part. However, he is apparently satisfied with the answer he gets even though, with the dexterity of any modern politician in a radio interview, Ziba avoids the issue and states the obvious. David might actually have realized without asking that the donkeys were for riding and the food for eating! David's immediate response is to hand over all Mephibosheth's property to Ziba, without hearing any further evidence, providing us perhaps with an indication of the failings in the handling of the justice department that Absalom had hinted at. The evidence that we shall see later on (19:24–30) certainly supports Mephibosheth's case and indicates that Ziba was at best mistaken and probably deliberately lying. Any support in times of danger and crisis is always welcome and material support perhaps especially so. But, as many other leaders have found throughout the centuries, support that comes with strings, expecting a return, can be dangerous in itself. Not all apparent friends are what they seem. David can perhaps be excused for his hasty decision because of the stress of the moment, but it shows that his weaknesses had not all been left behind in the crisis. He still found it difficult to resist pressure from those close by.

It is interesting that accounts of those whose friendship and loyalty to David are real and free from self-interest, Ittai, Zadok and Hushai, are followed by the mention of Ahithophel's disloyalty and then Shimei's enmity to David resulting from a continuing loyalty to Saul. In the middle of this we have the account of Ziba's arrival where his loyalty to David is ambiguous and his disloyalty to Mephibosheth is clear. It seems we are being asked to reflect on the nature of loyalty and the nature of friendship and of trust.

e. The real enemies are those who go against God's will (16:5–14)

Shimei makes no pretence to be a friend of David but declares himself rather to be delighted by David's downfall. He sees it as God's judgment on David's supposed involvement in the death of Saul's family. It may be that David's attempts to distance himself from the deaths of Saul and his family had not succeeded with this member of Saul's family. However, we do not know the timing of the events recorded in 2 Samuel 21:1–14 when seven of Saul's family were executed, and so Shimei's tormented opposition to David may have been a response to this. Shimei was clearly beside himself, in a way that is reminiscent of Saul's violent episodes, although he was together enough to remain at a safe distance on the other side of the valley as he hurled both missiles and abuse. Joab's brother Abishai in typical fashion sought permission to chop off Shimei's head – presumably to stop him saying such things – just as years before he had sought to kill Saul (1 Sam. 26:8)! David strongly dissociated himself not only from this particular action but from the whole approach of Joab and his brothers. We are perhaps being led to question whether, in one sense at least, Abishai and Joab are also being presented as enemies of David almost as much as Shimei is. David was clearly aware that his supporters who sought to lead him into ungodly behaviour were just as dangerous as those who overtly opposed him.

The attitude to Shimei's cursing is interesting. In nations surrounding Israel, life was dominated by the fear of curses, which were seen as a powerful means of manipulating circumstances and of causing people great harm. But for the believers in Yahweh, their conviction of his sovereignty was so great that curses as such could simply be ignored. Significantly, there is no biblical equivalent of the anti-curse rituals that abound in the literature of the Ancient Near East. If Shimei had really grasped a truth and this was God's judgment on David, then it was God himself and not Shimei's curse that was to be feared. David had not been directly responsible for killing Saul or his family, but the truth of the accusation that he was a *murderer* and a *scoundrel* must have hit home. However, if this was not God's judgment, if Shimei was not in line with God's will, then his curse was irrelevant. Indeed, the distress caused to David by the opposition of those like Shimei might eventually be eased by God's blessing. David was not sure whether the current situation would end positively for him or not, but he was completely convinced that in either instance God remained sovereign. There is perhaps a need for believers today to recapture the conviction that it is God and God alone who is sovereign. It is God who is to be both feared and trusted. Jesus said in Luke 12:4–5 that it is not 'those who kill the body' who are to be feared but the one who 'has authority to throw you into hell'. Of course enemies of various kinds can do us great damage, but we need to be far more afraid of offending against God's will than of any curses.

Eventually David and his accompanying forces arrived at their temporary destination, 'the fords in the wilderness' (15:28), where they would wait for further news before crossing the Jordan. Unsurprisingly, David and his men arrived exhausted, not only from the upheaval of the move and the difficulties of the journey but also from the emotional trauma of the events. If Absalom were to press forward his advantage and attack immediately, they would have little chance of resisting. With that thought in mind the story takes us back to Absalom's camp.

5. Civil war begins (16:15 – 17:29)

a. It is not a good idea to take God's support for granted! (16:15–19)

The descriptions throughout this section are very detailed; the reader is drawn right into the events and can picture very clearly all that goes on, including the reactions of the characters involved. It seems likely that the writer's own great skill is backed up here by eyewitness accounts. Absalom, as David had expected, moved quickly into Jerusalem and we enter his 'court' along with Hushai. Absalom knew just how close had been the friendship between Hushai and David and was naturally suspicious. However, as he had apparently convinced himself that his own actions were right, serving the interests of both God and Israel, he failed to notice any ambiguity in Hushai's statement that his loyalty would be with *the one chosen by the LORD* and *by all the men of Israel* (18).[12] Absalom's prideful confidence proved to be his downfall. He might be popular, particularly with his own supporters, but there had as yet been no national meeting of the tribes. The one chosen *by all the men of Israel* was still David, but it apparently never entered Absalom's head that he was not supported both by the people and by God.

In the past, David himself had fallen into the trap of assuming that his plans, made in the light of known facts and with good intentions, must therefore be the will of God. Absalom, with rather more questionable intentions, fell into the same trap. There is a further warning here for all readers to be on their guard against this and similar dangerous assumptions that in essence see God as there for our convenience. A similar issue arose for Joshua who, when fighting with the Canaanites, was faced with a powerful warrior. His question 'Are you for us or for our enemies?' (Josh. 5:13) seems perfectly fair, but the point of the reply is clear: 'Neither . . .

---

[12] Note the similarity here with David's ambiguous statement 'Why can't I go and fight against the enemies of my lord the king?' in 1 Sam. 29:8.

but as commander of the army of the LORD I have now come' (Josh. 5:14). God was not simply an extra section in Joshua's arsenal providing an overwhelming advantage of 'firepower' against any enemy. David had learned the lesson that he could not take God's support for granted, but Absalom apparently had not.

b. Consulting is good, but the advice of consultants cannot always be trusted (16:20 – 17:4)

Having accepted Hushai as a genuine supporter, Absalom sought specific advice about the next stage of his campaign from both Ahithophel and Hushai, so that he could compare the two and make his own decision about how to proceed. Ahithophel's first piece of advice was for Absalom to sleep with David's concubines. This would assert his own status and indicate symbolically that he had taken over David's power,[13] but in addition this act would let everyone know that there was no turning back. David would rightly see such an action as unforgivable. Absalom's supporters would then know that they, being associated with Absalom and his actions, had to fight to the end; the possibility of defecting to David's side was no longer available to them. In that sense, the *hands of everyone with* Absalom would *be more resolute* (21). The rights and feelings of the women were apparently irrelevant to all concerned. Ahithophel and Absalom seem to have been completely undeterred by the dehumanization involved and the fact that such action was completely forbidden by the law – even women captured in battle were given time to adjust to their new situation before being married off (Deut. 21:10–14). Absalom's concern about the abuse of his sister Tamar does not seem to have extended to these other women. Again, the only light as far as these women are concerned is that the wrongness of Absalom's action and the effect that it had on them is noted and understood by the writer (cf. 2 Sam. 20:3). These were real people and not objects to be owned and used at will.

Ahithophel's second piece of counsel (17:1–4) is prefaced by the note that his advice was seen as *like that of one who enquires of God* (16:23). He was so perceptive and insightful that he might have been a prophet. His advice about the concubines may have been immoral and illegal, but from the point of view of Absalom's self-interest it was good advice. The

---

[13] The taking over of the women of the previous ruler was a recognized indication in the Ancient Near East that power now lay with the new king.

implication is that what follows will also be good advice. Knowing that David would have had the stuffing knocked out of him by Absalom's treachery and perhaps more so by the extent of the popular acclaim received by Absalom, Ahithophel strongly advised that they should strike while the iron was hot and go all out to finish the job. They should take the *twelve thousand men*[14] who had already assembled and attack now. The reader, who has seen the exhausted state of David's army, can recognize immediately that this makes sense. *The elders of Israel*, or at least those of them who had accepted Absalom's claims (and apparently a significant number had), also recognized that it was good advice. If David could be killed in an initial attack, then further bloodshed might be avoided. But Hushai was also a respected counsellor so his opinion was investigated too.

c. The advantage of a good reputation; the danger of pride (17:5–14)

Hushai's task was difficult. He had to provide an alternative plan that was strong enough to persuade all concerned that it was more likely to succeed than Ahithophel's plan and yet would in fact give David a better chance of victory. He managed admirably. He reminded Absalom and his men of David's renowned skill in guerrilla warfare and warned that his reputation might cause panic to spread through the whole army in the event of a possible defeat of a small section of Absalom's troops. They were convinced. Hushai then presented his plan. It appealed to Absalom's pride (11), but he didn't see that it would make him vulnerable to David's troops. Surely, Hushai argued, if Absalom gathered troops from far and wide (the danger of setting out with an untrained army was ignored by both sides, probably deliberately by Hushai) and *with you yourself leading them into battle*, he was bound to be successful. What group could fail if Absalom were at their head! It may be significant that it was *all the men* rather than *all the elders* whom Hushai was able to persuade. But his advice was followed; Absalom decided not to move until he had called up enough of the part-time national guard to outnumber David's better-trained standing army. One can understand why Absalom's soldiers, aware since their childhood of David's reputation, thought that this was a good idea. However, the time taken to gather the large force from around the country also meant, as

---

[14] The *thousand* here may refer to a specific unit or cohort not necessarily containing anywhere near as many as 1,000 men.

Hushai had known it would, that David had time to rest, recover and regroup. The final result was still in question, but at least now David had a fighting chance.

The fact is noted in verse 14 that Absalom's decision to follow Hushai's advice was an answer to David's prayer and part of God's plan to ensure Absalom's failure. The writer wants us to be absolutely sure that Absalom was not 'the one chosen by the LORD' (16:18). God's involvement in history must be understood clearly. His sovereignty must be recognized not only by David but by all Israel. In many ways Absalom's rebellion made good sense and could be justified on the grounds that his leadership might benefit Israel and therefore would surely be what God wanted. But God had not been consulted. The plan had been worked out as if God was an irrelevance. Absalom's rebellion was against God just as much as, or perhaps more than, it was against David. We leave God out of the picture at our peril.

d. Success or failure often depends on apparently insignificant characters (17:15–22)

The story continues almost in the manner of a James Bond-style spy story. Hushai sent word to the two young men, Jonathan and Ahimaaz, using the ancient equivalent of a secure encrypted transcription, that is, a message carried by *a female servant*. Just in case Absalom did change his mind and take Ahithophel's advice after all, David was to move immediately beyond the Jordan and, by implication, also immediately prepare for war.

Hushai's part was played, Jonathan and Ahimaaz were ready, but in the meantime other unnamed characters briefly take centre stage. History is rarely made entirely by the stars and we do well to note the many, often unnamed, bit players without whom the stars would have no role. The Old Testament does not explicitly expound the teaching of 1 Corinthians 12 concerning the whole body having many equally significant parts, but the evidence is there nevertheless. David's eventual victory was made possible by the work of two unnamed women and almost thwarted by the quick thinking of an unnamed young man. The use of the two women shows, as so often in the Old Testament narratives, both an awareness and a critique of the prevailing worldview. Women were unlikely to be suspected because of society's assumption that they were incapable of the sophisticated thinking required for subterfuge, but in fact they were more than capable of all that was involved in the task.

Jonathan and Ahimaaz had stayed outside the town at En Rogel because *they could not risk being seen entering the city*. Presumably they could have entered the town as their fathers had done, but that would have meant enlisting with Absalom's forces which would have made it virtually impossible then to get away unnoticed. As it was, if they were discovered to be spying for David, it would mean instant death. Nevertheless, the female servant was willing to risk her life in carrying the message to them. In spite of their care to avoid attention, the two spies were spotted perhaps as they left their hiding place and their presence was reported immediately to Absalom. We don't know anything about the young man who reported them. He clearly recognized the two and understood the significance of their presence and surreptitious departure, and they apparently recognized him and grasped the significance of his having seen them. He also clearly had quick access to Absalom. Perhaps he was the son of some court or temple official, one of those whose hearts had been completely won over by the active, charismatic prince. It is left to our imagination to wonder what happened to this young man later on in the aftermath of Absalom's death.

Jonathan and Ahimaaz headed out towards the river but stopped to hide at Bahurim where they were aided by another woman, the unnamed wife of a local farmer or businessman, who hid them in the well and bravely diverted those who searched for them. Bahurim was Shimei's home town (16:5). Civil war can cause divisions in small communities as well as in the whole nation. Clearly Bahurim was not united either for or against David or Absalom. Eventually, Absalom's men gave up the hunt and the two spies were able to reach their destination and deliver the message. At once, David and his people crossed the Jordan and the immediate danger was over, at least for them. To take a large group of people across the narrow fords in a short space of time could cause havoc – as anyone will know who has faced the jams in trying to get out of a large car park through the only open exit after a sports event or other large attraction. If this had been attempted while they were under attack, defeat would have been inevitable, as Ahithophel had predicted. Now they could do it, in haste certainly (it was accomplished in a single night, 22), but without the added pressure of a pursuing force.

e. A sad end for a gifted man (17:23)

Once Ahithophel *saw that his advice had not been followed*, he was fairly certain that Absalom's cause was now lost. We are told, briefly and with a no-comment objectivity that only adds to the pathos, that he went to his home town, *put his house in order and then hanged himself.* He may have realized that David would probably, if only for political and public relations reasons, have forgiven his betrayal and not executed him, but apparently he could not live with himself under those circumstances. In general the writer of Samuel provides great insight into motivation and emotion. We are often given real understanding of where people are coming from, but in Ahithophel's case we are provided with no such insight, only with the bare facts.

There is no suggestion in the text that Ahithophel's action was appropriate or approved of, or that suicide could or should somehow be seen as a noble action or as anything other than a blameworthy taking of life. However, this action is only one among the many described that fail to take God, his character and his commands seriously and is certainly not presented as more serious than the others. There is understanding and perhaps a hint of sympathy as we are informed that he *was buried in his father's tomb.* He may have made an error of judgment which he himself saw as unforgivable, but for the rest of his life he had been a good servant of his God, his country and his king. He deserved a decent burial. It is always important not to concentrate so much on one mistake that we lose sight of the contribution of a whole life.

f. The importance of supporters (17:24–29)

Information about the actual military operations is sparse. Stories of particular people and what might be seen as minor events in the run-up to and aftermath of the campaign are told in great detail but the picture of the fighting is painted only with very broad brushstrokes. The writer is more interested in how this affected people than in what actually happened. It reads more like history retold as the troops relaxed around the campfire than official military records; more like the result of a newspaper or TV investigation than a judicial inquiry. This material is written for the people, not for a few academics. It is a great tragedy if and when large sections of the Old Testament are seen as beyond the reach of ordinary believers. We are introduced briefly to Absalom's general, Amasa, probably so that we recognize him when he appears in the narrative at a later stage (19:13; 20:4–13). As Joab had remained with David, it was necessary for Absalom to appoint a credible replacement and his choice was his cousin who was also Joab's cousin, the son of their aunt

Abigail.[15] The point of this detail is to show that like the nation and individual communities, even families are divided by civil war.

By the time Absalom gathered his troops and crossed over to Gilead on the east side of the river Jordan, David was already well ensconced in Mahanaim. This had been Ish-Bosheth's old capital and was well chosen as both easily defensible and a good base for attack. David's positive foreign policies were now bearing positive consequences as allies from Ammon, Lo Debar and Gilead brought him supplies. The mention of Shobi brings an interesting glimpse between the lines. He had apparently replaced his brother Hanun as leader of the Ammonites after Hanun's unfortunate encounter with David's men, but we have no information whatsoever as to how David managed to build bridges so that Shobi saw him as an ally. Makir from Lo Debar had been Mephibosheth's sponsor and it may have been David's earlier kind treatment of Mephibosheth that brought his support. He had presumably not heard that David had now confiscated all of Mephibosheth's property! This is the first mention of Barzillai the Gileadite but we hear more of him later on when David seeks to repay his kindness (19:31–40).

6. The end of the line (18:1 – 19:7)

a. There is a time to fight and a time to let others do the fighting for you (18:1–5)

Time has clearly moved on from the occasion when David was given a scathing rebuke for not taking his place with the army (2 Sam. 11:1; 12:27–28). In this case David's presence with the army would be an unnecessary danger and distraction. His physical powers were no longer what they once were. More significantly, this time the whole campaign revolved around David's personal safety. If he was killed, then the battle was over: there would be no point in fighting on. This was not a situation when the future of the nation was at stake, only the future of the king. The need to protect David on the battlefield could actually put his troops in further danger. David was apparently keen to go with them, but could see

---

[15] 1 Chr. 2:13–16 gives details of David's wider family and notes that Jesse had seven sons and two daughters, Zeruiah and Abigail. There is some confusion here about the identity of Nahash, who is not mentioned in Chronicles. It may be that Abigail is David's and Zeruiah's half-sister and this is the name of her mother, although Nahash in other instances is a male name. It has been suggested that as the name Nahash is also mentioned in the next verse, what we have here is a copyist's error replacing another similar name with Nahash when his eye fell in the wrong place.

the logic of their argument and, at their united insistence, agreed to provide *support from the city*. Sometimes the desire of elderly leaders to continue to take their place on the front line can cause all kinds of problems. It is important to recognize when it is time to begin to take a back seat in any situation; when to stop driving, or preaching, or chairing meetings or making the final decision. David provides a good example here. In this particular campaign, the *support from the city* was still a vital part of what was going on; taking a back seat is not the same as taking no seat at all! The troops must have been greatly encouraged as he waved them off when the three contingents, under Joab, Abishai and Ittai, marched through the gate of the city.

Just as David's safety was crucial to his campaign, so Absalom's safety was essential to his. If Absalom was killed, then his forces had no focus at all: they were fighting for no other cause than his kingship. Nevertheless David, even as he indirectly expresses real confidence that his troops will be successful, and knowing that the defeat of Absalom inevitably involves his removal from the scene, pleads with the generals to *be gentle* with him. David may not always have been a good father, but he was still a father. This was not a private request; it was made in the presence of the whole army. Everyone knew that David's desire was that Absalom be captured but not killed.

b. War inevitably involves suffering and death (18:6–15)

The actual battle is described in three brief verses. It took place in the forested area of Ephraimite territory and Absalom's nationally gathered army was crushed by David's much smaller group of trained troops under trained generals. More soldiers died because of their failure to cope with the environmental conditions than because of enemy attacks, and twenty thousand lives were wastefully destroyed. The land was not forested as we would understand it, but was a rough area with some trees and undergrowth and many hidden pitfalls. There was virtually nothing that could be used as 'bush tucker' if supplies were cut off. Groups were easily separated and the fighting would have been in many small battles rather than on one major front. In that context, the trained army, however outnumbered, was very much at an advantage. Twenty thousand died, probably mostly ordinary farm boys who had been swept along by the force of Absalom's charismatic reputation. Perhaps Ahithophel envisaged this result of the failure to take his advice. Perhaps in his prideful confidence the possibility of defeat never entered Absalom's head and he was as shocked as any by what he had brought upon the nation. We are told nothing of that; we are told only the pathetic and somewhat blackly comic story of Absalom's own death – brought about largely by his own pride.

Absalom, like an arrogant aristocrat insisting on driving his luxury car across a muddy bog where it was bound to get stuck, was riding his mule through a forest terrain for which it was most unsuitable. He had apparently made no attempt to prepare for the battle by cutting the long hair in which he took such great pride.[16] Presumably he wanted all his fans to be able to recognize him and acknowledge his kingly appearance. As Proverbs 16:18 notes, reflecting perhaps on this incident, 'Pride goes before destruction, a haughty spirit before a fall.' Absalom's head got caught in the trees, the royal mule moved on and he was left hanging there, his hopes of victory and his dignity both completely lost in the cause of his pride. His death was equally inglorious. Although the soldier who found him took David's request seriously and would have nothing to do with killing him, Joab had no such qualms and without compunction thrust *three javelins . . . into Absalom's heart* to ensure that there was no chance of his survival. The young soldier had no doubt that David would have found out about his action and his reluctance seems to have stemmed as much from concern for his own safety as from any moral scruples. Perhaps David's peremptory execution of those involved in the deaths of Saul and Ish-Bosheth had become legendary. The soldier makes a telling prediction about Joab's action: *you would have kept your distance from me*, he says (13). In other words, 'you would have left me to carry the can', thus providing rather a sad reflection on Joab's character. This man at least did not expect him to show any loyalty to his troops. However, perhaps his view is belied by the action of Joab's own armour-bearers – it may or may not be significant that Joab had ten in contrast to the one that Jonathan had perceived to be necessary (1 Sam. 14).[17] This group immediately followed Joab in stabbing Absalom, probably not so much to ensure his

---

[16] In fact the text does not mention his hair here (cf. 2 Sam. 14:26), but the tradition cited by Josephus (*Antiquities* 7.239), which sees his hair as the cause of his downfall, could easily be right. A luxuriant head of hair would certainly make it harder to release a head trapped in the branches.

[17] It is possible that Joab had so many armour-bearers not as a sign of his status but because his tendency to put quick results before the safety of his men had created enemies and he needed a number of bodyguards.

death as to ensure that neither Joab nor indeed any single individual could be identified as the one who might actually be blamed for Absalom's death. Their loyalty to Joab is some indication that to this group at least he had shown loyalty.

c. War involves difficult decisions (18:16–18)

Joab knew that if they took Absalom back to Mahanaim alive, then there was no way that David was going to bring himself to pronounce the death sentence, however much it was deserved or even however much the law called for it. Presumably he calculated that facing David's displeasure was in the long run likely to cause less harm for Israel than leaving Absalom alive, even if he had been imprisoned, to act as the focus of continuing opposition to David. With Absalom dead, it was possible that action could be taken that would assuage the people's doubts about David's capacity to continue in power. The writer records all these actions without comment. The reader is left to reflect on the rightness or wrongness of Joab's action and whether or not it was in fact in David's best interests. It involved the deliberate countering of David's instructions but it certainly meant the immediate end of the current conflict and undoubtedly saved many lives. One can indeed feel sympathy for those who in the chaos of the battlefield have to take such decisions.

As far as Absalom is concerned, his tremendous potential and his pride in his own abilities both came to nothing. He was remembered only by a pile of stones in the forest and a monument that he himself had erected. His lack of sons (presumably the unnamed three mentioned in 2 Samuel 14:27 all died in early childhood) meant that there was no chance that a son of Absalom could succeed him as heir apparent to his father's throne. The question of who would be appointed as David's successor, a question which some have seen as the key interest in this section of the narratives, thus far remains unanswered.

d. Good news and bad news; does public gain outweigh personal loss? (18:19–33)

The account of the way in which the news was brought to David adds little to our understanding of national events but provides a fascinating insight into the characters of those involved. Ahimaaz, who, once his spying mission was completed, had presumably remained with David's troops, wanted to be the one who carried the last message of the war to David just as he had been the one who carried the first. Joab, knowing David well and understanding how he would react, was concerned that the bearer of the message might be the one blamed, however unjustly, for the content of the message. Therefore he sent instead a Cushite.[18] It may be that Joab thought that an unrelated foreigner was more likely to be safe, but there is also a strong implication that he was unconcerned about the Cushite's fate. The safety of a foreign or possibly a mercenary soldier or perhaps a slave was irrelevant to him: political correctness was not on Joab's agenda. However, the way in which the incident is recorded indicates that even the life of a foreigner was on the writer's agenda and is on God's agenda. The Cushite was probably glad to be given the assignment. He knew nothing of the undercurrents and as far as he was concerned the news was excellent; David's enemies had been soundly defeated. Perhaps he even hoped for a reward. Ahimaaz, still wanting to play his part in the final scene, but unwilling to cross Joab, eventually obtained permission and outran the Cushite to bring David news of victory.

The picture of David sitting in the shelter of the wall *between the inner and outer gates*, constantly asking for news, constantly calling to the watchman up on the wall to look again, is both realistic and rather sad. His main concern is not for the cause but for Absalom. Whether this is a praiseworthy reaction or not is left somewhat ambiguous at this stage. Eventually the two runners are seen, and in time the first is recognized as Ahimaaz. He arrives and delivers the news of victory; he has assured his place in history. However, maybe realizing on hearing David's immediate question about Absalom that Joab's warning had been right, he baulks at bringing the news of Absalom's death. It was not until the arrival of the Cushite, who had had no such warning, that David knew that his worst fears were realized. Absalom was dead. The king (the fact that the whole fight had been about kingship is emphasized by the constant reference to David as the king) was totally and disablingly devastated. His statement *If only I had died instead of you* (33) may indicate that he had a strong sense of his own guilt in the matter, although it's not clear if his guilt was because he had failed as a king or because he had not handled Amnon and Absalom properly. The question of Absalom's guilt was not considered. David's kingship, even in his role as

---

[18] Cush was in the area south of Egypt which today forms part of Sudan and Ethiopia.

national judge, was apparently meaningless in comparison with the loss of his son. Perhaps as he'd sat there, probably for several days if not weeks – the timing of the campaign is never clarified – David had had time to think. It is possible that he came to the conclusion that power was not everything and the price of clinging on to power was too high to pay. In Luke 14:25–33 Jesus warns his disciples to think about the cost of any action, even discipleship, before they undertake it. Maybe there is an element of the same lesson in this story. We must be sure that the outcome of a battle and the possible gains are really worth the cost that must be paid. In this instance, David apparently had come to the conclusion that they were not.

e. Personal concerns versus public responsibilities? (19:1–8)

The king's grief was extreme and his behaviour perhaps paralleled that at the death of his first son by Bathsheba many years before. Any joy or even relief and satisfaction that his men might have felt at having successfully served their king and country was taken away. Instead they felt *ashamed*. David might have retained his crown but he had apparently abdicated from all his responsibilities as king. There is certainly no question of his providing his men 'support from the city' (18:3) as they returned.

Anyone taking up leadership responsibilities must realize there are times when personal considerations must be set aside. This does not mean that family responsibilities can be avoided. The whole account of David's life shows that his neglect of his family was blameworthy, and Paul in 1 Timothy 3 and elsewhere makes it clear that one evidence of leadership potential is that proper attention is given to responsibilities within the family. Nevertheless, there is a balance to be maintained. The expression of David's grief was excessive and to a large extent self-indulgent. Joab's fierce denunciation of his behaviour (5) may seem harsh, but was probably very necessary. David's behaviour could have quickly turned the vague disquiet at his failings as a king into a full-scale and unquenchable surge of opposition. Absalom had not defeated David, but David might defeat himself. Joab's words did nudge David out of his quagmire of self-pity enough to retake his place in the city gate. In local towns the gateway was the normal site for public meetings and justice hearings, so David's presence there was a sign to the people that normal life had been resumed. He was available to consider their needs. He was indeed king of Israel.

243

7. Peace and the aftermath of war (19:9–43)

a. Winning the peace can be a greater challenge than winning a war (19:9–14)

The inevitable confusion, discomfort, recriminations and self-justification within the country are described wonderfully. In modern South Africa, it has been suggested, it is hard now to find those who will admit to having supported apartheid. In Israel at this point it was certainly hard to find those who would admit to having supported Absalom. The facts were clear; they had *anointed* Absalom *to rule over* them, but once he was dead, there was widespread recognition of the need to bring David back and return things to normal as soon as possible. David, once the first agonies of his grief for Absalom had subsided, regained his love of a challenge. He began his reconciliation attempts with his own tribe of Judah and recruited Zadok and Abiathar, who, having remained in Jerusalem, would be in a good position to know what had gone on there and who were the best people to work with, to manage the process. There were apparently to be no recriminations.

His positive approach to Amasa, Absalom's general, would reassure all those who had fought on Absalom's side that rather than being punished they could be affirmed. The model of reconciliation is one well worth noting by those involved in internal power struggles today, whether in countries, families or churches. Bringing senior members of the former opposition forces into government is one way of indicating that those now in power really do see the conflict as over. Amasa's replacement of Joab as the main military commander in the nation was an interesting strategy on David's part. It served several purposes. It played a major part in winning *over the hearts of the men of Judah* (14), that is, in winning them back from their allegiance to Absalom. Also it served as a way of punishing Joab. It is inconceivable that David had not heard about Joab's part in Absalom's death. This action would let everyone know that such deeds would be punished, but it would not actually bring David into direct conflict with Joab – or at least that was the theory.

b. The importance of turning enemies into friends (19:15–23)

The return of David and his entourage to Jerusalem took much more time and was much more formal and sedate than their rather chaotic flight. The journey back across the Jordan was used as a time to build bridges in more ways than one, and David's spiritual insight as well as his diplomatic skill again comes into view. The people of Judah came out in force to escort David back across the river. With hindsight, David's attempt to stimulate Judah to support him by emphasizing his relationship to them might have also stimulated the rivalry with the northern tribes that caused so much trouble later on. But at this time that is not the point at issue. Unsurprisingly Ziba, Mephibosheth's steward, was also there, perhaps seeking to reinforce David's picture of him as a useful man to have around, someone who was worth rewarding. He must have known that it would not be long before Mephibosheth was able to meet with David and put forward his own point of view. Ziba knew that if he was accepted by David in front of all the crowds, it would be more difficult for David to speak out against him later on.

Shimei was a more unexpected arrival, bringing a thousand other Benjaminites with him *from Bahurim*[19] in a show of mass support for David. The calm, rational man pictured here who has no problem in permitting himself to *fall prostrate before the king* seems very far removed from the ranting character of the earlier encounter. The similarities with Saul's great mood swings are quite pronounced. Shimei seems to have been alone when he staged his attack on David as he fled from Jerusalem (16:5–14). He may also have been acting independently and with a genuine repentance for his previous behaviour now. However, it is possible that the town, which we know had not all opposed David (17:18), had put pressure on Shimei to apologize and had come along to make sure that he did. If so, then their implicit fear that David might punish the whole town for Shimei's offence proved to be unfounded. Abishai, in his usual violent fashion, wanted David to make an example of Shimei because *he cursed the Lord's anointed* (21). He probably used the phrase deliberately, suggesting that David could no longer defend Shimei's cursing on the grounds that he might just have caught something of God's intention. Shimei had claimed that it was God who had 'given the kingdom into the hands of . . . Absalom' (16:8), but events had proved him wrong. David should now prove his kingship by executing Shimei. David immediately dissociated himself once more from the approach of Abishai and his brothers, making it clear that it was they rather than Shimei who were his 'adversaries' (cf. 19:22, ESV) in making such a suggestion. They thought that kingship meant

---

[19] It would be interesting to know whether the woman who had protected Jonathan and Ahimaaz at Bahurim (2 Sam. 17:18–22) was with them.

domination and that power needed to be indicated by an aggressive display of strength. David in his better moments, one of which we see here, knew that he didn't need to take that kind of action to prove his kingship. It is a temptation, even within Christian circles, to feel that the best way for leaders to assert their authority is by a show of strength. It is to be hoped that we can be as strong as David in resisting such a temptation.

Perhaps in making the statement *Don't I know that today I am king over Israel?* (22) his thoughts went back to the commission and covenant he had received in 2 Samuel 7. His kingship was given by God and was to be demonstrated by care for all the people, not by gratuitous shows of violent revenge. This was a day of celebration, almost a second coronation day. On that day, not even Shimei was to die; what is more, he was given a sure promise that he would not be executed by David on a future occasion.

A rather sad postscript to this incident is recorded in 1 Kings 2:8–9, where David charges Solomon with making sure that Shimei is violently punished after all. This may indicate that David's action here was not an exercise of spiritual wisdom but a purely political public relations exercise while his own personal desire for revenge simmered underneath all along. However, only a very cynical reader would abstract that from 2 Samuel 19, and it seems much more likely that David's vindictiveness stemmed rather from the fact that his spiritual insight failed along with his other powers as he fell into the confusion of old age (1 Kgs 1:1ff.).

c. Giving and receiving (19:24–39)

The expected encounter with Mephibosheth was perhaps not quite what David had envisaged and brought him a dilemma. Mephibosheth provided irrefutable evidence that far from rejoicing at David's downfall he had been in mourning since David had left. Ziba had lied. Mephibosheth's next statements may simply have been the culturally appropriate response to David. However, they may be seen as presenting Mephibosheth as reflecting the character of his father, Jonathan. He suggests that money is actually an irrelevance to him and in doing so he gives David a way out. David's final decision, to divide the land equally between Ziba and Mephibosheth, appears to reflect weakness rather than justice. Yet again we see David's inability to deal with face-to-face confrontation with people with whom he has some kind of a relationship. However, it may have seemed to David the best way forward under the circumstances. Given that Ziba had looked after the property since Saul's death with no help from Mephibosheth, perhaps David's original decision to restore the land to him without compensating Ziba had been somewhat less than fair. In any case, Mephibosheth does not contest this decision. Sometimes the best way forward is to let sleeping dogs lie and it is not neccooarily a display of weakness to take that line.

The description of David's meeting with Barzillai adds little to our understanding of Israel's history, but it is a fascinating cameo nevertheless. David knew he was beholden to Barzillai and he wanted it to be known that he was not stinting in the expression of his gratitude to those who had helped him. Barzillai understood that. He was rich and he was old and he had neither the need nor the desire for any help from David, but just as he was generous in material things he was generous in allowing David his chance to distribute largesse. It is indeed 'more blessed to give than to receive' (Acts 20:35) and sometimes, as in Barzillai's case, the gift to others of the opportunity to give to us is a real demonstration of such blessedness. The apparently generous approach that always wants to give to others can in fact mask an inherent selfishness. In this instance, Kimham, perhaps a younger son or grandson of Barzillai, was more than happy to emigrate across into Israel under David's sponsorship and to take up a role in the court. Kimham's presence as a kind of envoy would provide diplomatic advantages to both parties as well as evidence of David's generosity to his allies.

d. A fresh start needs the cooperation of all concerned (19:40–43)

It should have been a happy time all round. There were to be no repercussions of the rebellion and order was restored in Israel. However, the underlying tensions and resentments between Judah in the south and the northern tribes that had been simmering since the death of Saul began to emerge. The debate over who had the right to bring David back and who was the most loyal was probably the excuse rather than the reason for a demonstration of all the unlovely elements of tribalism and racism that we see here. David's reign had brought security and prosperity to the land, but the unity between the tribes had clearly not penetrated far beneath the surface. There is no resolution of the tension at this point: we are simply left with the two sides at each other's throats. The reader is prepared not only for the account of Sheba's rebellion, but also for the wider splits that eventually result from the oppressions of the latter part of Solomon's reign.

It was a day of victory for David, but victory in one area by no means ensures victory in all areas of a nation's life. Seeking after power was not the monopoly of princes, kings and generals. There was just as much jostling for status among the tribes. Perhaps if the people had shown as much generosity to one another here as David had shown to those who had opposed him, then the history of the nation of Israel which is described in the books of Kings might have been very different. One can see similarities between the attitude of the tribes at this point and that of the different parties in the church at Corinth. Paul's instructions about the nature of love in 1 Corinthians 13 would most certainly have helped to show the people of Israel 'the most excellent way' (1 Cor. 12:30). There is a warning and a challenge here to all modern believers. Factions and special-interest groups seeking for precedence within local churches, denominationalism, patronizing attitudes and all other forms of infighting are as unpleasant and ugly today as they were in David's post-rebellion Israel.

8. Sheba's rebellion (20:1–26)

a. It is important to choose carefully the causes we fight for (20:1–2)

In some ways the account of Sheba's rebellion can be seen as a rather minor supplement to the story of Absalom's revolt. The timing is unclear and it may have been a little later in David's reign, although Joab's murder of Amasa links the two stories, and the *happened to be there* of 20:1 indicates an immediate follow-on. In spite of the tribal tensions that emerged at its conclusion, the original civil war had not been tribally based. It was a dispute about which of two men, not just from the same tribe but from the same family, should be king. There were those from all the tribes who took part on both sides. Nevertheless, Sheba, a dissident from Saul's family, took advantage of the tension and called for the non-Judean tribes to unite against David, suggesting that he should be seen as king only of Judah. The ease with which the rebellion was overcome indicates that it was something of an overstatement to suggest that *all the men of Israel*[20] *deserted David*. It may be that they followed Sheba only in

---

[20] The term 'Israel' is used in two different ways: in the first place for the whole nation consisting of all the tribes, and in the second place for the kingdom in the north consisting of ten tribes that, at God's direction, broke away at the time of Rehoboam (1 Kgs 11:26 – 12:24). Its use for the non-Judean tribes at this

the sense that they also were travelling back up north to their homes rather than going back to Jerusalem with David. Although the northern men wanted to show their pride in their own heritage, and to insist that their allegiance to a king who was Judean in no sense meant that they gave allegiance to Judah or accepted in any way the priority of Judah, it seems that their hearts were not really with Sheba. It is sadly often the case that people can be led into supporting one line of action by falsely linking two concepts. The argument goes like this: 'You strongly oppose A (in this case, Judean supremacy or, say, pornography). People who support A also support B (the kingship of David or, say, the movie trade). This means that if you support B, you could be seen as also supporting A. Therefore you must reject David's kingship or, for example, you must never go to the cinema and you must fight with all your might against those who do.' One should be very careful about giving in to that kind of illogical argument. It does not aid the original cause and in general does not bring glory to God.

b. The honour of the powerful versus the rights of the powerless (20:3)

We have already noted (see on 2 Sam. 15) that the fate of David's ten concubines, which may be seen as an incidental irrelevance to the main storyline, was neither incidental nor irrelevant – certainly not to the women concerned and also not to the writer or to God. It may be thought that living as widows for the rest of their lives might come as a welcome relief from their existence as unconsidered pawns in the power struggles between men. But being *kept in confinement* (3) was not the normal fate of widows and the words have something of an ominous ring to them. It appears that the choice of remarriage, which would normally be available to any who had been given a certificate of divorce and sent away (Deut. 24:1), was not available to them. In this case, David's 'honour' was apparently more significant than their freedom. Because of Absalom's mistreatment of them, no doubt seen by him as a political necessity but seen by the women as more like rape, these women could no longer be part of David's household. However, those who had been in David's harem could not be allowed to marry outside of it as anyone who 'took over' one of David's women could be seen as attempting to take over David's power.

---

point may be anachronistic, used by the editors to aid clarity. In fact at that time the tribe of Benjamin remained with Judah under Rehoboam's control, so the use of Israel here in contrast just to Judah adds a little to the complication.

David probably felt that in providing for the women's material needs he had done his duty, but there is an implicit critique in the text of this attitude and the worldview that supports it. David's God is 'a defender of widows' who 'sets the lonely in families' (Ps. 68:5–6). These women were individuals created and cared for by a sovereign Lord and it was unacceptable that they should be treated as pawns in this way. We must be very sure that any action that seeks to protect the reputation of leaders does not do so at the expense of others who do not have the same protection as the powerful.

c. Rebellion and betrayal can take different forms (20:4–13)

In the account of the rebellion that came next, the interest is again in people rather than in the course of the battle and we read only of the beginning and end of Joab's campaign. Interestingly, Sheba himself is not one of the people that the text focuses on. We know nothing of him except that he was a Benjaminite and that he died at Abel Beth Maakah. Even if Sheba did not have as much underlying support as he had hoped for, if the damage to the united nation was to be limited it mattered that he was taken out of the picture as soon as possible before loyalties began to harden even further. Ahithophel's advice to Absalom is well noted by David! Amasa, David's new general, is therefore given just *three days* to rally the Judean troops and return so he can lead the army into the attack. Perhaps Amasa, in his inexperience, did not appreciate just how important the timescale was; perhaps he took time because he wanted to make sure that he did this, his first major job as commander of the joint forces, properly; or perhaps he was just not able to act as quickly as David was used to. In any case, time ran out. Sending for Joab in the crisis would have meant a real loss of face, both for David and for Amasa, so it was to Abishai that David turned. Abishai's task was probably to lead an advance party rather than actually to replace Amasa as general. The irony is that Abishai was placed in charge of *Joab's men*; nobody was really in any doubt as to where these men's allegiance lay. Amasa, still technically in charge, met up with them at the *great rock in Gibeon* (8), where Joab, without warning or compunction and in the midst of a brotherly embrace, murdered him. The gruesome details are provided so that the reader will understand just how unacceptable Joab's behaviour was.

Joab had apparently never wanted to be king and probably therefore did not see himself as a power-seeker. However, his driving ambition was such that he was completely unable to accept anything other than a place as David's chief general. To maintain that place he had ruthlessly murdered Abner and now he did the same to Amasa. Uriah's death had been at David's command; Abner's could be justified in Joab's mind at least as revenge for the death of his brother; Absalom's death was perhaps justified on political grounds; but for the death of Amasa there is no excuse whatsoever. This was murder pure and simple. It is just possible that Joab thought that Amasa deserved to die because of his support for Absalom, but there is no real indication of that in the text and it is clearly seen as no excuse for Joab's action. By usurping David's function and taking on the role of judge and jury, Joab was just as guilty of betrayal as Amasa had ever been and maybe just as guilty of rebellion as Sheba. David knew of Joab's violent tendencies and had, even though it was rather late in the day, made an attempt, by replacing him with Amasa, to put some kind of sanction on him. Joab was having none of it and it is interesting that David made no further attempt to rein in Joab's activities. Instead he gave up and left him to Solomon to deal with (1 Kgs 2:5–6). The consequences of David's failure to deal with Joab in the beginning, and of the hold Joab gained over him when Uriah was murdered, were tragic, not least for Amasa. Any refusal to make tough decisions or carry out difficult actions because of a desire not to offend someone of significance within the community, or because of a wish for certain things not to be revealed, is likely to end up causing more trouble than is saved.

Once Amasa is dead, Joab leaves him lying where he fell and gets on with the job in hand, dealing with Sheba. It is as if Amasa is of no consequence at all for Joab. He *lay wallowing in his blood in the middle of the road* (12). The writer seems to be deliberately drawing attention to the wrongness of this. Even enemies deserve more respect than that, and Amasa was by no means an enemy of Israel. The traffic jam as the following soldiers stopped when they approached Amasa's body may have been nothing more than the natural curiosity tinged with fear that causes drivers to slow down as they pass road traffic accidents. However, it may also be an indication that the soldiers understood and disapproved of Joab's action and were unwilling to go on until further action was taken. Clearly there was no time for a proper burial, but it was only when Amasa was placed decently in a field and covered over that the men were willing to move on. Perhaps the men were willing to move on once the body was hidden because there was no more to see, but the implication is that something more than that was involved. Illegal and immoral action to preserve the status of generals is no more acceptable than illegal action to preserve the status of kings. It is possible that at this point the people were more conscious than their leaders of what God really wanted.

d. A wise woman limits the violence of a ruthless general (20:14–26)

The final incident in this section has the feel, as have many of the other accounts, of an eyewitness report, and, like those other accounts, was probably told and retold around the campfire as a salutary tale. Sheba does not seem to have collected vast numbers of followers as he *passed through all the tribes*. He, and the probably fairly small group of Bikrites who were the only ones who really did follow him, ended up besieged inside the town of Abel somewhere in the northern area.[21] Joab's rigour in the pursuit of what he saw as his duty was well known. He had no qualms about causing the death of innocent parties as long as his own objectives, in this case the annihilation of Sheba and with him the threat of secession by the northern tribes, were achieved. As the siege ramp was built and the battering ram put in place, all those inside must have quaked. Once more, it was a woman who saved the day for them. There are parallels here with the 'wise woman' found in chapter 14. Abel seems to have had a reputation as a centre for wisdom (18) and this woman apparently carried on the tradition. She seems to have been accepted as a spokesperson for the town and had no problem convincing the inhabitants to follow her advice. Women leaders and prophets were rare in Old Testament times, but where they did exist there seems to have been no opposition to them carrying out their functions, whether in formal settings as with Deborah and Huldah (Judg. 4; 2 Kgs 22:14ff.), or more informally as here. Not only was she unafraid to talk to Joab, she also understood something of his character. He would use all means, however destructive, to achieve his end. However, if that end could be achieved more easily and more quickly by less violent means, then he was happy to go along with it. He may also have been aware that the woman's arguments, with their theological import – these were the Lord's *peaceful and faithful* people that he was intending to destroy – would have appealed strongly to David. Sheba was therefore executed by the townspeople themselves and, as there was no doubt that

---

[21] The site of the town cannot be identified with certainty. It seems that the name of the town was simply Abel (18), with Beth Maakah added to give more detail which may have been helpful to the original readers but is now obscure.

the rebellion would be over now it had lost its focus, the gathered army went home and Joab returned to Jerusalem to face, or as it turned out not to face, the consequences of his treatment of Amasa.

Rather than being punished, once more *Joab was over Israel's entire army* (23). The writer almost certainly is aware of the irony involved as he makes this statement, but he uses the opportunity to provide an update for the readers on the make-up of David's government.[22] Terrible things have happened, but life goes on and administrators, priests and historians are still needed to carry out their duties.

Questions to ponder

1. Why do the books of Samuel dwell so much on the stories of Absalom when Chronicles ignores them completely?
2. How should David have dealt with Absalom after he killed Amnon?
3. Was Joab right to 'interfere'?
4. Was Absalom's rebellion inevitable? Should it be seen as God's way of giving David a wake-up call?
5. Why was David so quick to set Mephibosheth aside?
6. Was David's treatment of Shimei appropriate?
7. Did Ahithophel really have no other choice than to kill himself?
8. Is subterfuge an acceptable tactic for believers in a civil war?
9. Was Joab right to kill Absalom?
10. Is there any action that David could have taken to release tribal tensions?
11. After a civil war, how far should one go in letting bygones be bygones?
12. Is Joab a hero or a villain? What do we learn from the ambiguous presentation of his story?
13. These stories provide a realistic picture of David's strengths and weaknesses. Is he presented as an example to follow or a pattern to be avoided – or both?

---

[22] The last update was given in 2 Sam. 8:15–18. There have been one or two changes since then, notably the omission of David's sons as advisors.

2 Samuel 21 – 24

10. Filling in the gaps?

Many documents and other resources were used as sources for the books of Samuel, and scholars have identified a range of difficulties in the composition of the text. Nevertheless, those who have brought all the sources together have produced a narrative that in its final form is very readable, largely chronological and certainly comprehensible as far as the average reader is concerned. In particular, 2 Samuel 9 – 20 is seen as relating a single continuing story with descriptions of many events, episodes and encounters used in an orderly and extremely creative way to produce a coherent whole. The first chapter of 1 Kings picks up the story where 2 Samuel 20 leaves off and continues the story of the kingdom of Israel. Chapters 21–24 of 2 Samuel are slightly different. It is as if the editors found a number of other documents or incidents that were important enough to include but that didn't quite fit in with the structure of the other narratives. The six sections are thus largely independent of one another and their timing is not always easy to determine. However, they very helpfully shed further light on the life and times of David.

1. Consequences of a violated covenant (21:1–14)

At some point during the reign of David a certain incident occurred. The events themselves are fairly clear. There was an extended time of famine. David enquired of God, and was told that this was a judgment on the nation for Saul's failure to abide by an ancient covenant with the Gibeonites (Josh. 9). Therefore, the Gibeonites were owed recompense and so it was decided that seven of Saul's descendants should be put to death. The grief-stricken mother of two of these men protected the bodies from wild animals until they were eventually buried properly alongside the bones of Saul and Jonathan. Once all this was done, the famine ended. The timing of the events is less sure. The information that David *spared Mephibosheth son of Jonathan* (7) seems to indicate that this happened after the incident recorded in 2 Samuel 9 when Mephibosheth joined David's court. However, Shimei's opposition to David makes more sense if it came after these executions, and so in fact does David's search for further descendants of Saul in 2 Samuel 9. It seems hard to believe that he was not aware of these seven and their whereabouts. However, the story itself and any possible meaning is not really affected by whether it came early or late in David's reign.

a. It is important that God's people be seen as trustworthy (21:1–2)

Famine was seen as a normal part of life. Sometimes harvests were good, sometimes less good and sometimes really bad. It was part of the lot of a farming society to cope with whatever came along. There is no indication that Israel was expected to be exempt from the vagaries of nature any more than Christians today should expect to be exempt from the trials and difficulties of modern life (cf. Jas 1; 1 Pet. 4:12). It was only when the famine had been going on for three years that David began to suspect that this might involve some kind of judgment on the nation. Not all adverse weather conditions were viewed as a direct consequence of human behaviour, but God was seen as sovereign Creator and his right to use the resources of his world to make a point, his right to give or to withhold rain, was undoubted (cf. Amos 4:7).

We are not told how it was that God's view on the matter was sought, whether from a prophet, the use of the ephod or by some other means. However it was done, there seems to have been no doubt in anyone's mind as to the accuracy of the conclusion. The problem was that Saul, in some otherwise unrecorded incident, had apparently included the Gibeonites in his attempt to rid the nation of foreign opposition. Saul's motives had been good. Out of *zeal for Israel and Judah* (2) he had tried to clear the land of non-Israelites, as he had been commissioned to do. But it is not acceptable, even in completing worthwhile tasks, to set aside other principles. The Gibeonites had, way back in the time of Joshua, negotiated an alliance with Israel. A covenant was made under which Gibeon was guaranteed freedom from attack and its people were made bonded labourers. The implication here is that the Gibeonites remained in a subservient position within Israel and assumed that the covenant of peace was still in force. The breaking of any kind of covenant was always seen as a serious matter. God is a God of faithfulness and truth and it mattered that his people illustrated his character by their own trustworthiness.[1] Israel, through Saul, had committed a grave offence against the Gibeonites and they deserved to be avenged.

One wonders why it took so long before the judgment was instituted. It would also be interesting to know more details of what Saul did,[2] and indeed what was happening among the Gibeonites currently that perhaps brought the old covenant into focus. But as in so many cases, in these narratives we are given only the details that enable the writer's point to come across. The point in this case seems to be, first, that it is very important to keep promises, and, second, that God takes seriously the rights of all members of society, even those who are normally considered as insignificant. It mattered that some action was taken, that some kind of reparation was made that would let Gibeonites and Israelites alike recognize that the Gibeonites were of value to God and that their rights should be upheld. David's responsibility was now to determine what recompense should be made.

b. Taking and avoiding responsibility (21:3–6)

Often, in ancient times, the offended party was given some say in the punishment to be awarded. Interestingly, this same concept has been revived in recent years. The Israelite law lays down the kind of restitution to be made in a range of circumstances, but it does not support the custom of allowing the victim to choose the punishment. It may be that in forcing the Gibeonites to choose, David was opting out of his own God-given responsibility. The Gibeonites were placed in a very difficult position. They had to say something or they could be held responsible for the continuing famine, but they were clearly still seen as outsiders by their Israelite neighbours and would not have wanted to make the situation worse. In fact, the Gibeonites showed great diplomacy. It appears that many of them had been killed but they probably knew that demanding the death of equal numbers of Israelites would serve only to make the attitude

---

[1] Amos 1:9 indicates that the breaking of treaties was seen as a very serious matter for foreigners as well.

[2] Clearly the Gibeonite community still remained, so any destruction by Saul had been only partial.

of their neighbours towards them much more negative. They asked therefore for the death of seven descendants of Saul. Seven, a small number but the symbol of completeness, could appropriately indicate that the debt was indeed repaid. For David the removal of seven potential threats might be seen as a very positive side effect of this incident and this may or may not have been a relevant factor. Anyway, David gladly agreed to their suggestion in spite of the fact that the Old Testament forbids the punishment of children for crimes committed by their parents (Deut. 24:16; cf. Ezek. 18), and that David had himself made an oath to Saul that his descendants would not be killed (1 Sam. 24:21–22). David does not come out entirely well from this incident. It is ironic that his method of absolving the nation from the guilt caused by the breaking of a promise was to break another promise.

c. A grief observed (21:7–14)

The victims were chosen: *Armoni and Mephibosheth*, the two sons of Saul's concubine Rizpah (2 Sam. 3:7),[3] and the five sons of Merab, Saul's eldest daughter who had originally been promised to David (1 Sam. 18:17–19) before she married Adriel. It may be that Merab herself had actually died by this time, but Rizpah was devastated by what happened. It is probable that she recognized and accepted the concept of corporate responsibility and family solidarity which meant that no-one would question the justice of Saul's sons and grandsons bearing the punishment for his decisions. But recognizing that an action is necessary does not take away the personal agonies of those involved. The deaths of her sons could be seen as having saved many more Israelites from death resulting from the famine, but they were still her sons and she could not allow their bodies to be violated.[4] Once again we see the writer's awareness of the emotions and feelings of women. Rizpah's action apparently helped David to understand that what appeared to be politically necessary actions nevertheless had consequences for individuals. He felt compassion for Rizpah and possibly a sense of guilt for his own part in the proceedings. Her concern for the bodies of her loved ones made him remember that the bodies of Saul and Jonathan, although kept protected by the people of Jabesh Gilead, had never received a proper burial. Perhaps his action in

---

[3] We cannot tell which Mephibosheth was the elder: the son or the half-brother of Jonathan. It was not unusual to have two family members with the same name.

[4] Apparently bodies were normally left exposed after an execution.

burying the executed men along with the bodies of Saul and Jonathan brought comfort to Rizpah's grieving heart.

This story does not fit comfortably with modern readers who really prefer happy endings. However, for those who lived during these times, although these events would have caused great grief to the people directly involved, the logic would have been understood. There would not have been the same offence to moral scruples that is perhaps caused to us. We have a dilemma here. On the one hand, we must be careful not to assume that things which cause problems or raise questions in the twenty-first century would or should have done so three thousand years ago in the society where the events are placed. On the other hand, if our problem is not with the behaviour of the human characters but with the apparent reactions of God, then it does remain a problem and has to be taken seriously. But in this case, should we see God's action as that of an unjust or capricious deity? I think not, and the text certainly does not present it in that way. If there is a problem, it is more in our unwillingness to recognize the reality of judgment than in anything else. This incident is presented to show that God does judge the behaviour of societies as well as of individuals. It also shows that God works within the context of particular cultures and that although those cultures may be critiqued and believers encouraged to work for change, he will not, in general, intervene to prevent the normal practices of those cultures being carried out. David was made aware of the problem but his decision to 'solve' the problem in a way contrary to the law was allowed to stand. In this instance, God acts first in judgment and later (14) in grace, but both of these are worked out in the context of the understanding of those who lived at that time.

2. Battleground heroics (21:15–22)

Four separate incidents are recorded within these eight verses, each noting the death of a Philistine hero at the hand of an Israelite warrior. They are all presented in a formulaic pattern and are probably extracts from a larger document perhaps detailing military exploits in general. Three of the Philistines are spoken of as being of exceptional size and this may indicate some kind of genetic condition within one of the Philistine tribes.[5]

---

[5] Some suggest that the third of these incidents, where in the Hebrew 'Goliath the Gittite' is killed by Elhanan (see e.g. ESV), is the original story on which that of David's killing of Goliath is based, and the parallel account in Chronicles, where it is Goliath's brother Lahmi who is killed by Elhanan, has been changed to avoid

a. A time to retire? (21:15–17)

The first incident is told in some detail. Presumably it took place towards the end of David's reign. Certainly the energy and ability of the younger David are not evident here. He may have been able to kill Goliath many years before but now he was in danger of losing his own life to another Philistine warrior. However, Joab's brother Abishai *came to David's rescue* (17). His life was saved, but his men insisted that he should no longer take an active part in warfare. The writer's intention may be to show that everyone has a different part to play and that the time comes when certain roles have to be handed over to those who are now more competent in those particular areas. David still had a very significant function as a focal point for Israel's life and confidence; he was indeed still *the lamp of Israel*. His men still felt dependent on him; it mattered to them that he should not be killed in battle. It is possible that the mention of Abishai as the one who rescued him is significant given David's somewhat tortuous relationship with Zeruiah's sons. Abishai saved David's life but perhaps in doing so also added to the burden of dependence that hampered David's relationship with the brothers.

b. No-one is indispensable (21:18–22)

The point of including the last three records seems to be partly to make sure that the reader understands that the war with the Philistines took place over an extended period of time and included many battles. It also makes clear that although the Philistines had some remarkable soldiers fighting for them, the Israelites also had many warriors who were quite capable of dealing even with these powerful men. It was a very different situation at the end of David's reign from the time years before when there was not a single Israelite soldier brave enough to face Goliath (1 Sam. 17). We should not underestimate David's contribution in giving training and confidence to the army of Israel. In chapter 23 we are provided with a list of the 'mighty warriors' of Israel, and this section gives some information about how they gained their reputation. There may also be an emphasis that although David was the 'lamp of Israel',

---

this implication. However, the arguments here are fairly subjective. It is of course possible that there were two Goliaths; the use of the same name for different members of the same family is common in many cultures. It is also possible that Chronicles is correct and that a couple of words have been lost in the Samuel version. The editors of Samuel, whose ability to understand, organize and present texts is undoubted, were clearly aware of both stories and saw no inconsistency.

they were not dependent on him and certainly not on the sons of Zeruiah. There were plenty of heroes in the nation. Later Israelite soldiers should take courage; there was no need for them to be afraid of anyone, not even giants. In more recent times, John Bunyan picked up the same idea, suggesting that for the Christian pilgrim, neither 'hobgoblin, nor foul fiend, can daunt his spirit' because 'he knows he at the end shall life inherit'.[6]

3. A psalm of thanksgiving (22:1–51)

David was known as a great poet and musician. It is, therefore, appropriate that one of his psalms should be included within the account in Samuel that deals with his life and times. There is no reason to doubt that this was a psalm written by David as well as used by him. There are few clues to the timing of the psalm, although it appears to be well into David's reign but before the encounters with Bathsheba and Uriah. David was never completely free from enemies, but the phrase in verse 1 is parallel to that in 2 Samuel 7:1 and may indicate that David wrote the psalm around the time that he learned of God's special covenant with him. It makes no mention of any identifiable incidents within David's reign and may in fact have been chosen precisely because of its general nature as a psalm of thanksgiving.

There are only very minor differences between this psalm and Psalm 18 and the heading there is almost certainly taken from the text here. There are also a number of links between this psalm and Hannah's song in 1 Samuel 2.[7] Both reflect on God as the Rock and both speak of God's power to turn human concepts of power upside down and to enable the weak to triumph. It is possible that they should be seen as 'bookends' holding the whole account together. Certainly the extended theological reflections found in both passages mean that the account of Israel's history and the way in which Israel's God, Yahweh, is at work within that history is sandwiched between these statements about the nature and character of God and about his relationship with those who worship him. It may be seen as a personal reflection on David's part, but it has great relevance to all followers of Yahweh.

---

[6] John Bunyan, from the hymn 'He who would valiant be'.
[7] R. P. Gordon identifies some of these links (Gordon [1986], p. 309).

a. David's psalm (22:2–51)

The contents of the psalm can be divided up as follows:

vv. 1–4: God the Rock who is worthy of praise
vv. 5–7: The circumstances that threatened
vv. 8–16: God the overwhelming Lord of nature
vv. 17–20: God the powerful rescuer
vv. 21–25: God the rewarder of righteousness –
    David revels in his righteousness
vv. 26–30: God the faithful enabler
vv. 31–37: God the perfect, unique provider
vv. 38–39: David revels in his victories
vv. 40–46: God the triumphant conqueror
vv. 47–51: God the Rock who is worthy of praise

b. David's God (22:2–20)

The psalm centres on God in relationship. It begins (2–4) with a proclamation of God not just as rock and deliverer, but as *my rock, my fortress . . . my deliverer.* David's God is totally trustworthy, totally dependable, totally safe. He takes the initiative in keeping safe from their enemies those who acknowledge how *worthy* he is *of praise.* It is tempting to assume that verses like these imply that the believer will be kept free from any kind of trouble, but the next section makes it clear that that is not so (5–7). There were times in David's life, as there are times in all our lives, when he felt totally overwhelmed by danger. The imagery is striking: *The waves of death swirled about me . . . The cords of the grave coiled around me.* The appropriate action, indeed the only possible action, in those circumstances is to do as David did. He *called out to* his *God.* And his God – the *my* of verse 7 is again significant – heard him.

David was absolutely confident that even in the midst of the most overwhelming *torrents of destruction,* God was still present, still listening, still responding. Because God is greater than any human understanding, the language of uncontrollable earthquakes and storms (8–16) is appropriate to describe his reactions to the abuse of his people. David's enemies might have seemed *powerful* and *too strong for* him (18), but his God was infinitely stronger and more powerful. When God comes into the picture, the perspective changes and enemies seem much smaller. God *reached down from on high and . . . drew* him *out of deep waters* (17), where he had felt completely enclosed and oppressed, into *a spacious place* (20) where he did not. And why did God rescue David? *Because he delighted in* him. Because God took joy in their relationship.

c. The confidence of youth (22:21–25)

Psalm 103 follows on from the meditations of the less confident and more repentant David found in Psalms 51 and 32, and in verse 10 concludes that God 'does not treat us as our sins deserve or repay us according to our iniquities'. However, this psalm recorded in Samuel comes from the pen of one who has not yet understood his own potential for failure and sin (21–25). He is aware of and rejoices in his own trust in God and his own desire, reasonably successful so far, to keep God's ways, indeed in his own *righteousness* (21). He concludes that God's help for him must have been given on this basis and that the reward he has undoubtedly received, the help he has undoubtedly had, must have come because of this righteousness. The more mature David is much more aware of the God of grace, but there is nevertheless something attractive about the confidence expressed here. David knows the majestic wonder of the God who rewards the righteous, even though he has at this stage still to learn the wonder of the God who meets with and works with those who have failed. David's confidence in himself may have been somewhat misplaced, but his confidence in his God was not. As experience taught him that one of his greatest enemies was his own sinful nature, a powerful foe who would certainly prove too strong, it also taught him that even this enemy was not too powerful or too strong for God to be able to deal with. It would be too easy to dismiss this young confident believer as arrogant, but that would be to judge his inexperience too harshly. Older, wiser observers, more aware of human weakness, sometimes need to wait for experience to teach the lessons rather than seek to stamp out supposed arrogance, and need to make sure that it really is wisdom and not cynicism that makes them want to insist that the lesson be learned now.

d. God of the swift and the stumbling (22:26–51)

David's insight into human nature may be limited at this stage but the insight into God's nature is profound. In verses 26–46 we have a protracted reflection on the nature of God that expands on the one found in verses 1–3. We learn that God takes people seriously and does reveal himself to them in accordance with their own attitude to him (26–28). He encourages those who trust him and ties up in knots those who seek to deceive him. We learn that human behaviour does matter to God but that he can transform circumstances and enable his people to do more than they ever thought possible (29–30, 33 37). David may have been the 'lamp of Israel' (21:17) but it was Yahweh who was his *lamp*. God knows what he is doing and has the power to do it (31–32). We learn that God will enable his servant to deal with all enemies that come along, no matter how strong (38–46). All of these lessons are constantly reaffirmed even in the later psalms where David is well aware that he has been far from 'blameless before him' (24). There is irony in this section: unintended irony in verse 28 when David confidently states that God's *eyes are on the haughty to bring them low*, little knowing how much this will apply to himself later, and intended irony when we read that God will not only make *my feet like the feet of a deer*, but will also make it possible that *my ankles do not give way* (34, 37). God is there for both the swift and the stumbling.

And the God who does all this, who avenges and empowers, who exalts and rescues, who *shows unfailing kindness* to his followers, is the living Lord, *God, the Rock, my Saviour*, who deserves all the praise we can give (47–51).

4. David's 'last will and testament' (23:1–7)

a. The legacy that David wanted to leave (23:1)

This passage is more likely to be a prepared final statement from David than his actual 'last words'. Such statements were not unusual in the Ancient Near East and within Israel itself. Jacob, Moses and Joshua all made similar speeches (Gen. 49; Deut. 32 – 33; Josh. 23 – 24). This statement was probably intended to be read at David's funeral and would have been treated very seriously as David's last wish. It doesn't really fit well in the main narratives of Samuel, but one can see why the editors did not want to omit it. Israelite readers would have been as eager to know what David said at this time as the modern media is to reveal any pronouncements made by royalty or great celebrities. Made at the end of David's reign, it follows on well from the psalm in chapter 22 which was almost certainly written in the early years of his kingship.

The statement is presented as an oracle and David, already well known as a poet, unusually moves into prophetic mode. This is what he wanted the people to remember as they reflected on his life and his years as king.

In the modern West there is sadly something of a tendency to discount the words of those who are nearing the end of a long life and often the lessons of experience can be lost. Our last wills and testaments concentrate on how our material possessions are to be distributed. Maybe we should recapture the tradition of preparing a statement that may leave a more significant and lasting legacy.

David's statement begins as tradition dictated with an introduction of himself. It is interesting that he describes himself first of all not as David the king but as *David son of Jesse*. He goes back to his roots, recognizing that all he has gained in the meanwhile has been given to him by God. He speaks to them first and foremost as a fellow Israelite. Yes, he has been *exalted* and *anointed*, but it is God, *the Most High*, who has done the exalting and the anointing. David is only *the man* with whom Israel's great God has been working. This is a very different David from the confident youngster who penned the psalm recorded in the previous chapter. Perhaps as he wrote, David was conscious of the ways in which he had fallen short of the high expectations of kingship or perhaps he had come to see that there were things more significant and more lasting than power. In either case, he focuses not on his anointing as king but on his parallel calling to be 'the sweet psalmist of Israel' (ESV). It is David the poet, as much as if not more than David the king, who wants to bring this message; a message directed to all the people but particularly to those who follow him as ruler.

b. God is the Rock, in youth and in old age (23:2–3a)

It was important that the people realized that these words had been given to David by God himself. He was speaking as one who had been very conscious of the presence of God from his youth, especially from the day Samuel had anointed him and 'the Spirit of the LORD came powerfully upon' him (1 Sam. 16:1–13). It was that same *Spirit of the LORD* who was enabling him to speak now. God who is *the Rock of Israel* gave him the words. The quadruple parallelism (2–3) shows how significant this point was to him. He again, as he had done long before in the psalm recorded in chapter 22, describes God as a Rock. This may be one of the reasons why Psalm 18 was chosen as the one to function in Samuel as a sample of David's poetry. David had grown older but God had not changed; he was still David's and Israel's secure foundation, still their Rock.

c. True leadership (23:3b–7)

After such a profound introduction the message itself is very simple: a ruler who *rules in the fear of God* (3) brings tremendous blessing on himself and his people.[8] David may be speaking prophetically at this point, but his poetic heart runs away with him as he uses the evocative imagery of creation, perhaps deliberately avoiding anything that might speak more directly of wealth and power. Who has not revelled in the morning light on a cloudless day or rejoiced in the sparkling brightness of the sun reflecting off the droplets left from a recent rainstorm (4)? That kind of wondrous rejoicing can also come from a ruler who rules well. The avoidance of the term 'king' is almost certainly deliberate; nevertheless it is of future kings that he speaks. David has learned hard lessons and he wants to make sure that his heirs are aware of these in advance. He has not had much success with his sons so far, but because of God's covenant grace he still has hope for those who will succeed him.

The second half of the oracle (5–7) could be seen as a development of the confident youthful David whom we saw in 22:21–25 rejoicing in his own righteousness, but that would miss the point. David here is not claiming his own righteousness but stating the fact that because of God's own gracious action in making with him *an everlasting covenant*, he and his house are indeed *right with God*. His heirs start from a good base, certainly *arranged and secured in every part* (5). He makes clear their potential for being kings who rule well, who do bring the kind of blessing that David has spoken of. They have no excuse for failure. However, knowing that the covenant is with him and his house but that any given individual descendant could be excluded by his own actions, David is quite clear: *evil men are all to be cast aside like thorns*. Their reigns will be as useless to their people as a thornbush to a farmer.

d. Standing in God's grace (23:1–7)

His last words, whether applied to kings, to the nation as a whole or even to ordinary Israelites, are at the same time wonderfully encouraging and frighteningly challenging. The message has a strong New Testament ring to it also. Paul in 1 Corinthians 15:10 recognized, just as David does here, that 'by the grace of God I am what I am, and his grace to me was not without effect'. Both David's descendants and modern believers have been

---

[8] This passage has links with Ps. 72 which also explores, though in more detail, the concept of what it means to be a righteous king.

given the grace to stand. But the challenge is still there for us to 'see to it that no one falls short of the grace of God and that no bitter root grows up to cause trouble and defile many' (Heb. 12:15). If David's descendants or we as modern believers turn away from the grace of God, then we will most certainly fall. David's basic convictions have not changed between the psalm of chapter 22 and the oracle of chapter 23. He is still clear about the Deuteronomic teaching that those who serve well and with righteousness will be blessed and that God will always protect and be present with those who are in covenant relationship with him.

5. The honours list (23:8–39)[9]

Throughout the books of Samuel there is an awareness that no leader stands alone, that each is dependent on the advice, help and support of many others. It is appropriate, therefore, before the account moves on from the reign of David, to list some of those who have played a significant part in David's development of Israel into a secure and successful nation. A few names are already known to us, but many are unknown outside of this chapter or its parallel in 1 Chronicles 11: that they are listed here reminds readers – not least the descendants of these men who would have delighted in finding the names of their own particular ancestors in the Scriptures along with those of the ancestors of the whole nation – that everyone who plays a part in God's kingdom is significant. The decision to close this list with Uriah (the list in Chronicles has sixteen names after him)[10] is almost certainly a deliberate but low-key way of drawing attention to the fact that even kings like David had their failures. It could also have been a way of implying that these *mighty warriors* may be heroes, but they are not to be given the trust of the people that should be accorded only to God himself.

a. These also served (23:8–12, 18–39)

Two sets of warriors are listed, the Three and the Thirty. Membership of these elite groups seems to have been dependent on specific military

---

[9] A number of fairly minor textual problems occur within this chapter: the number of footnotes in some versions is an indication of this.

[10] There are some other slight differences between this list and that found in Chronicles. This may be the result of copying errors, of the lists being compiled from the main record at different times so that different names were included, or because some people had alternative names and different alternatives were used. Probably all three of these factors come into play at some point. Certainly this list seems to focus on the first part of David's reign whereas Chronicles covers a wider range of time.

exploits rather than on any office held. In that sense they are ancient equivalents to the British Victoria Cross medal or the American Medal of Honor. It may be that the extra numbers stem from the fact that 'three' and 'thirty' are general terms and refer to groups of flexible numbers.[11] However, in this case it seems more likely that they are accurate figures, standing for titles of honour given to limited numbers of people, with new names being added but only as the older soldiers were killed or retired from active service.[12] Thus it was possible for generals like Abishai and Benaiah to be *held in greater honour* (19) than those who were members of the Three or the Thirty and even to be in command of them without being members of the groups (19, 23). There is some slight confusion over the numbers because, as well as the renowned three, there were also three who were with David on a specific occasion who were also known as *three mighty warriors* but who may or may not have been at some time members of the official group of Three.

The second half of the section is simply a list of names, notably including Joab's brother Asahel,[13] Ahithophel's son Eliam[14] and Uriah the Hittite.[15] In the list are several who, like Uriah or his parents, appear to have joined Israel as immigrants. The first part gives more detailed accounts of specific actions of some of the warriors that led to them gaining a reputation for courage or skill. Josheb-Basshebeth,[16] Eleazer and Shammah were noted for fighting against the odds, for killing many enemies and for standing firm under great difficulties. Shammah was so committed that he even defended a field of lentils (8–12). We know nothing about these three major heroes of the nation other than what we are told here. It is possible that the editors, in choosing their material, were making the point that although all of those who, like these three, assisted in the building of the nation are significant, nevertheless physical prowess and military power are not the only or maybe even the most significant means of serving God.

---

[11] Cf. comment on 'thousand' on p. 234, n. 14.

[12] It is not easy to work out exactly who is involved in the thirty-seven mentioned (39) as there are only thirty named in the list apart from the unknown number of sons of Jashen (32). It may be that those mentioned earlier in the chapter are assumed to be included and perhaps Joab as well, whose name is notable by its absence.

[13] Killed by Saul's general Abner (2 Sam. 2).

[14] Possibly the father of Bathsheba (2 Sam. 11:3).

[15] Killed in battle at David's instigation (2 Sam. 11).

[16] Some manuscripts of the Septuagint have 'Ish-Bosheth' instead of *Josheb-Basshebeth*.

There are three further incidents from the heroic records of the nation that are brought in here. The second tells us that *Abishai the brother of Joab* (18), whom we have met several times before (notably 1 Sam. 26; 2 Sam. 2 and 16), once stood out against *three hundred men*. The third gives more details of the career of *Benaiah son of Jehoiada* (20). He was a senior officer in David's army (2 Sam. 8:18; 20:23) who later replaced Joab as general after Solomon instructed him to execute Joab (1 Kgs 2:35). We learn here that he once *killed a lion*[17] on *a snowy day* – probably remembered as much because of the rarity of snow as for the killing itself – and had the better of a hand-to-hand combat with *a huge Egyptian*. These records add something of a personal touch. One can imagine these stories being told again and again to young soldiers, inspiring them as they too set out to fight for their nation and their God.

Verse 18 is slightly ambiguous. It seems that at one point Abishai had the famous Three under his command but was not actually one of them. It could also imply that he was one of the three mighty warriors, not the Three, who served David in the first of these incidents. This happened well before David came to the throne at the time when he was hiding from both Saul and the Philistines in the cave at Adullam (1 Sam. 22:1).

b. Costly gifts deserve significant acknowledgment (23:13–17)

Between these lists the writer includes a story about David. The scene is evocatively described in a style more like that of 2 Samuel 9 – 20 than the rest of these lists. One can almost feel the dryness in David's throat as he speaks of his thirst and his particular longing for a drink from the sweet water of the well that he remembers so vividly from his childhood in Bethlehem. We can sense the nervous excitement of his three warriors as they dare one another to enter Bethlehem, at this point a Philistine stronghold, and get the water for David. At first sight David's reaction in tipping the water away and refusing to drink seems ungrateful and thoughtless. However, in actual fact, *he poured it out before the Lord* (16). It had been brought to him as a present, an offering that his men had risked their lives for. It was too special simply to drink. It was worthy to be a special drink offering presented to Yahweh. Such an offering would usually be of fine wine (cf. Exod. 29:40–41; Num. 15:7, 10), but this water

---

[17] This may have been a mountain lion or a symbolic way of describing a Moabite warrior.

could serve the same purpose. His action was honouring rather than dismissive of the men who gave. Their gift was for David but he recognized that their service was for God.

In fact, this whole section is to honour those who gave. The presents brought to church leaders, sometimes at great cost, can be accepted with an easy gratitude. It is perhaps more important that we take time to acknowledge the contributions of 'the Three' and 'the Thirty' who serve within our communities today. These might not be the official leaders, they might not be known outside their particular context, but they are those who serve with courage, with perseverance and with commitment. Sometimes they may do so out of a desire to meet the needs of a leader, but they and the leader both need to realize that it is God himself who really should be the recipient of their gifts. Annual commissioning services that recognize the service of all who minister within a church, not just the official leaders, can have real significance within the community.

6. Consequences of a foolish action (24:1–25)

The last chapter of 2 Samuel, probably included partly as an introduction to the description of the building of the temple on the site of Araunah's threshing-floor (cf. 2 Chr. 3:1), is one of the hardest for modern readers to get to grips with. There are a number of reasons for this, not least the statement in verse 1 that because *the anger of the LORD burned against Israel . . . he incited David against them,* telling him to do something that, apparently obviously to Joab if not at first to David, was a very wrong thing to do. David was to *take a census.* What exactly was going on here? What was so wrong with taking a census anyway? There were several occasions in Israel's history when the tribes were numbered with no obvious ill effects (e.g. Num. 26). And what does it mean for God to incite? James 1:13 tells us that no-one should claim he or she is being tempted by God, 'for God cannot be tempted by evil, nor does he tempt anyone'; but there is a strong implication here that that is just what God was doing. How could that be?

a. The danger of focusing on numbers (24:1–8)

The answer to the question about the census itself becomes clearer when we realize that it was the *fighting men* that David was counting. He wanted to know how big his army was; how many soldiers he could depend on.[18] Joab may have reacted against this primarily on pragmatic grounds. In most instances the army had a job to do and it had to be done, however many soldiers were available. To count the men could imply that the army as it stood was not up to the job, that there were certain tasks that could be undertaken only if there were more soldiers available. That could seriously damage morale. It was Joab's job to make the men confident that they were quite a big enough army to do anything that God called them to do. And that brings in the other problem with the census: a failure to recognize God's power. This is possibly the main point that Joab was making and it is almost certainly the issue that the text is highlighting. God is the one who calls his people to serve him and sometimes calls them to fight. Any victory is given by God. The story of Gideon, presumably known to David, should have been enough to teach him that it is irrelevant how many soldiers are fighting when a battle is at God's behest and on God's behalf. Jonathan knew this when he spoke of God's ability to save 'whether by many or by few' (1 Sam. 14:6). David apparently had temporarily lost sight of God's power and was becoming both proud of and reliant on his own power, exhibited in the number of fighting men in his army. It is important for all godly leaders to demonstrate faith both in their teams and in God. The church, both local and universal, really is the people of God, really is able to function in the way that God has called her to act, really has been given the necessary resources. Our trust, like David's and Israel's, should be in God himself and not in the probably prideful display of all the resources that he has provided. The number of *fighting men* available is no measure of the power of God's people any more than the size of the buildings or the amount of money in the treasury. The New Testament conviction that kingdom values turn upside down the values of the world is found here in incipient form.

b. Temptation is not the cause of our downfall – sin is

The question concerning God's role in apparently egging David on is made more complex by the fact that in the parallel account in 1 Chronicles 21[19] it

---

[18] It has also been suggested that he wanted to change the structure of the army and the way in which the army was called up. This would explain Joab's interest. Kirkpatrick (1889) makes the suggestion that Joab's motivation was 'fear of exciting disaffection among the people by a scheme to increase the burdens of military service'.

[19] There are a number of other differences between the two accounts. Some of the differences in numbers may result from the fact that, as Chronicles states (1 Chr. 27:24), no records were kept and therefore those given can only have come from oral tradition.

is Satan[20] and not God who is described as inciting David to act. Was it God or was it Satan? It is important here not to import into our understanding of Satan all that is associated with the New Testament presentation of the evil spirit who stands in opposition to God. In the Old Testament, Satan, whose name means 'Accuser', is pictured as just that, a kind of supernatural public prosecutor within the heavens who calls upon God as judge to make sure that people really do get their just deserts. There are hints, on all three occasions where the term is used in the Old Testament,[21] that Satan enjoys his job and that may be the reason why the term came to be used for the devil himself. However, in all three instances Satan could be seen as functioning within the sphere of God's purposes.

Samuel and Chronicles almost certainly both obtained their material from the same national record, but we have no way of knowing which one is the original. In Samuel, the writer, who knows that God is in control of all things and who wants to emphasize the fact that what was happening here was a punishment from God, does so by his statement that *the anger of the LORD burned against Israel, and he incited David* (1). He does not want the reader to become distracted by any focus on Satan's part in the matter. Chronicles has a slightly different emphasis and purpose so the Chronicler is happy to acknowledge the role of the Accuser. It is also possible, if not completely satisfactory, to come to terms with the difference between Samuel and Chronicles by saying that it was Satan who actually did the tempting but God allowed it and can therefore be described as being behind it. In any case, when James says 'no-one should say "God is tempting me"' (Jas 1:13), his point is that God never desires our downfall or our hurt and we should never imply that God is to blame for our yielding to temptation. The fault is ours alone. It is made clear in 1 Corinthians 10:13[22] that God does allow us to face temptation, but only in ways that are for our benefit. The person who has faced up to a temptation and conquered it is far stronger than the one who has never faced the difficulty in the first place. It was important that David and Israel faced up to their problem of pride.

---

[20] The fact that the Chronicles reference has no definite article means that it could be translated simply as 'an adversary'.

[21] Job 1 – 2 and Zech. 3:1–2 are the other two occasions.

[22] 'No temptation has overtaken you except what is common to mankind. And God is faithful; he will not let you be tempted beyond what you can bear. But when you are tempted, he will also provide a way out so that you can endure it.'

In any event, two things are clear. First, both Israel and David were caught up in this sinful act. God's anger was against Israel. Israel as much as David was being punished. Perhaps David's action symbolized the attitude of the whole nation. He was caught up in the nationalistic pride in the power and size of their army. The dependence on human support rather than on God's provision was something that involved the whole nation. It was true that God's provision might often come through the work of the army, but that was not the point. Second, David might have been *incited*, but there is no question that he did have a choice in the matter. The intervention of Joab and the commanders makes that clear. David is held fully accountable for his actions and there is no doubt in the mind of the writer that that is right and just. It is interesting that on this occasion Joab (3) is the one who is standing against David and seeking to rein in his inappropriate enthusiasms. By this role reversal the writer helps us to see another side of Joab's complex character; to recognize that Joab himself, although he had no compunction in going against God's law on many occasions, nevertheless was, at least sometimes, motivated by a genuine desire to serve God.

c. Decisions have consequences for which those who make the decisions are responsible (24:9–14)

This time, Joab was overruled, the census took place, the *able-bodied men who could handle a sword* (9)[23] were counted and the results were brought back to David. At this point, and apparently not until this point, ten months after his first decision, *David was conscience-stricken*. Perhaps as the results were coming in it began to dawn on David that both he and the people had begun to take an unhealthy pride in their own achievements. If so, then David's action actually helped him to realize how wrong it was to depend on numbers and one can perhaps understand better why God might have incited him to conduct the census.

Whether or not his conscience had been stimulated by a previous visit from the prophet Gad[24] cannot be determined, but it was not long before Gad came to convey to David the answer to his prayer that God might *take*

---

[23] The increase in the prosperity of the country since Saul came to power is indicated by the assumption here that swords, which had been so scarce that only Saul and Jonathan had one (1 Sam. 13:19–22), were now freely available. The change is remarkable and helps to explain how tempting it must have been for David to want to count his swordsmen.

[24] Gad had worked alongside David in a ministry comparable to Nathan's since the early days of David's exile (1 Sam. 22:5).

away his *guilt.* It would be possible for David's relationship with God to be restored, but his sin could not be ignored. This is God's world. He is a God of justice and of righteousness as well as of mercy and of grace. God's people have to learn to take God, his character and his requirements seriously. In many ways this sixth passage in the final section of Samuel acts as a parallel to the first passage where action is taken against Saul for his crime against Gibeon. It seems likely that the writers are emphasizing that, on the one hand, kings, and by implication all leaders, cannot simply change the rules to suit themselves and, on the other hand, that the actions of all leaders will often have far-reaching effects on the people they lead. This was true for Saul and it remained just as true for David.

So David is faced with an unenviable choice. What had happened was wrong and would have consequences. The nation had been involved in the sin and the nation would be affected by the consequences. In the past, David had tried to opt out of making difficult decisions. Ironically, this time he is to be the one who chooses what the consequences are going to be. The terms 'punishment' and 'judgment' are not used in Gad's prophecy, but it seems clear that that is what is being talked about. There is no doubt that it is coming, but David is asked to decide whether it should be by famine, war or plague. In today's world there is, at least in the affluent West, a prevalent conviction that somehow actions and consequences can be separated, that it is possible to find a way round anything, that someone, somewhere, ought to make it all go away. But allowing people to believe that consequences can be avoided, that they can have their cake and eat it, ultimately does no-one any favours. David learned, to the nation's cost as well as to his own, that responsibility is real, that God, generally, will not prevent the consequences of actions from taking effect. In this instance David does not shirk his responsibility and he chooses plague. There is no indication that there is a right or a wrong answer in this instance. It could be that if the army of which he had been so proud did its job properly, then three months of being chased by enemies might cause less suffering and death than three days of plague. Perhaps a younger, more confident David might have chosen that option. However, his answer is an indication that he has grasped where the sin of the people lay. They and he had trusted in human strength rather than in God. Now, even when it is punishment rather than blessing that is in question, he would rather receive it at God's hands than be at the mercy of human opposition. His conviction remains that God is a God of mercy, who will judge and who will punish, but who will limit the suffering if it is possible to do so.

d. God still listens, cares, answers, acts (24:15–25)

The facts are bleakly stated: the plague arrives and many people die. The results of David's census are ironically no longer valid. The disease spreads throughout the land but has run its course by the time it reaches Jerusalem. The picture of *the angel of the LORD* here leaves us with more questions. Was this another functionary in the heavenly courts parallel to the accuser of 1 Chronicles 21? How, when and where did David see the angel? Is this in fact a symbolic way of talking about the progress of the disease or was it a visible messenger? David's prayer in verse 17 implies that he was not aware of the events of verse 16 which indicate that the plague was over. This does seem strange if David had seen the angel for himself. Chronicles, which has a strong interest in anything to do with the temple, implies that God's decision to spare Jerusalem from the full impact was as a direct result of David's prayer, sacrifice and purchase of the site on which the temple was eventually built. Here, where the continuing emphasis is on the power of God, David's part is not given quite as much significance. It may be that David's prayer influenced God's decision, but it is clearly indicated that the decision was God's, resulting from the fact that he *relented concerning the disaster* (16).

In verse 18 we read of Gad's instruction to David to *build an altar to the LORD on the threshing-floor of Araunah the Jebusite*. The description of the purchase of the threshing-floor provides a fascinating insight into negotiation techniques of the time. Araunah's offer to give not just the land but also everything that was needed for the offering may have been genuine or may have been part of the culturally acceptable procedure. In any case, David wanted everyone to be clear that he accepted his responsibility, that this was his offering, recognizing both his own sin and his own thankfulness to God. It mattered that he paid the full price. The account ends in exactly the same way as the story of the consequences of Saul's sin, with the statement that God *answered his prayer on behalf of the land* (25; see also 2 Sam. 21:14). All sin has consequences and must be dealt with, but once dealt with life goes on. God still wants to relate to his people; the future remains full of hope. God is still listening, still caring, still answering, still powerful. It is a good concept on which to end the first half of the account of the Israelite monarchy and to lead into the next stage of the story.[25]

Questions to ponder

1. What do you make of the link between famine and treaty-breaking? Is it valid today to make such links with weather conditions?
2. Was Saul's family treated fairly in this instance (21:1–14)?
3. Does 2 Samuel 21:15–17 provide support for the introduction of a retirement age?
4. Is David's psalm at the end of Samuel meant to balance Hannah's song at the beginning of 1 Samuel? Is it a true reflection of David's experience?
5. Does the list of Israel's heroes really have significance in today's world? Are there appropriate ways for us to recognize the heroes and heroines of today's church?
6. Does God really incite his people to commit offences? What would be the equivalent today of taking a census of the fighting men?
7. Can being 'incited', whether by God or by Satan, ever be seen as a reason for refusing to take responsibility for our own actions?
8. In what ways might God's displeasure with our behaviour, as a believing community or as a society in general, be revealed today? What should we do about it?
9. So what then is the theme (or themes) of the books of Samuel?
10. Why are the books of Samuel included in God's Word?

---

[25] The fact that Araunah's threshing-floor became the site of the temple could be seen as another major preparation for the continuing story but although Chronicles brings this out, in Samuel and Kings the connection is not made.

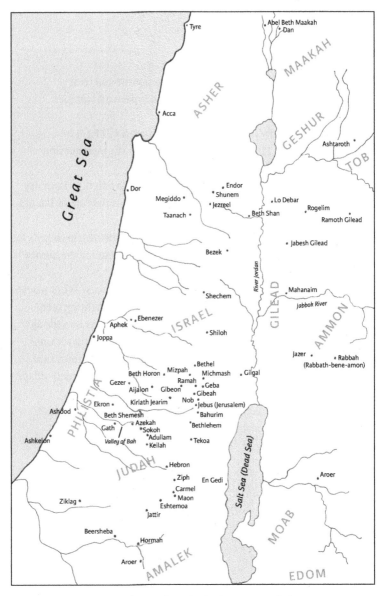

1 and 2 Samuel: places and peoples (scale: 1 cm = c. 16 km)

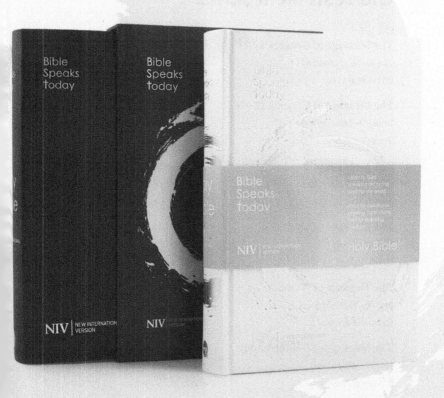

The Bible Speaks Today: Old Testament series

The Bible Speaks Today:
New Testament series

The Message of Matthew
The kingdom of heaven
Michael Green

The Message of Mark
The mystery of faith
Donald English

The Message of Luke
The Saviour of the world
Michael Wilcock

The Message of John
Here is your King!
Bruce Milne

**The Message of the Sermon
on the Mount (Matthew 5 – 7)**
Christian counter-culture
John Stott

The Message of Acts
To the ends of the earth
John Stott

The Message of Romans
God's good news for the world
John Stott

The Message of 1 Corinthians
Life in the local church
David Prior

The Message of 2 Corinthians
Power in weakness
Paul Barnett

The Message of Galatians
Only one way
John Stott

The Message of Ephesians
God's new society
John Stott

The Message of Philippians
Jesus our joy
Alec Motyer

**The Message of Colossians and
Philemon**
Fullness and freedom
Dick Lucas

**The Message of
1 and 2 Thessalonians**
Preparing for the coming King
John Stott

The Bible Speaks Today:
Bible Themes series

The Message of the Living God
His glory, his people, his world
Peter Lewis

The Message of the Resurrection
Christ is risen!
Paul Beasley-Murray

The Message of the Cross
Wisdom unsearchable, love indestructible
Derek Tidball

The Message of Salvation
By God's grace, for God's glory
Philip Graham Ryken

The Message of Creation
Encountering the Lord of the universe
David Wilkinson

The Message of Heaven and Hell
Grace and destiny
Bruce Milne

The Message of Mission
The glory of Christ in all time and space
Howard Peskett and Vinoth Ramachandra

The Message of Prayer
Approaching the throne of grace
Tim Chester

The Message of the Trinity
Life in God
Brian Edgar

The Message of Evil and Suffering
Light into darkness
Peter Hicks

The Message of the Holy Spirit
The Spirit of encounter
Keith Warrington

The Message of Holiness
Restoring God's masterpiece
Derek Tidball

The Message of Sonship
At home in God's household
Trevor Burke

The Message of the Word of God
The glory of God made known
Tim Meadowcroft